Research on Mathematical Methods in Economics

—— Topological，Differential and Conformal Geometry of Surfaces

经济领域的数学方法研究

——曲面拓扑、微分几何和共形几何视角

朱南丽　诺卜特·阿坎博（Norbert A'Campo）著

西南财经大学出版社
Southwestern University of Finance & Economics Press
中国·成都

图书在版编目(CIP)数据

经济领域的数学方法研究:曲面拓扑、微分几何和共形几何视角:英文/朱南丽,(瑞士)诺卜特·阿坎博(Norbert A'Campo)著.—成都:西南财经大学出版社,2021.6
ISBN 978-7-5504-4928-2

Ⅰ.①经… Ⅱ.①朱…②诺… Ⅲ.①经济数学—研究—英文
Ⅳ.①F224.0

中国版本图书馆 CIP 数据核字(2021)第 104997 号

经济领域的数学方法研究——曲面拓扑、微分几何和共形几何视角
JINGJI LINGYU DE SHUXUE FANGFA YANJIU——QUMIAN TUOPU、WEIFENJIHE HE GONGXINGJIHE SHIJIAO
朱南丽 诺卜特·阿坎博(Norbert A'Campo) 著

责任编辑:王利
封面设计:何东琳设计工作室
责任印制:朱曼丽

出版发行	西南财经大学出版社(四川省成都市光华村街 55 号)
网　　址	http://cbs.swufe.edu.cn
电子邮件	bookcj@swufe.edu.cn
邮政编码	610074
电　　话	028-87353785
照　　排	四川胜翔数码印务设计有限公司
印　　刷	四川五洲彩印有限责任公司
成品尺寸	170mm×240mm
印　　张	12.75
彩　　插	1 页
字　　数	306 千字
版　　次	2021 年 6 月第 1 版
印　　次	2021 年 6 月第 1 次印刷
书　　号	ISBN 978-7-5504-4928-2
定　　价	75.00 元

2017 年 3 月 Norbert A′Campo 教授在云南财经大学开讲
经济领域的数学方法高层培训，来自全国的专家学者济济一堂

本书作者朱南丽与 Norbert A′Campo 教授在由昆明理工大学
与丘成桐团队合作成立的工程数学中心讨论留影

推荐语

共形几何是融黎曼曲面、微分几何、代数拓扑等诸多数学分支于一体的新兴数学分支,在计算机图形学、影视特效、动漫游戏、医学影像处理、人脸表情识别,以及装备制造、智慧城市等涉图处理领域取得技术突破性应用,显示出令人瞩目的发展前景。

朱南丽博士和 Norbert A'Campo 教授合作撰写的《经济领域的数学方法研究》,在对共形几何理论进行深入清晰剖析的基础上,将其理论成果首次引入经济领域,用于对经济特别是金融问题进行研究,为共形几何理论的推广与应用拓展提供了富有价值的学术尝试,相信会对经济领域的有关研究和问题解决产生深远的影响。

该书对共形几何在我国特别是经济领域的推广应用具有开拓意义,是数学理论结合领域应用的意深思精力作,特诚推荐该书。

——中国工程院院士 赵沁平

《经济领域的数学方法研究》向经济尤其是金融领域的研究引入共形几何数理方法，为经济领域的学者们从基础开始逐级深入学习了解共形几何理论体系梳理出清晰架构，并进一步示范了这个体系的方法在经济问题尤其是金融问题探索与求解中的应用与效率提升案例。通过阅读本书，有志于在经济尤其是金融问题研究中运用共形几何方法以提高研究效率的学者们，可以从基础理论的详细推导中明析共形几何的理论根源与思想精髓，夯实向自身研究领域拓展应用的理论基础，厚积而薄发。

——国家级多个荣誉称号获得者、专家 钟昌标

朱南丽博士和 Norbert A′Campo 教授合作撰写的这本书，从数学理论中一个精深的分支——共形几何的经济领域应用视角，在对 Conformal Geomerty（共形几何）的基础理论进行清晰细致剖析的基础上，将此数理理论成果引入经济领域的问题研究与解决。全书逻辑思路清晰，目标明确，为共形几何的理论推广与应用拓展提供了非常好的学术尝试。本书对共形几何在我国经济研究的应用推广具有开拓意义，是数学理论联系经济领域应用的实力著作，我非常乐意为该书进行推荐。

——教育部新世纪优秀人才 李小平

序

从事现代经济领域的理论研究，需要有扎实的数学功底。数学方法向经济领域的应用拓展为经济问题的建模与深入研究提供了强大的技术利器，促使近现代经济学领域取得一次次重大突破。该书尝试从一个新颖的视角——共形几何视角对有助于经济尤其是金融领域问题解析的数学方法进行系统性基础研究。

在共形几何中，所有单连通曲面都能共形变换成某种标准空间——球面空间、平面空间、双曲空间。依据这种认知，任何曲面都是三种标准几何（球几何、欧式几何、双曲几何）中的一种，于是大部分三维数字几何处理任务便都能转化成为二维标准空间中的任务，这为优化计算庞杂繁复的以 HJM 和 BJM 等市场模型为例的经济问题提供了新的更为高效的解析方法。

该书从掌握经济领域相关研究所需的共形几何理论基础开始，由基础微分几何逐步展开至黎曼几何，严谨、细致地对这一架构下的 Geometry of Manifolds（流形几何）、双曲几何（罗巴切夫斯基几何）、微分拓扑曲面、黎曼曲面等进行了系统阐述。同时，还引入在经济尤其是金融领域的研究问题求索中运用此系列数学方法的应用场景，从微分几何在经济尤其是金融领域的应用，推进至共形几何在经济尤其是金融领域的应用，对 SABR 模型、无套利几何、随机时间下的共形模型等进行了深入讨论。

恭喜朱南丽博士与世界级数学大师诺卜特·阿坎博(Norbert A'Campo)长期互动学习和紧密合作结出硕果。期待该书能为有志于在经济尤其是金融问题研究中运用共形几何方法提高研究效率的学者提供扎实全面的方法引导。

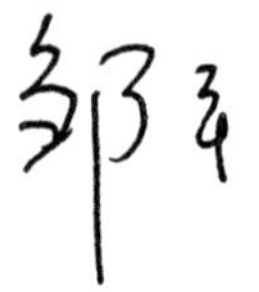

［云南省委高校工委原副书记
云南省教育厅原党组副书记、云南省教育厅原副厅长(正厅级)
昆明理工大学教授、博士生导师］

2021年6月于昆明

前　言

在经济与金融领域的研究中，数理基础无疑是至关重要的一个部分。共形几何(Conformal Geometry)是数学中很多学科的交叉领域，比如黎曼曲面理论、微分几何、代数曲线、代数拓扑、偏微分方程、复分析等。共形几何方法因其性能卓越而被应用于工程和医疗等领域，包括电影特效、动漫游戏、数字制造、人脸识别、物联网协议、医疗导航、美容手术、癌症诊断、阿尔茨海默病预防等。随着我们对其认知的逐步加深，共形几何的应用也在向更多领域延伸。本书内容聚焦于共形几何的基础知识及其在经济领域的应用，就相关研究进行了细致的展开分析与讨论。

共形几何正式被引入我国学术界是在20世纪90年代前后。主要由国际微分几何大师、菲尔兹奖和沃尔夫奖双料得主、中国科学院院士丘成桐先生和其弟子顾险峰教授等共同创立发展的计算共形几何成为一门新兴的跨领域学科，并且发展异常迅猛。Norbert A'Campo 教授早在1978年便受吴文俊先生之邀第一次访华。时隔34年，Norbert A'Campo 教授在2012年受丘成桐先生之邀第二次访华。也正是经由丘先生，笔者有幸结识了 Norbert A'Campo教授，而我们的讨论和互动便由此开启。2017年，在云南省外国专家局大力支持下，受钟昌标先生之邀，Norbert A'Campo 教授到访云南财经大学，为来自全国的经济领域教授、博士们开设系列培训讲座。正是这次学术盛会启迪了本书的撰写初衷。随着与 Norbert A'Campo 教授的讨论日渐深入，我们决定合作完成本书。

诚挚希望本书呈现的内容能够对有意在此领域进行探索的学者有所裨益，也希望我们能把这个领域内的思考与探索推向更加深入。

朱南丽

2021 年 6 月于昆明

Contents

1 Introduction / 1

2 Basic Differential Geometry / 3

2.1 Fields on open sets in real vector spaces / 3

2.2 Closed forms are locally exact / 20

2.3 Fixed Point Theorems / 23

2.4 The abstract field $\mathbb{C}$ versus the $\mathbb{R}$-algebra $\mathbb{C}$ of complex numbers / 27

2.5 Coordinates and local smooth Rigidity Theorems / 33

2.6 Differentiation in Banach spaces / 39

2.7 Sard's Theorem / 41

2.8 Morse Lemma, Morse functions / 46

3 Geometry of Manifolds / 50

3.1 Differential manifolds / 50

3.2 Fields on manifolds / 56

3.3 Integrability condition of Frobenius / 59

3.4 Foliations on manifolds / 64

3.5 Topology of connected, compact surfaces / 67

4 Hyperbolic Geometry / 72

4.1 Hyperbolic plane $\mathbb{H}=\mathbb{H}I$ / 72

4.2 Intermezzo: Higher Cross Ratios / 85

4.3 Hyperbolic trigonometry / 92

4.4 Hyperbolic Area / 107

4.5 A compact hyperbolic surface of genus $g \geqslant \mathbf{2}$ / 109

4.6 The Riemann Sphere $\mathbb{C} \cup \{\infty\}$ / 112

5 Examples of Geometry / 114

5.1 The Space of Norms / 114

5.2 Combinatorial Geometry / 116

5.3 Spaces of Involutions / 117

6 Differential Topology of Surfaces / 118

6.1 **0**- and **1**-deRham cohomology of surfaces / 118

6.2 Hyperbolic plane again, now $\mathbb{H}=\mathbb{H}_J$ / 122

6.3 Reminder: Multi-Linear Algebra / 125

6.4 Reminder: Holomorphic functions in one complex variable / 127

6.5 J-Laplace operator and metric / 134

6.6 J-surfaces / 136

7 Riemann Surfaces / 140

7.1 Riemann surfaces as z- and as J-surface / 140

7.2 Natural structures on the space $\mathbb{J}(TS)$ / 141

7.3 J-fields and Integrability in higher dimension / 146

7.4 Integrability of fibred J -fields / 147

7.5 Analysis of Laplace operators on J -surfaces / 149

7.6 Topology of the two point Green function / 155

8 Differential Geometry in Economics and Finance / 157

8.1 SABR model / 157

8.2 Geometry of no arbitrage / 162

9 Conformal Geometry in Economics and Finance / 165

9.1 Models with Zero Instantaneous Spot Rate / 166

9.2 Conformal Symmetries and Lorentz Transformations / 168

9.3 Conformal Diffusion / 171

9.4 Time Homogeneity and Hyperbolic (Lorentz) Evolution / 173

9.5 The Conformal Model under Stochastic Clock / 178

References / 180

后　记(Postscript) / 189

1 Introduction

These are extended lecture notes of courses at the University of Basel over many years, a series of lectures that has started at the Center of Engineering Mathematics, Kunming University of Science and Technology, December 2014, and are continued at Yunnan University of Finance and Economics, the Erwin Schrödinger International Institute for Mathematics and Physics, Vienna, the International Centre for Theoretical Sciences of the Tata Institute of Fundamental Research, Bangalore, a CIMPA School at Banaras Hindu University, Varanasi. The aim is a study of surfaces from the topological, differential, metrical and conformal view-point, and leads to the applications in Economics.

First sections introduce basic concepts such as differential of a function and also various fields: vector fields, 1-and 2-differential forms, path integral of 1-forms, exterior differential of forms, almost complex structure by J-fields. Poincaré lemma for 1-forms. Morse Lemma. Morse functions on manifolds. Frobenius Integrability Criterion. Classification of compact connected oriented surfaces by genus or Euler number. Stokes Theorem and *deRahm* cohomology. Brouwer, Kakutani, Banach and Schauder Fixed Point Theorems. Coordinates and basic smooth local Rigidity Theorems. The abstract field of complex numbers $\mathbb{C}$ and the $\mathbb{R}$ -algebra of complex numbers $\mathbb{C}$.

Two interpretations $\mathbb{H}_I$, $\mathbb{H}_J$ of the hyperbolic plane $\mathbb{H}$ as space of geometric objects: $\mathbb{H}_I$, the interior of the surface with boundary representing surjective ring-homomorphism from $R[X]$ to a field up to automorphism of the target field or $\mathbb{H}_J$, representing oriented linear complex structures on the real plane. Hyperbolic trigonometry.

Riemannian metric, its isometric torsion free connection on vector fields and its curvature, using the Ansatz of Koszul. Gauss-Bonnet Theorem. Conformal structure on surfaces via J-fields. Local rigidity of J-field and integrability to complex local coordinate on J-surfaces. J-fields in higher dimensions and the obstruction to integrability by the Nijenhuis tensor. A specialisation and simplification of the Nijenhuis tensor in case of families of J-surfaces over a smooth complex base.

Riemann surfaces. Examples of Riemann surfaces with a hyperbolic metric. Hyperbolic metric on compact conformal surfaces of genus $\geqslant 2$ and Uniformisation Theorem for compact Riemann surfaces by a perhaps new continuity method. Riemann's Theorem on holomorphic 1-forms and Existence Theorem. Reconstruction of Riemann Surfaces from the field of meromorphic functions. Holomorphic line bundles. Čech and Dolbeault Cohomology. Riemann-Roch theorem. Teichmüller spaces as leafs of a foliation on the space of J -fields, together with a construction of the Weil-Petersson Kähler structure. Holomorphic embeddings of Riemann surfaces in projective spaces. The Theorem of Wei-Liang Chow and Riemann surfaces as projective varieties. The Teichmüller Curve and its universal functorial property. The Jacobian of a Riemann surface. Bergman metric and a stratification of Teichmüller space. Energy of canonical embeddings. Figure 1 shows Genus 5 Cube and compact surface of very high genus in the 3 dimensional real torus from equations computed. We will cover the first part of all these contents in this book.

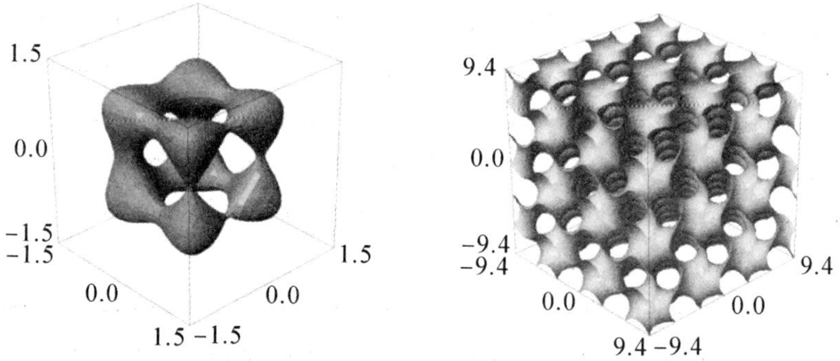

Figure 1 Genus 5 "Cube" and compact surface of very high genus in the 3 dimensional real torus from equations computed and plotted with SAGE

2 Basic Differential Geometry

2.1 Fields on open sets in real vector spaces

Let V be a real vector space of finite dimension and equipped with a norm function $\| \ \|_V : V \to \mathbb{R}$. A norm function allows estimations of vectors, defining convergence of sequences in V , and provides a topology on V . Remember, a real valued function $\| \ \|_V : V \to \mathbb{R}$ on a real (or complex) vectorspace is a *norm* if the following properties for $\lambda \in \mathbb{R}$, $u, v \in V$ or $\lambda \in \mathbb{C}$, $u, v \in V$ hold:

—"Detects equality", $\| u - v \|_V > 0$ if and only if $u \neq v$,

—"$(\lambda, |\lambda|)$ - Homogeneous", $\| \lambda u \|_V = |\lambda| \, \| u \|_V$,

—"Sub-additivity", $\| u + v \|_V \leqslant \| u \|_V + \| v \|_V$.

Associated to a norm $\| ? \|_V$ on V is the distance function Dist : $V \times V \to \mathbb{R}$ by $Dist(u, v) = \| u - v \|_V$.

More generally, a *distance function* on a set X is a two point function Dist : $X \times X \to \mathbb{R}$ satisfying for $a, b, c \in X$

—"Detects equality", $\mathrm{Dist}(a,b) \geqslant 0$ and $\mathrm{Dist}(a,b) = 0$ if and only if $a = b$,

—"Symmetry", $\mathrm{Dist}(b,a) = \mathrm{Dist}(b,a)$,

—"Triangular inequality", $\mathrm{Dist}(a,c) \leqslant \mathrm{Dist}(a,b) + \mathrm{Dist}(b,c)$.

A distance function on a set X provides a *topology* on X . A *topology* T on a set X is a subset $T \subset P(X)$ in the power set $P(X)$ of the set X . A set X endowed with a topology $T \subset P(X)$ is called the *topological space* (X, T) . Elements in $A \in T$ are called *open* subsets in (X, T) or in X if the topology is not explicitly mentioned. In order to be a topology on the set X the subset $T \subset P(X)$ satisfies the axioms:

—$\emptyset, X \in T$,

—if $(A_i)_{i \in I}$ is a finite family with $A_i \in T$ then $\cap_{i \in I} A_i \in T$,

—if $(A_i)_{i \in I}$ is any family with $A_i \in T$ then $\cup_{i \in I} A_i \in T$.

In words, the above properties say that a union of open subsets in a topological space is again an open subset, and that a finite intersection of open subsets in a topological space is again an open subset. The provided topology T on a *metric space* (X, Dist) is constructed in three steps: first declare the so called *open balls* , i.e. subsets $b_{\text{Dist}}(a,r) := \{b \in X \mid \text{Dist}(a,b) < r\}$, $a \in X, r \in \mathbb{R}$, to be elements in the set T , second declare unions of open balls to be elements in T , and finally (please) do the third step by verifying that T is indeed a topology on X .

A distance function Dist on a vector space V is constructed using a norm on V if and only if the following properties for $u, h \in V$ and $\lambda \in \mathbb{R}$ hold:

—$\text{Dist}(u, u + h)$ only depends upon h ,

—$\text{Dist}(u, u + \lambda h) = |\lambda| \text{Dist}(u, u + h)$.

The first property says that distances are invariant under translation, the second says that distances are positively homogeneous.

In case where the distance function on a vector space V is constructed from a norm $\| \ \|_V$, an open ball in V with center $p \in V$ and radius $r \geqslant 0$ is the subset $b_V(p,r) = \{q \in V \mid \| q - p \|_V < r\}$. A subset U in V is *open* if it is a union of open balls. The collection of open subsets in V is the topology on V induces by the given norm. If the real or complex vector space is of finite dimension, two different norms provide equal topologies.

Let U be an open subset in the vector space V . Of central importance is the notion of field on U . There are many kinds of fields, so we proceed by giving the first basic examples.

A *vector field* on U is a map $X: U \rightarrow V$. For a vector field we denote the value of the map X at the point $p \in U$ by $X_p \in V$.

Let V^* be the vector space of all linear maps $L: V \rightarrow \mathbb{R}$. An element of V^* is called a *linear form* on V . Some times we say more shortly form on V . The vector space V^* is called the *dual vector space* of the vector space V .

A 1-*differential form* on U is a field given by a map $\omega: U \rightarrow V^*$. Again we denote by $\omega_p \in V^*$ its value at the point $p \in U$.

A real valued function $f: U \to \mathbb{R}$ or a complex valued function $f: U \to \mathbb{C}$ with numerical values can also be seen as a "field of numbers" on U.

Let $f: U \to \mathbb{R}$ be a function. Let $p \in U$ be a point. We wish to study the behaviour of the function f near the point $p \in U$. In order to do so we consider a number $r > 0$ such that the ball $b_V(p,r) := \{q \in V \mid \| p - q \|_V < r\}$ with center p and radius r is contained in U. Such a positive radius r exists since we have assumed U to be an open sub-set in V. The behaviour of the function f near p, we say also the local behaviour of f at p, is encoded in the map $p + h \in b_V(p,r) \mapsto f(g + h) \in \mathbb{R}$. Very important is the following notion of *differentiability* of f at p.

We say that a function f is differentiable at p if for $p + h \in b_V(p,r)$ a three term expansion of $f(p + h)$ exists

$$f(p + h) = A + L(h) + R(h)$$

that satisfies the following typical properties for each term:

—The first term A is independent of h, so $A \in \mathbb{R}$ is a number.

—The second term $L(h)$ is the value at $h \in V$ of a linear form $L \in V^*$.

—The third term $R(h)$ is the value at $h \in V$ of a map $R: V \to \mathbb{R}$ with the property

$$R(h) = 0, \quad \lim_{h \to 0, \| h \|_V \neq 0} | R(h) | / \| h \|_V = 0.$$

Remember, the dual vector space V^* of the real vector space V is the vector space of all linear maps $L: V \to \mathbb{R}$. So, for $h \in V$ and $L \in V^*$ by $L(h) \in \mathbb{R}$ is denoted the value of L at h.

The last property of the term $R(h)$ is expressed in words by saying that $R(h)$ is relative to h arbitrarily small. This condition on the term $R(h)$ can be expressed using quantifiers on positive numbers ϵ, δ in the following way: For every $\epsilon > 0$ there exists $\delta > 0$ such that for all $h \in V$ with $\| h \|_V < \delta$ the inequality $| R(h) | < \epsilon \| h \|_V$ holds.

The first observation is that the first term A is the value $f(p)$ of the function f at the point p. Indeed, evaluating the three term expansion for $h = 0$, one gets $f(p) = f(p + 0) = A + 0 + 0$ since $L(0) = R(0) = 0$.

Next observation is that the linear form L that appears in the second term of the three term expansion is independent of the expansion. Indeed, let

$$f(p+h)=A+L(h)+R(h) \quad ,$$
$$f(p+h)=A+L'(h)+R'(h)$$

be two expansions satisfying the above typical properties. It follows that the difference

$$L(h)-L'(h)=(L-L')(h)=R'(h)-R(h)$$

is linear in h and also relative to $\|h\|_V$ arbitrarily small, hence $L=L'$ since $L-L'$ is a linear form on V. Indeed, suppose the contrary: let $u\in V$ be with $L(u)\neq L'(u)$; we would have

$$\lim_{s\to 0, s>0} |(L-L')(su)|/\|su\|_V = |(L-L')(u)|/\|u\|_V\neq 0$$

contradicting that $R'(h)-R(h)=L(h)-L'(h)$ is relative to $\|h\|_V$ arbitrarily small.

Since now the linear form of the second term is well defined it deserves a name and a notation. We call the linear form $L\in V^*$ the *differential* of the function f at the point p , see Figure 2. We denote the differential of f at the point p by $(Df)_p\in V^*$.

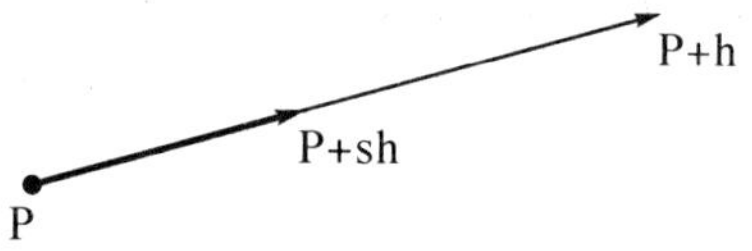

Figure 2 Directional derivative of a function

The value $(Df)_p(u)$ is also called the derivative at p of f in the direction of $u\in V$ and can be computed by the limit

$$(Df)_p(u)=\lim_{s\to 0, s>0}\frac{1}{s}(f(p+su)-f(p)) .$$

A norm function on V admits at $0\in V$ for all $u\in V$ a directional derivative, but is at $0\in V$ not differentiable.

Let the function $f: U\to\mathbb{R}$ be differentiable at every point of U. In short we say that f is differentiable. From the differentiable field of numbers f we get a field of linear forms. Indeed, the map

$$p\in U\mapsto (Df)_p\in V^*$$

is a 1-differentiable form that we denote by df. So df is a field defined on $U\subset V$ with values in V^*.

From a function f we get by differentiation the field $df: U \to V^*$. The value of df at p is the linear form $(Df)_p$. It seems to be self explanatory to call df the *differential* of the function f, but be aware that not all 1 differential forms appear this way as differential of a function. Even locally, as we will see, not all differential 1-forms appear as differential of a function.

There are many ways as we will see later to make out of two fields a third one. Here an example: let $\omega: U \to V^*$ be a 1-differentiable form and let $X: U \to V$ be a vector field. We get a field of numbers, a function $f := i_X \omega$ by putting $f(p) = (i_X \omega)_p := \omega_p(X_p)$. The operation i_X is called the *insertion* of the vector field X. Let $f: U \to \mathbb{R}$ be a differentiable function and let $X: U \to V$ be a vector field. We get a third field Xf of numbers, so a function by putting $(Xf)(p) := (df)_p(X_p)$. Note: $Xf = i_X(df)$. The function Xf is called the derivative of f in the direction of X. Other notations are common, for instance $d_X f$.

The action of vector fields on functions $f \mapsto Xf$ satisfies the Leibniz rule:

$$X(f \cdot g) = (Xf) \cdot g + f \cdot (Xg)$$

where here the dot $\cdot$ stands for the multiplication of functions. Multiplication of functions will however mostly be written without this dot. The Leibniz rule without the dot. looks as

$$X(fg) = (Xf)g + f(Xg).$$

We want also the notion of differentiability of vector valued functions.

So, let W be a second normed finite dimensional vector space with norm $\| \ \|_W$. A map $f: U \to W$ is differentiable at a point $p \in U$ if a three term expansion with the following typical properties for each of the three terms

$$f(p+h) = A + L(h) + R(h)$$

exists. The typical properties are: $A \in W$, $L \in \mathrm{Hom}(V, W)$ is a linear map $L: V \to W$ and finally $R: V \to W$ is a map such that $\|R(h)\|_W$ is relative to $\|h\|_V$ arbitrarily small. Again, A has to be the value $f(p)$ of f at p, the linear map L is well defined independent of the expansion and is denoted by $(Df)_p$. Now df is a field on U with values in $\mathrm{Hom}(V, W)$, the vector space of linear maps from V to W.

As example, from a vector field X on $U \subset V$ we get by differentiation the field

$$dX: U \to End(V) \quad , p \mapsto (u \in V \mapsto (DX)_p(u) \in V)$$

which is a field of endomorphisms of the ambient vector space V.

A map $f: U \to W$ is twice differentiable, if f is differentiable and the map $df: U \to \mathrm{Hom}(V, W)$ is also differentiable. Inductively on $k = 1, 2, \cdots$ we define a map $f: U \to W$ to be k-times differentiable if f is differentiable and the map $df: U \to \mathrm{Hom}(V, W)$ is $(k-1)$-times differentiable. We call a map $f: U \to W$ *smooth* if f is k-times differentiable for all $k \in \mathbb{N}$.

In this text we consider only smooth fields, functions, maps,... except if we explicitly state the contrary.

Let $(x_1, x_2, \cdots, x_n)$ be a basis for the vector space V^* of linear forms on V. The restrictions of the functions $x_i: V \to \mathbb{R}$ to the open subset $U \subset V$ are functions on U that we again denote by the symbols x_i. A number $a \in \mathbb{R}$ can be considered as the constant function on U that takes only the value a. As example for $p \in U$ the expression $x_1 - x_1(p)$ denotes a function on U that vanishes at p.

Theorem 2.1 *Let $U \subset V$ be an open subset in a real vector space V of finite dimension n. Let $(x_1, x_2, \cdots, x_n)$ be a basis of V^*. Let $p \in U$. Let f be a smooth function on U with $f(p) = 0$. Then there exist smooth functions $g_1, g_2, \cdots, g_n$ on U such that*

$$f = (x_1 - x_1(p))\, g_1 + (x_2 - x_2(p))\, g_2 + \cdots + (x_n - x_n(p))\, g_n.$$

If moreover $(Df)_p = 0$ holds, the function g_i in the above expansion satisfy $g_i(p) = 0$, $i = 1, \cdots, n$.

Proof: We assume that the open set U is star shaped with p as center. This means that for all $q \in U$ the segment $\{ tq + (1-t)p \mid t \in [0,1] \}$ lies in U. Moreover we assume that the coordinate functions are centred at p, i.e. $x_i(p) = 0$. Let $(e_1, e_2, \cdots, e_n)$ be the basis of V with $x_j(e_i) = \delta_i^j$ and $q = q - p = \sum_i x_i(q) e_i$. With these notations for $q \in U$, remembering $f(p) = 0$, one expands

$$f(q) = f(q) - f(p) = \int_0^1 (Df)_{tq+(1-t)p}(q-p)\, dt =$$

$$(Df)_p(q-p) + \int_0^1 ((Df)_{tq+(1-t)p} - (Df)_p)(q-p)\, dt =$$

$$\sum_i x_i(q) \left((Df)_p(e_i) + \int_0^1 ((Df)_{tq+(1-t)p} - (Df)_p)(e_i)\, dt \right) =$$

$$\sum_i x_i(q)\, g_i(q)$$

with

$$g_i(q) = (Df)_p(e_i) + \int_0^1 ((Df)_{tq+(1-t)p} - (Df)_p)(e_i)\, dt.$$

Hence $f = \sum_i x_i g_i$. Clearly $g_i(p) = 0$ if $(Df)_p = 0$ holds. Remove the assumption U to be star shaped by using a smooth partition of unity.

Before going on, please consider the following exercises.

Exercise 1: *Let X be a set having three elements and let $D: X \times X \to \mathbb{R}$ be a distance on X. Show that there exists an isometric embedding of the metric space (X, D) into the Euclidean plane. Let $Y = \{a, b, c, d\}$ be a set having four elements. Let $D: Y \times Y \to \mathbb{R}$ be the distance function given by $D(d,a) = D(d,b) = D(d,c) = 1$, $D(a,b) = D(b,c) = D(c,a) = 2$. Show that no isometric embedding of (Y, D) in an Euclidean space of any dimension exists. Find a norm on a two-dimensional vector space inwhich (Y, D) isometrically embeds.*

Exercise 2: *Let V, W be a finite dimensional vector spaces with norms $\| \ \|_V$ and $\| \ \|_W$. On $Hom(V, W)$ we define the operator norm*

$$\| A \|_{Operator} \overset{\text{def}}{=} \text{Max}\{ \| A(v) \|_W / \| v \|_V \mid v \in V, v \neq 0 \}.$$

Show that this maximum is achieved.

The following exercise was proposed with a * for the freshman 1959 at the University of Utrecht by Professor Frederik van der Blij (1923–2018), a Dutch mathematician.

Exercise 3: *Let $f: \mathbb{R} \to \mathbb{R}$ be a function, that is continuous at $0 \in \mathbb{R}$. Assume that $\lim_{h \to 0, h \neq 0} \frac{f(2h) - f(h)}{h}$ exits. Show that f is differentiable at 0.*

Exercise 4: *Let $sq: Hom(V, V) \to Hom(V, V)$ be the map defined by $sq(A) \overset{def}{=} A \circ A$. Compute $(Dsq)_A(H)$, $A, H \in Hom(V, V)$. For $V = \mathbb{R}^2$ with standard Euclidean norm and $A = \begin{pmatrix} 0 & 1 \\ 1 & 1 \end{pmatrix}$ compute the operator norms of A and of $(Dsq)_A$.*

Exercise 5: *Let $exp: \text{Hom}(V, V) \to \text{Hom}(V, V)$ be the exponential map*

$$\exp(A) \overset{def}{=} \sum_{n=0}^{n=\infty} \frac{1}{n!} A^n.$$

Show that the exponential mapping is differentiable. Do not try to compute its differential, *but compute instead* $(Dexp)_A(H)$ *for* $A, H \in Hom(V,V)$ *assuming* $A \circ H = H \circ A$ *or* $A \circ H = -H \circ A$.

Exercise 6: *For a vector space of finite dimension V over the field of real numbers, let* $Det: Hom(V,V) \to \mathbb{R}$ *be the determinant function. Compute* $(DDet)_{Id}(H)$ *as* $Trace(H)$. *Hint: Study first the cases of* $Dim(V) = 1, 2, 3$.

Exercise 7: *For* $H \in Hom(V,V)$ *let H also denote the constant vector field on* $Hom(V,V)$ *with value H. Compute the function* $i_H dDet$.

Exercise 8: *Let V be the vector space* $\mathbb{R}^2$. *Let* $A \in Hom(V,V)$ *have* 0, 1, 2 *or* ∞ *many 1-dimensional eigenspaces and let* $v \in V$ *be a non eigenvector, if possible. Draw by a sketch the curves* $t \in \mathbb{R} \mapsto exp(tA)(v) \in V$. *Consider* $A: V \to V$ *as a vector field on V. The corresponding differential equation for parametrized curves* $\gamma: \mathbb{R} \to V$ *is* $\dot{\gamma}(t) = A(\gamma(t))$, $\gamma(0) = v$. *Extend the list of the above sketched curves in order to get a complete list of all possible sketches of solutions of the differential equations like* $\dot{\gamma}(t) = A(\gamma(t))$, $\gamma(0) = v$.

Exercise 9: *Let X, Y be vector fields on U. Show that the additive commutator of the actions of the vector fields X and Y on smooth functions satisfies again the Leibniz rule. More precisely, we call* $[X,Y]f \overset{def}{=} X(Yf) - Y(Xf)$ *the additive commutator and check the rule* $[X,Y](f \cdot g) = [X,Y]f \cdot g + f \cdot [X,Y]g$.

Gottfried Wilhelm Leibniz (1646–1716) was a German mathematician and philosopher.

Exercise 10: *Let X, Y be vector fields on U. Show the existence of a uniquely defined vector field Z with* $Zf = [X,Y]f$ *for all smooth functions f on U. We denote by* $[X,Y]_{Lie}$ *this vector field Z. The operation* $(X,Y) \mapsto [X,Y]_{Lie}$ *is called the Lie bracket of vector fields.*

Marius Sophus Lie (1842–1899) was a Norwegian mathematician.

Exercise 11: *Continuation. Show for a smooth function f and vector fields X, Y on U the properties:*

$$[fX, Y]_{\mathrm{Lie}} = f[X,Y]_{\mathrm{Lie}} - (Yf)X$$
$$[X, fY]_{\mathrm{Lie}} = f[X,Y]_{\mathrm{Lie}} + (Xf)Y.$$

Conclude that $([X,Y]_{Lie})_p$ *does not only depend on the values* X_p, Y_p *of the vector fields X, Y.*

Hint: In case $X_p \neq 0$, *choose a function f with* $f(p) = 1$ *and* $(Df)_p(Y_p) \neq 0$.

Exercise 12: *Let X, Y, Z be vector fields on U. Show the Jacobi identity:*

$$[X, [Y, Z]_{\text{Lie}}]_{\text{Lie}} + [Z, [X, Y]_{\text{Lie}}]_{\text{Lie}} + [Y, [Z, X]_{\text{Lie}}]_{\text{Lie}} = 0.$$

Carl Gustav Jacob Jacobi (1804–1851) was a German mathematician.

Exercise 13: *For a function f denote by m_f the operation on the space of functions consisting of the "multiplication by" f. So, $m_f(g) = fg$. We say that a vector field F compensates m_f if the commutator $[F, m_f]$ is the identity operator on functions. Which functions are compensated by a vector field?*

Exercise 14: *Let $f: U \to \mathbb{R}$ be a smooth function on an open subset in a real vector space V of finite dimension n. Let at $p \in U$ the function f and the higher order differentials up to order k vanish. Show that f admits an expansion $f = \sum_e (x - x(p))^e g_e$ where $e = (e_1, e_2, \cdots, e_n)$ are the integral multi-exponent with $0 \leqslant e_i$, $|e| = \sum_i e_i = k$, the g_e are smooth functions on U, $x_1, x_2, \cdots, x_n$ are a basis for V^*, and $(x - x(p))^e$ denotes the product $\prod_i (x_i - x_i(p))^{ei}$.*

Hint: first expand $f = \sum (x_i - x_i(p)) g_i$ and apply inductively the statement to the functions g_i.

Exercise 15: *Keeping the notation from the previous exercise, let $M_k(p)$ be the ideal in the ring of smooth real functions $C^\infty(U, \mathbb{R})$ on U consisting of those functions that vanish at p as also all higher differentials up to order k. Show that $m_p \overset{def}{=} M_0(p)$ is a maximal ideal. Show $M_k(p) = m_p^{k+1}$. Compute the dimensions of the vector spaces $M_{k-1}(p)/M_k(p)$. Identify $M_0(p)/M_1(p)$ with V^*.*

We have seen that a vector field X defines an operation of derivation on functions, the operation of insertion i_X and also defines a differential equation. Solutions of the latter are parametrized curves. What can we do with a 1-differential form?

We have already seen that a 1-differentiable form ω together with a vector field X yields a function: $i_X \omega$. What more can we do?

Let $\omega : U \to V^*$ be a 1-differentiable form. Let $\gamma : [a, b] \to U$ be a continuously differentiable curve in U. The *path integral* of ω over γ is defined by:

$$\int_\gamma \omega \overset{def}{=} \int_a^b \omega_{\gamma(t)} (\dot{\gamma}(t)) \, dt$$

which is a number. Here $\dot{\gamma}(t) \in V$ is the speed vector of γ at instant t:

$$\dot{\gamma}_{(t)} \stackrel{\text{def}}{=} (D\gamma)_t(1)$$

i.e. the differential $(D\gamma)_t : \mathbb{R} \to V$ of γ at the point $t \in [a,b]$ evaluated at the vector $1 \in \mathbb{R}$.

The path integral $\int_\gamma \omega$ does not depend on the parametrization, as long the re-parametrization respects the orientation.

The path integral is additive with respect to catenation of paths. So, the path integral is also well defined for paths that are piece-wise continuously differentiable.

The path integral $\int_\gamma df$ where the 1-form is the differential of a function evaluates to the difference of the values of the function at the endpoints:

$$\int_\gamma df = \int_a^b (df)_{\gamma(t)} (\dot{\gamma}(t))\, dt =$$

$$\int_a^b \frac{d}{dt}(f \circ \gamma(t))\, dt = [f \circ \gamma]_a^b = f(\gamma(b)) - f(\gamma(a))$$

In particular for a closed path, i.e. a path with $\gamma(a) = \gamma(b)$, one has $\int_\gamma df = 0$.

The path integral over a closed path of a 1-differential form does not evaluate in general to 0.

In order to give examples, we consider on $\mathbb{R}^2$ the coordinate functions

$$x, y : \mathbb{R}^2 \to \mathbb{R}.$$

The functions x, y are defined as follows. Let $e_1 = (1,0)$, $e_2 = (0,1) \in \mathbb{R}^2$ be the two standard basis vectors. Every vector $u \in \mathbb{R}^2$ can be written in a unique way as a linear combination $u = ae_1 + be_2$, $a, b \in \mathbb{R}$. We define the functions x, y on $\mathbb{R}^2$ by $x(u) = a$, $y(u) = b$. The differentials of the functions x, y are the 1-differential forms dx, dy. The function $y : \mathbb{R}^2 \to \mathbb{R}$ has at $p \in \mathbb{R}^2$ the typical expansion $y(p + h) = y(p) + y(h) + 0$ so we get $(dy)_p(h) = y(h)$.

1. Let ω be the 1-differential form on $\mathbb{R}^2$ given by $\omega = xdy$. This very short and dense notation expands by evaluating at a point p and vector h to the number $\omega_p(h)$, $p, h \in \mathbb{R}^2$, given by:

$$\omega_p(h) = x(p)((dy)_p(h)) = x(p)y(h).$$

Evaluating the path integral of ω on the closed path γ defined by

$$\gamma(t) \stackrel{\text{def}}{=} \cos(t)e_1 + \sin(t)e_2,\ t \in [0,2\pi],$$

with $\dot{\gamma}(t) = -\sin(t)e_1 + \cos(t)e_2$, one gets

$$\int_\gamma \omega = \int_0^{2\pi} x(\gamma(t))\,(dy)_{\gamma(t)}\,(\dot{\gamma}(t))\,dt = \int_0^{2\pi} \cos(t)^2 dt = \pi \neq 0.$$

If we denote by $\partial B_p(r)$ the counter clockwise oriented boundary of the closed Euclidean ball with center $p \in \mathbb{R}^2$ and radius $r \in \mathbb{R}_{>0}$ we have

$$\int_{\partial B_p(r)} \omega = \pi r^2 \neq 0.$$

We conclude by the first computation $\int_\gamma \omega = \pi$, that the 1-differential form ω is not the differential of a function on $\mathbb{R}^2$.

We conclude by the second computation $\int_{\partial B_p(r)} \omega = \pi r^2$, that for no nonempty open subset U in $\mathbb{R}^2$ the restriction ω_U of the form ω to U is the differential of a function on U.

In short, the 1-differential form ω is at no point locally the differential of a function. Even shorter we say, the 1-differential form ω is locally not the differential of a function.

2. Let U be the punctured plane $U \stackrel{\text{def}}{=} \mathbb{R}^2 \setminus \{0\}$. Let $\rho : U \to \mathbb{R}$ be the radius function $\rho \stackrel{\text{def}}{=} (x^2 + y^2)^{1/2}$. Put $\alpha \stackrel{\text{def}}{=} \frac{x}{\rho}dy - \frac{y}{\rho}dx$. For $p \in U$ let B_p be the open euclidean ball of radius $\rho(p)$. We have the inclusion $B_p \subset U$. Let $\text{angle}_p : B_p \to [-\pi/4, \pi/4]$ be the function where $\text{angle}_p(q)$ equals the counter-clock wise oriented Euclidean angle in radians between the rays emanating from the origin through p and q. We notice, that its differential $d\text{angle}_p$ equals to the restriction of α on B_p. So for every closed path in B_p its path-integral of α evaluates to 0. In short, the 1-differential form α is locally the differential of a function. Nevertheless,

$$\int_{\partial B_p(r)} \alpha = 2\pi \neq 0, r > \rho(p), p \in U$$

and α can not be globally on U the differential of a function.

Let $U \subset V$ be an open subset in a vector space V. We say that a 1-differential form $\omega : U \to V^*$ is exact, if there exists a function f on U with $\omega = df$. We say that a 1-differential form $\omega : U \to V^*$ is *locally exact*, if for every $p \in U$ there exist an open subset U' of U containing p and a function f on U' such that we have for the restriction of $\omega_{|U'}$ to U' the equality $df = \omega_{|U'}$.

The 1-form ω of the first example is not exact, and also not locally exact. The 1-form of the second example is locally exact, but not exact.

Exercise 16: *For* $p \in \mathbb{R}^2$ *put*

$$\alpha(p) = \frac{x - x(p)}{((x - x(p))^2 + (y - y(p))^2)^{\frac{1}{2}}}dy - \frac{y - y(p)}{((x - x(p))^2 + (y - y(p))^2)^{\frac{1}{2}}}dx.$$

Let $\gamma : [0,1] \to \mathbb{R}^2$ *be a smooth closed curve. Define on* $C = \mathbb{R}^2 \setminus \gamma([0,1])$ *the function*

$$Ind_\gamma : p \in C \mapsto \int_\gamma \alpha(p) \in \mathbb{R}.$$

The value $Ind_\gamma(p)$ *is called the index of the loop* γ *with respect to the point* p. *Assume moreover that the curve* γ *is simply closed. Show that the function* Ind_γ *takes only two values* 0 *and* 1 *or* 0 *and* -1. *Show that* $C_0 = \{p \in C \mid Ind_\gamma(p) = 0\}$ *is connected as also* $C_1 = C \setminus C_0$. *Show that* C_1 *is homeomorphic to the open disc in the plane.*

The above exercise is a proof for the smooth Jordan Curve Theorem. For a proof of the continuous Jordan Curve Theorem see[63].

Theorem 2.2 Smooth Jordan Curve Theorem. *Let* $\gamma : [0,1] \to \mathbb{R}^2$ *be a smooth simply closed curve. The complement of the image of* γ *has two connected components.*

We wish to have an infinitesimal criterion for local exactness. First we define the so called exterior derivative of $d\omega$ of a 1-differential form on $U \subset V$.

The exterior derivative $d\omega$ will be a field on U with values in $\Lambda^2(V)$. So first we define $\Lambda^k(V)$, $k \in \mathbb{N}$. In case $k = 0, 1$ we put $\Lambda^0(V) = \mathbb{R}$ and $\Lambda^1(V) = V^*$. In case $k = 2$ we define $\Lambda^2(V)$ as the vector space of all maps

$$\Lambda^2(V) \stackrel{\text{def}}{=} \{B : V \times V \to \mathbb{R} \mid B \text{ bi-linear and anti-symmetric}\}.$$

In case $k > 2$ we define $\Lambda^k(V)$ as the vector space of all maps

$$\Lambda^k(V) \stackrel{\text{def}}{=} \{B : V^k \to \mathbb{R} \mid B \text{ multi-linear and alternating}\}.$$

A field on U with values in $\Lambda^k(V)$ is called a *k-differential form* on U. Such a field is a real function in case $k = 0$.

We turn back to the definition of the exterior differential $d\omega$ of a

1-differential form ω. In order to do so, we have to define the number

$$(d\omega)_p(u,v) \in \mathbb{R},\ p \in U,\ u,v \in V.$$

For $p \in U$, $s \in \mathbb{R}$, $s > 0$, $u,v \in V$ let $P_p(u,v,s)$ be the parallelogram in V with corners p, $p+su$, $p+su+sv$, $p+sv$. Let $\partial P_p(u,v,s)$ be its oriented boundary from p to $p+su$ to $p+su+sv$ to $p+sv$ back to p, see figure 3. For s small enough we have $P_p(u,v,s) \subset U$ since U is open. We define the required number by

$$(d\omega)_p(u,v) \overset{def}{=} \lim_{s\to 0, s>0} 1/s^2 \int_{\partial P_p(u,v,s)} \omega.$$

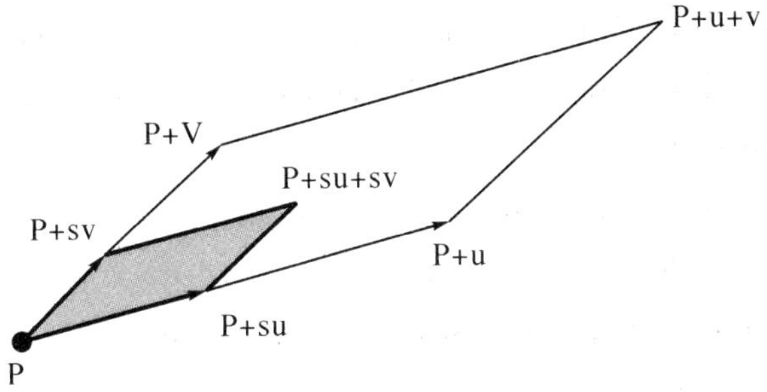

Figure 3 Exterior differential of 1-differential form

For a function f on U we have the important basic fact:

Theorem 2.3

$$d(df) = 0$$

Proof: Since $\partial P_s(p,u,v)$, $s > 0$, is a closed path, we have the vanishing

$$\frac{1}{s^2}\int_{\partial P_p(u,v,s)} df = 0$$

even before taking limits.

It is important to note that the above proof works as soon as $df : U \to V^*$ is continuous, i. e. the function f is *continuously differentiable*. But, if the function f is twice differentiable we can deduce more:

Theorem 2.4 *The differential* $(D(df))_p : V \to V^*$ *is symmetric.*

Before giving a proof, we recall basic facts from linear algebra. Here V is a finite dimensional real vector space. A vector $u \in V$ can also be considered as a linear form on V^* by declaring $u(L) \overset{def}{=} L(u)$, $L \in V^*$. Hence we get a canonical map

$$u \in V \mapsto (L \in V^* \mapsto L(u) \in \mathbb{R}) \in V^{**}$$

which is a canonical inclusion $i: V \hookrightarrow V^{**}$ in general and which is an isomorphism of vector spaces in case of finite dimension. This isomorphism i allows the identification $V^{**} = V$.

According to a theorem of Pál Erdős (1913–1996), a Hungarian mathematician, and Irving Kaplansky (1917–2006), a Canadian mathematician, a vector space V is isomorphic to its dual V^* if and only if the dimension of V is finite. More precisely, their proof shows that if V is of infinite dimension, a strict inequality of cardinals $\mathrm{Dim}(V) < \mathrm{Dim}(V^*)$ holds. From the inequalities $\mathrm{Dim}(V) < \mathrm{Dim}(V^*) < \mathrm{Dim}(V^{**})$ that hold only if V is of infinite dimension, follows that a vector space V and its bi-dual V^{**} are isomorphic if and only if the vector space V is of finite dimension.

We recall that the transpose ${}^tB$ of a linear map $B: V \to W$ is the linear map

$${}^tB: W^* \to V^*,\ L \in W^* \mapsto L \circ B \in V^*.$$

Assume V to be of finite dimension. The natural inclusion

$$i: V \to V^{**},\ u \in V \mapsto (L \in V^* \mapsto L(u) \in \mathbb{R}) \in V^{**}$$

is an isomorphism that allows to identify the spaces V and V^{**}. The transpose of a linear map $A: V \to V^*$ from V to its dual V^* is again a linear map ${}^tA: V^{**} = V \to V^*$ from V to its dual V^*.

A linear map $A: V \to V^*$ defines a bilinear map $B_A: V \times V \to \mathbb{R}$ by putting $B_A(u,v) \overset{\text{def}}{=} (A(u))(v)$. Not always we have the following symmetry property: $B_A(u,v) = B_A(v,u)$, $u,v \in V$. If so, we say that B_A and also that A itself are *symmetric*.

A linear map $A: V \to V^*$ can be decomposed in a unique way $A = A^+ + A^-$ as a sum of two terms where the first term

$$A^+ \overset{def}{=} \frac{1}{2}(A + {}^tA)$$

is symmetric and the second term

$$A^- \overset{def}{=} \frac{1}{2}(A - {}^tA)$$

is anti-symmetric.

For U, V, f, as above, the Hessian $(H_f)_p$ at a point $p \in U$ is the symmetric bilinear form $(H_f)_p : V \times V \to \mathbb{R}$ defined by

$$(H_f)_p(u,v) \stackrel{\text{def}}{=} ((D(df))_p(u))(v).$$

For a twice differentiable function we have a four term expansion:

$$f(p+h) = f(p) + (Df)_p(h) + \frac{1}{2}(H_f)_p(h,h) + R_p(h)$$

where the Rest term $R_p(h)$ is relative to $\|h\|_V^2$ arbitrarily small.

Ludwig Otto Hesse (1811–1874) was a German mathematician.

Proof: We check,

$$(((D(df))_p)^-(u))(v) = (d(df))_p(u,v) = 0$$

so the anti-symmetric part of $(D(df))_p$ vanishes, hence $(D(df))_p$ is symmetric.

We present some computations, that use explicitly the linear structure on U. The above definition of $d\omega$ has used parallelograms, so it has used the linear structure of V. Let V be an n-dimensional vector space, that is equipped with the basis $e_1, e_2, \dots, e_n$. The corresponding linear coordinate functions $x_1, x_2, \cdots, x_n : V \to \mathbb{R}$ are implicitly defined by the unique linear combination

$$u = x_1(u)e_1 + x_2(u)e_2 + \dots + x_n(u)e_n, \ u \in V$$

of u with respect to the basis $e_1, e_2, \dots, e_n$.

The differentials $dx_i : V \to V^*$, $p \in V \mapsto (dx_i)_p \in V^*$ of the coordinate functions are constant maps. The field dx_i takes on V only one value in V^*. It follows $D(dx_i) = 0$ in $\mathrm{Hom}(V, V^*)$. Moreover, the linear forms $(dx_i)_p \in V^*$ constitute at every point $p \in U$ a basis of V^*. A 1-differential form ω on an open subset U in V can hence be written as a linear combination

$$\omega = a_1\, dx_1 + a_2\, dx_2 + \dots + a_n dx_n$$

where the coefficients a_i are functions $a_i : U \to \mathbb{R}$. It follows by the Leibniz product rule:

$$(D\omega)_p = (Da_1)_p dx_1 + (Da_2)_p dx_2 + \dots + (Da_n)_p dx_n : V \to V^*, p \in U.$$

By testing on the basis vectors e_i one obtains for a function $f : U \to \mathbb{R}$ at $p \in U$:

$$(Df)_p = (Df)_p(e_1)(dx_1)_p + (Df)_p(e_2)(dx_2)_p + \dots + (Df)_p(e_n)(dx_n)_p$$ hence

$$df = \frac{\partial f}{\partial x_1}dx_1 + \frac{\partial f}{\partial x_2}dx_2 + \cdots + \frac{\partial f}{\partial x_n}dx_n$$

where we have used the traditional notation of partial derivatives

$$\frac{\partial f}{\partial x_i}(p) \overset{def}{=} (Df)_p(e_i) = i_{e_i}df.$$

We have defined for a 1-differential form ω its exterior differential $d\omega$ by

$$(d\omega)_p(u,v) \overset{def}{=} \lim_{s\to 0, s>0} \frac{1}{s^2}\int_{\partial P_s(p,u,v)} \omega.$$

In order to evaluate this limit as $s \to 0$ of an integral depending on s, we use the three term expansion of the integrand $\omega : U \to V^*$ at the point p.

$$\omega_{p+h} = \omega_p + (D\omega)_p(h) + \text{Rest}_p(h).$$

The integral expands accordingly. The first term contribute 0 since contributions from opposite sides of the parallelogram $P_s(p,u,v)$ cancel. Note that the second term can be used to define the 1-differential form α on U by putting

$$q \in U \mapsto (D\omega)_p(q-p) \in V^*.$$

Observe for $q = p + h$ the identity $\alpha_{p+h} = (D\omega)_p(h)$.

It follows that the integral for $s > 0$ of the second term evaluates to

$$\frac{1}{s^2}\int_{\partial P_s(p,u,v)} \alpha$$

and

$$\lim_{s\to 0, s>0} \frac{1}{s^2}\int_{\partial P_s(p,u,v)} \alpha =$$

$$(da_1 \wedge dx_1 + da_2 \wedge dx_2 + \cdots + da_n \wedge dx_n)_p(u,v).$$

This evaluation is anti-symmetric in u,v since the orientations of the boundaries of the parallelograms $P_s(p,u,v)$ and $P_s(p,v,u)$ are opposite and moreover this evaluation yields the anti-symmetric part of the bilinear form $(u,v) \in V \times V \mapsto ((D\omega)_p(u))(v) \in \mathbb{R}$.

The third term defines also a 1-form ρ on U by

$$q \in U \mapsto \rho_q \overset{\text{def}}{=} \text{Rest}_p(q-p) \in V^*.$$

The integral

$$\int_{\partial P_s(p,u,v)} \rho$$

is relative to s^2 arbitrarily small, so its contribution vanishes after taking the limit s

$\to 0.$

We conclude:

$$d\omega = da_1 \wedge dx_1 + da_2 \wedge dx_2 + \cdots + da_n \wedge dx_n.$$

In particular for a 1-form $\omega = df$ that is the differential a twice differentiable function f, we have from $d\omega = d(df) = 0$, that

$$0 = \sum_{1 \leqslant i \leqslant j \leqslant n} \left(\frac{\partial^2 f}{\partial x_i \partial x_j} - \frac{\partial^2 f}{\partial x_j \partial x_i} \right) dx_i \wedge dx_j$$

and

$$\frac{\partial^2 f}{\partial x_i \partial x_j} - \frac{\partial^2 f}{\partial x_j \partial x_i} = 0$$

hold. Indeed, $0 = i_{e_j}(i_{e_i} d(df)) = \frac{\partial^2 f}{\partial x_i \partial x_j} - \frac{\partial^2 f}{\partial x_j \partial x_i}$. Remember the notation $\frac{\partial}{\partial x_i}\left(\frac{\partial}{\partial x_j} f\right) = \frac{\partial^2 f}{\partial x_i \partial x_j}$. The above proves the important result due to Alexis Claude Clairaut, French mathematician, astronomer and geophysicist (1713 – 1765), and Karl Hermann Amandus Schwarz, German mathematician (1843–1921):

Theorem 2.5 *For a twice differentiable function f that is defined on an open subset in $\mathbb{R}^n$ the operations $f \mapsto \frac{\partial f}{\partial x_i}$ of partial differentiation commute, i.e. the following identities*

$$\frac{\partial^2 f}{\partial x_i \partial x_j} = \frac{\partial^2 f}{\partial x_j \partial x_i}$$

hold.

We turn back to a previous example. A computation shows for the 1-form $\omega = xdy$ on $\mathbb{R}^2$ from the first example

$$(d\omega)_p(u, v) = x(u)\, y(v) - x(v)\, y(u) =$$

$$\det \begin{pmatrix} x(u) & x(v) \\ y(u) & y(v) \end{pmatrix} = \pm Area(P_1(p, u, v)).$$

As example, taking $u = e_1, v = e_2$ yields $(d\omega)_p(e_1, e_2) = 1 \neq 0$. This example shows that no restriction to a non-empty open set of ω is exact.

Before going on, please consider the following exercises.

Exercise 17: *The choice of two points A, B in the Euclidean plan E defines on $E \setminus \{A, B\}$ the vector fields X, Y given by $X_p \stackrel{def}{=} A - p$, $Y_p \stackrel{def}{=} B - p$. Let the curve $t \in$*

$[0,+\infty) \mapsto \phi_X(t,p) \in E$ *solve with initial condition* $\phi_X(0,p)=p$ *the differential equation of the vector field X. Accordingly, the curve* $t \in [0,+\infty) \mapsto \phi_Y(t,p) \in E$ *solves the differential equation of Y. Does for* $t,s>0$, *and p not on the line through* A,B *the following hold:*

$$\phi_Y(s,\ \phi_X(t,p)) = \phi_X(t,\ \phi_Y(s,p))?$$

This question models politics in the capital or at home , if one is aiming at two different goals, but still fights about priority. Compute the bracket $[X,Y]_{Lie}$. *For which points* $p \in E \setminus \{A,B\}$ *does* $([X,Y]_{Lie})_p = 0$ *hold?*

Exercise 18: *Let* $\gamma : \mathbb{R} \to \mathbb{R}^2$ *be a periodic path with* $\|\dot{\gamma}(t)\|_{Euclidean} = 1$ *and* $T \mapsto \int_0^T x(\gamma(t))\, y(\dot{\gamma}(t))\, dt$ *bounded. Show that the curve* γ *has at least two flexes per period. A flex is a point where the speed* $\dot{\gamma}(t)$ *and acceleration* $\ddot{\gamma}(t)$ *vectors become linearly dependent.*

Exercise 19: *Let* $Q=(A, B, C, D)$ *be an oriented quadrilateral in the Euclidean plane E with side lengths* a,b,c,d. *Study the positions of Q in E for which the path integral* $\int_Q xdy$ *takes its maximal or minimal value. Is there always a position with* $\int_Q xdy = 0$? *Is the space of positions connected?*

Exercise 20: *Let* $U \subset V$ *be an open subset in a vector space V. Let* ω *be a 1-differential form on U,* $p \in U$, $u,v \in V$. *We wish to compute* $(d\omega)_p(u,v)$. *Let X,Y be vector fields on U with* $X_p = u$, $Y_p = v$. *First we consider the functions* $f \stackrel{def}{=} i_X\omega$, $g \stackrel{def}{=} i_Y\omega$, $h \stackrel{def}{=} i_Z\omega$ *where* $Z \stackrel{def}{=} [X,Y]_{Lie}$. *The value at p of the function* $Xg - Yf - h$ *is the number* $(d\omega)_p(u,v)$. *One can eliminate the point p and write.*

$$d\omega(X,Y) + \omega([X,Y]_{\text{Lie}}) = X\omega(Y) - Y\omega(X)$$

Show for a function f and vector fields X,Y :

$$d\omega(fX,Y) = fd\omega(X,Y) = d\omega(X,fY).$$

2.2 Closed forms are locally exact

The infinitesimal property $d\omega = 0$, i.e. to be closed, implies local exactness for a 1-differential form ω .

Theorem 2.6 *Let $U \subset V$ be an open subset in a real vector space of finite dimension and $\omega : U \to V^*$ a closed 1-differential form. Let $B_p(r) \subset U$ be a ball (for a norm on V). Then there exists a function $f : B_p(r) \to \mathbb{R}$ with $df = \omega$.*

Proof: Let $f : B_p(r) \to \mathbb{R}$ be the function defined by $f(q) \overset{\text{def}}{=} \int_{[p,q]} \omega$, $q \in B_p(r)$, where $[p,q] : [0,1] \to B_p(r)$ is the path $[p,q](t) = p + t(q-p)$. The main difficulty is to prove $(Df)_q = \omega_q$, $q \in B_p(r)$. First we prove

$$\int_{\partial\Delta(p,q,q+h)} \omega = \int_{[p,q]} \omega + \int_{[q,q+h]} \omega + \int_{[q+h,p]} \omega = 0$$

which would follow from Stokes Theorem, if applied to the triangle $\Delta(p,q,q+h)$ and its oriented boundary. Not having the Stokes Theorem at our disposal, we proceed differently.

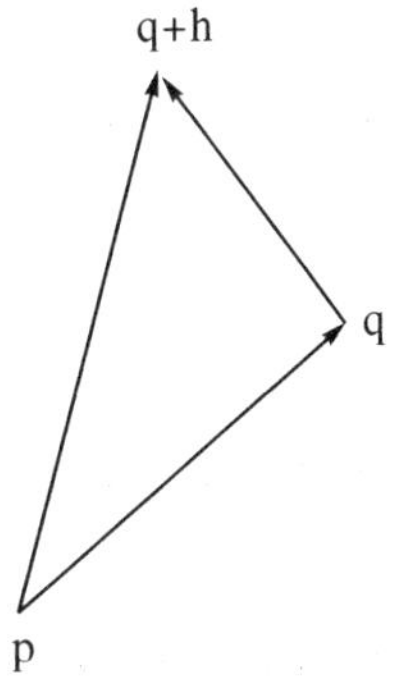

Figure 4 **Construction of** f

We subdivide the triangle $\Delta(p,q,q+h)$ by drawing N lines equidistant parallel to each of the sides, see figure 4. The lines divide the triangle in $(N+1)^2$ congruent triangles, all being a scaling of $\Delta(p,q,q+h)$ by the factor $\frac{1}{N+1}$. We have $(N+1)$ sub-triangles with an edge on $[q,q+h]$. We put the remaining $(N+1)^2-N-1=N^2+N$ two-by-two together and obtain $(N^2+N)/2$ parallelograms, each of them a translate of the parallelogram $P_p(q-p, q+h-p, 1/(N+1))$.

The path integral of ω over the boundary of $\Delta(p,q,q+h)$ is the sum of the path integrals over the boundaries of the $N+1$ sub-triangles and the N^2+N sub-parallelograms. The path integral over the boundary of a subparallelogram is bounded in absolute value by $C_1/(N+1)^3$ since we have $d\omega = 0$.

The path integral over the boundary of a sub-triangle

$$\Delta' = \Delta'\left(p',\ p' + \frac{q-p}{N+1}, p' + \frac{q+h}{N+1}\right)$$

is in absolute value bounded by $C_2/(N+1)^2$. Indeed,

$$\int_{\partial\Delta'} \omega = \int_{\partial\Delta'} \omega_{p'} + \int_{\partial\Delta'} \omega - \omega_{p'} = 0 + \int_{\partial\Delta'} (\omega - \omega_{p'}).$$

Hence the path integral of ω over the boundary of $\Delta(p, q, q+h)$ is in absolute value bounded by Maximum$\{C_1, C_2\}/(N+1)$. This bound holds for all N, so the path integral vanishes.

We can make a three term expansion for f at q:

$$f(q+h) = f(q) + \int_{[q,q+h]} \omega = f(q) + \omega_q(h) + \text{Rest}(h).$$

Now we see $(Df)_q = \omega_q$ after having checked, that the term

$$\text{Rest}(h) = -\omega_q(h) + \int_{[q,q+h]} \omega = \int_0^1 (\omega_{q+th} - \omega_q)(h)\,dt$$

is arbitrarily small relative to h.

Exercise 21: *Let ω be a closed 1-differential form on the punctured space $\mathbb{R}^3 \setminus \{0\}$. Show that ω is exact.*

Exercise 22: *Let α be a 1-differential form on $\mathbb{R}^2$. Assume $\alpha_p \neq 0$ at a point $p \in \mathbb{R}^2$. Show that a triple (U, f, g) consisting of open neighborhood U of p and two functions $f, g: U \to \mathbb{R}$ with $\alpha_{|U} = gdf$ exists.*

Exercise 23: *Consider $\alpha = dx + ydz$ on $\mathbb{R}^3$. Observe, the form $\alpha \wedge d\alpha$ is a volume form on $\mathbb{R}^3$. Conclude that even locally no functions f and g with $\alpha = gdf$ exist.*

We do not study the higher differential forms as introduced by Élie Cartan, a French mathematician (1869–1951), [20,21,22]. See the books of Henri Cartan, a French mathematician (1904–2008)[23,24] and Paul Malliavin, a French mathematician (1925–2010)[66]. Differential calculus provides a very powerful toolbox. As illustrations we propose in the two next sections the one (punch-) line proof of Nelson James Dunford and Jacob Theodore Schwartz of the Brouwer fixed point theorem and a study of real commutative division algebras.

2.3 Fixed Point Theorems

The Brouwer fixed point Theorem is a fundamental seminal result in Topology. It has many consequences and generalizations.

Theorem 2.7 Luitzen Egbertus Jan Brouwer. *Every continuous mapping f: $B^d \to B^d$ with domain and target the closed Euclidean unit ball $B^d \subset E^d$ has a fixed point , i.e. there exists $p \in B^d$ with $f(p)=p$.*

Proof: The following proof is by contradiction. Assume f to be a continuous self map of B^d without fixed point. The closed ball B^d being compact, the continuous function $p \in B^d \mapsto \| f(p) - p \|_{\text{Euclid}} \in \mathbb{R}$ achieves its minimal value $\epsilon > 0$. Approximate up to $\epsilon/3$ the map f by the restriction of a continuously differentiable map $g : E^d \to E^d$ with $g(B^d) \subset B^d$. Now, this restriction has no fixed point either. So, without loss of generality we may moreover assume that the map f is continuously differentiable.

Let $R : B^d \to B^d$ be the map where $R(p) \in B^d$, $p \in B^d$, is the intersection point of the half ray from $f(p)$ that passes through p with the boundary sphere ∂B^d of B^d. The map R is continuously differentiable, maps B^d to its boundary and satisfies $R(p) = p$ if p belongs to the boundary. The map R is a differentiable retraction of B^d to its boundary ∂B^d. Let $x_1, x_2, \cdots, x_d$ be orthonormal coordinate functions on E^d. Put $R_i(p) = x_i(R(p))$. The functions x_i and R_i coincide on the boundary of B^d.

Now see the contradiction given by the following line which uses twice Stokes's Theorem and the linear dependency of the differentials dR_i due to the identity $\| R(p) \|^2_{\text{Euclid}} \equiv 1$ on B^d and hence

$$\frac{1}{2} d \| R(p) \|^2_{Euclid} = R_1 dR_1 + \cdots + R_d dR_d \equiv 0$$

on B^d. The punch-line in question yields the contradiction:

$$0 \neq \int_{B^d} dx_1 \wedge dx_2 \wedge \cdots \wedge dx_d = \int_{\partial B^d} x_1 \wedge dx_2 \wedge \cdots \wedge dx_d =$$

$$\int_{\alpha B^d} R_1 \wedge dR_2 \wedge \cdots \wedge dR_d = \int_{B^d} dR_1 \wedge dR_2 \wedge \cdots \wedge dR_d = 0.$$

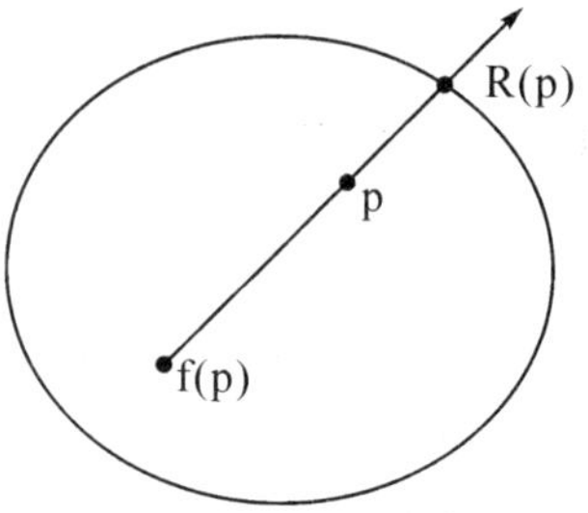

Figure 5 The retraction R in the proof of Brouwer's Theorem.

Figure 5 shows the retraction R in the proof of Brouwer's Theorem. See Nikolai V. Ivanov comments about the above proof of Brouwer's theorem[53]. Luitzen Egbertus Jan Brouwer (1881–1966) was a Dutch mathematician.

Exercise 24: *Let X: $\mathbb{R}^2 \to \mathbb{R}^2$ be a smooth vector field. Assume that the differential equation $\dot{\gamma}(t) = X_{\gamma(t)}$ admits a periodic solution $\gamma: \mathbb{R} \to \mathbb{R}^2$. Show that the vector field vanishes at some point $p \in \mathbb{R}^2$.*

Exercise 25: *Let $K \subset \mathbb{R}^n$ be compact non-empty and convex. Then a continuous map f: $K \to K$ has a fixed point.*

Hint: The space K is homeomorphic to a ball in Euclidean space $\mathbb{R}^m$.

Exercise 26: *Let B be the closed unit ball in the Banach space $C^0([0,1], \mathbb{R})$ of all continuous real function on $[0,1]$ with the supremum norm. Construct a fixed point free continuous map f: $B \to B$.*

Exercise 27: *Let $K \subset C^0([0,1], \mathbb{R})$ be a convex compact non-empty subset and let f: $K \to K$ be a continuous map. Prove that the map f has a fixed point.*

Exercise 28: Schauder fixed point Theorem. *Let $(E, \| \ \|_E)$ be a normed real vector space of any finite or infinite dimension and let $K \subset E$ be compact, non-empty and convex. Then a continuous map f: $K \to K$ has a fixed point.*

Hint: Construct for $\epsilon = \frac{1}{n}, n \geq 1$, a finite subset $A_n \subset K$ such that each point in K is at distance ϵ from A_n. Let $B_n \subset K$ be the convex hull of A_n. Construct a continuous map f_n: $B_n \to B_n$ with $\| f_n(b) - f(b) \| \leq \frac{3}{n}$. The maps $f_n: B_n \to B_n$ have fixed points, hence by a subsequence argument, it will follow that the map $f: K \to K$ too has a fixed point. One possible way of constructing the map f_n: $B_n \to B_n$

would be to map first $p \in B_n$ *to the compact convex subset in* B_n *consisting of those points* $q \in B_n$ *that realize the minimal distance* $Inf_{b \in Bn} \parallel b - f(p) \parallel_E$. *Then proceed as in the proof of the Kakutani fixed point Theorem, see here below.*

Juliusz Schauder (1901–1943) was a Polish Mathematician.

Exercise 29: Perron-Frobenius Theorem. *Let* $A: \mathbb{R}^n \to \mathbb{R}^n$ *be a linear map that maps the set* $\{u \in \mathbb{R}^n \mid u \neq 0, x_i(u) \geqslant 0\}$ *into the set* $\{u \in \mathbb{R}^n \mid x_i(u) > 0\}$. *Show that there exist a unique vector* $u \in \mathbb{R}^n$ *with* $x_i(u) \geqslant 0$, $\sum_i x_i(u) = 1$, *and* $A(u) = \lambda u$, $\lambda \in \mathbb{R}$. *Show that the eigenvalue* λ *is of multiplicity* 1. *Moreover, show that the eigenvalue* λ *dominates strictly the absolute values of the other eigenvalues of A.*

Hint: define a self map $\bar{A}$ *of the compact convex set* $\{u \in \mathbb{R}^n \mid x_i(u) \geqslant 0, \sum_i x_i(u) = 1\}$; *the use of the so called Hilbert metric, see a further section, is of great help.*

Oskar Perron (1880–1975) was a German mathematician. Ferdinand Georg Frobenius (1849–1917) was a German mathematician. The Perron-Frobenius Theorem is the fundament of the Google Search Machine.

The following generalization of the Brouwer Fixed Point Theorem is due to 角谷静夫 Kakutani Shizuo, (1911–2004), a Japanese-American mathematician[55].

Theorem 2.8 Kakutani fixed point Theorem. *Let* $K \subset V$ *be a nonempty convex compact subset in a finite-dimensional real vector space. Let* $CC(K)$ *be the space of non-empty, convex and compact subsets in* K, *the topology on* $CC(K)$ *being the Hausdorff topology. Let* $f: K \to CC(K)$ *be continuous. Then there exists* $p \in K$ *satisfying* $p \in f(p)$.

The Hausdorff topology on $CC(K)$ can be defined in terms of a metric. Let D_V be a Euclidean metric on V. For $A \in CC(K)$ and $\epsilon \geqslant 0$ let A_ϵ be the intersection of K with the union of the closed D_V-balls $B(a, \epsilon)$, $a \in A$. For $A, B \in CC(K)$ define the Hausdorff distance $D_{\text{Hausdorff}}(A, B)$ as the smallest ϵ for which the inclusions $A \subset B_\epsilon$ and $B \subset A_\epsilon$ hold.

The proof will use the following geometric statement, that is in particular true for the Euclidean distance D_V on V:

Theorem 2.9 Minimal Ball Lemma. *Let $A \subset V$ be non-empty, convex and bounded subset in an Euclidean Vector space V with Euclidean norm D_V. There exists a unique closed Euclidean ball $B(c(A), r)$ of minimal radius r that contains A. Moreover $c(A) \in A$. The map c: $CC(K) \rightarrow K$ is continuous.*

Proof: Such balls of minimal radius r exist since A is assumed to be bounded, see figure 6. If A is a subset of two such balls with centers c, c' one has $A \subset B(c, r) \cap B(c', r)$. But, unless $c = c'$, the inclusions

$$A \subset B(c,r) \cap B(c',r) \subset B\left(\frac{c+c'}{2}, r'\right), r' = \sqrt{r^2 - \delta^2} < r,$$

for $\delta = \text{dist}(c, c')/2$, contradict the minimality of r. Last inclusion reflects a special property of the Euclidean distance due to the Pythagoras Theorem. This proves Uniqueness of the center $c = c(A)$. Again from the Theorem of Pythagoras follows that the center $c(A)$ belongs to A. Indeed, assume $c(A) \notin A$ but $A \subset B(c(A), r)$ with minimal r. Let $c' \in A$ realize the minimal distance $t > 0$ from $c(A)$ to A. Then $A \subset B\left(c', \sqrt{r^2 - t^2}\right)$ contradicting the minimality of r. Continuity of the map c is clear.

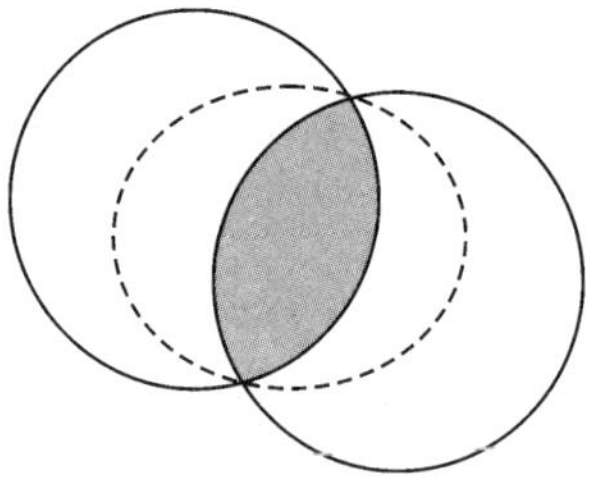

Figure 6　Uniqueness of Euclidean balls of minimal radius

Proof: Kakutani's Theorem. The composition of $c: CC(K) \rightarrow K$ with the map f is a continuous map $c \circ f: K \rightarrow K$ that has a fixed point $p \in K$ by Brouwer's Theorem. So, $p = c(f(p)) \in f(p)$ by the previous Theorem.

The above proof of the Minimal Ball Lemma works also for compact, convex, non-empty subsets in a Hilbert space. It follows that Kakutani's Theorem holds for convex compact subsets in a Hilbert space. Kakutani's Theorem is used in Game Theory and Econometrics, showing the existence of the Nash Equilibrium. John Forbes Nash Jr. (1928–2015) was an American mathematician.

The following theorem works for complete metric spaces and contracting maps. No compactness is assumed.

Theorem 2.10 Banach Fixed Point Theorem. *Let* (X,d) *be a complete not empty metric space. Let* $f: X \to X$ *be a contracting map, i.e. there exist* $\lambda \in [0,1[$ *such that for* $p, q \in X$ *the inequality* $d(f(p), f(q)) \leqslant \lambda d(p,q)$ *holds. Then the map* f *has a unique fixed point.*

Proof: Let $p \in X$. The inductively defined sequence $(p_k)_{k \in \mathbb{N}}$ of points in X by putting $p_0 = p$ and $p_{k+1} = f(p_k)$ is a Cauchy sequence. The map f being Lipschitz continuous, it follows that the limit point $q = \lim_{k\to\infty} p_k$ is a fixed point since

$$f(q) = f(\lim_{k\to\infty} p_k) = \lim_{k\to\infty} f(p_k) = \lim_{k\to\infty} p_{k+1} = q.$$

Fixed points q, q' coincide since $d(q,q') = d(f(q), f(q')) \leqslant \lambda d(q,q')$ only holds if $q = q'$.

2.4 The abstract field $\mathbb{C}$ versus the $\mathbb{R}$-algebra $\mathbb{C}$ of complex numbers

A *division algebra* over a field k is a pair (V, m) consisting of a k-vector space V of finite dimension and a bilinear map $m: V \times V \to V$ such that for all $u, v \in V$ with $u \neq 0$ and $v \neq 0$ the image $m(u,v)$ satisfies $m(u,v) \neq 0$. A division algebra (V,m) is called *commutative* if the map m is symmetric, i.e. if $m(u,v) = m(v,u)$, $u, v \in V$, holds. A division algebra (V,m) is called *associative* if $m(m(u,v), w) = m(u, m(v,w))$, $u,v,w \in V$, holds.

Let k be a field. The pair (V,m) with $V = k$ and m being the multiplication of k is a k-division algebra, that moreover is associative and commutative.

The field of complex numbers $\mathbb{C}$ is commonly constructed as the real associative commutative division algebra (V,m) where V is the $\mathbb{R}$-vector space of expressions $a + bi$, $a, b \in \mathbb{R}$, with the multiplication

$$m(a + bi, a' + b'i) = (aa' - bb') + (ab' + a'b)i.$$

It is convenient to identify a real number a with the complex number $a + 0i$. Also it is convenient to think of the symbol i as the complex number $0 + 1i$. Observe $0 + bi = m(b + 0i, 0 + 1i)$. The product $m(u,v)$ of two complex numbers u, v will be written as uv.

This construction induces on $\mathbb{C}$ even more structure then just the structure of a field $(\mathbb{C}, +, .)$, namely a topology $T_{\mathbb{C}}$ that is given by an absolute value.

Remember, the order relation $\leqslant$ on $\mathbb{R}$ is encoded in the multiplication: one has $a \leqslant b$ if and only if the difference $b - a$ is a square number. Hence, also the topology of $\mathbb{R}$ is encoded in its field structure. The topology $T_{\mathbb{R}}$ is given by the absolute value

$$t \in \mathbb{R} \mapsto |t| \overset{\text{def}}{=} \text{Maximum}\{\pm t\} \in \mathbb{R}.$$

This allows us to think of $\mathbb{R}$ as a field with the topology $T_{\mathbb{R}}$ that is given by the absolute value $|\ |$. The absolute value satisfies the multiplicative property $|ts| = |t||s|, t, s \in \mathbb{R}$, and the triangular inequality $|t + s| \leqslant |t| + |s|$, $t, s \in \mathbb{R}$.

Since the order relation on $\mathbb{R}$ is encoded in its multiplication every field automorphism ϕ of $\mathbb{R}$ will be strictly monotonously increasing and continuous. Moreover $\phi(t) = t$ holds for every rational number t. Hence, ϕ is the identity since the rationals are dense in $\mathbb{R}$.

Every real vector space V has a canonical topology, namely the coarsest topology T_V on V such that all linear maps $L: (V, T_V) \to (\mathbb{R}, T_{\mathbb{R}})$ are continuous. The canonical topologies on real vector spaces have the property that every linear map $A: V \to W$ between real vector spaces V and W is continuous for the canonical topologies T_V and T_W on V and W.

In case of vector spaces V of finite dimension, the topology T_V is given by a norm. Let $L_1, \cdots, L_n$ be a basis L of the dual space V^*. The topology T_V is given by the norm

$$u \in V \mapsto \| u \|_{V,L} = \text{Max}_{1 \leqslant i \leqslant n} |L_i(u)| \in \mathbb{R}.$$

The norm $\| \ \|_{V,L}$ depends upon the chosen basis, but not its topology T_V.

The above construction of the field of complex numbers $\mathbb{C}$ as the real division algebra $\mathbb{C} = (V, m)$ provides a topology $T_{\mathbb{C}} = T_V$. Also an involution appears: the map $a + bi \in \mathbb{C} \mapsto a - bi \in \mathbb{C}$ is an automorphism of fields and is commonly called the complex conjugation. Moreover the map

$$a + bi \in \mathbb{C} \mapsto |a + bi| \overset{def}{=} \sqrt{(a + bi)(a - bi)} = \sqrt{a^2 + b^2} \in \mathbb{R}_{\geqslant 0}$$

is an absolute value $|\,|$ on $\mathbb{C}$ that is multiplicative and that satisfies the triangular inequality. The topology $T_{\mathbb{C}}$ is given by this absolute value. Moreover, multiplication together with the complex conjugation define a Hermitian scalar product $(u, v)_{\mathbb{C}} = u\bar{v}$.

From now on we adopt the convention that the term *field of complex numbers* denoted by $\mathbb{C}$ is constructed as an $\mathbb{R}$ division algebra. So the field $\mathbb{C}$ is endowed with the canonical topology of its underlying real vector space. Also the field $\mathbb{C}$ comes with the involution given by complex conjugation.

If we want to consider very exceptionally the field $\mathbb{C}$ without these extra structures we adopt the term *abstract field of complex numbers*.

At this point one may ask if the topology $T_{\mathbb{C}}$ is encoded in the structure of the abstract field $(\mathbb{C}, +, .)$ of complex numbers? If the answer would be positive, then any automorphism of the field $\mathbb{C}$ would preserve the topology $T_{\mathbb{C}}$.

The answer to the above question is negative! Indeed, very negative, more precisely:

Theorem 2.11 *The group $Aut(\mathbb{C}, T_{\mathbb{C}})$ of $T_{\mathbb{C}}$-continuous automorphisms of the field $\mathbb{C}$ has two elements, namely the identity and the complex conjugation.*

Proof: Let $\phi : \mathbb{C} \to \mathbb{C}$ be a $T_{\mathbb{C}}$-continuous automorphism of the field $\mathbb{C}$. Observe, $\phi(1+0i) = 1+0i$, also observe $\phi(r+0i) = r+0i$ for rational numbers r, so also for real numbers r by continuity. The polynomial $t^2+1=0$ of degree 2 has at most two roots in any commutative field and $0 \pm 1i$ are two roots in $\mathbb{C}$. The polynomial has real coefficients fixed by ϕ, so ϕ permutes the two roots $0 \pm 1i$. Hence $\phi(0+1i) = 0 \pm 1i$. Clearly $\phi(a+bi) = \phi(a) + \phi(b)\phi(i) = a \pm bi$.

Theorem 2.12 *The group $Aut(\mathbb{C})$ of automorphisms of the abstract field $\mathbb{C}$ of complex numbers has the cardinality of the power set $\mathrm{P}(\mathbb{R})$ i.e. of the set of all subsets in the set of real numbers.*

Proof: A transcendence basis of $\mathbb{C}$ is a subset $\beta \subset \mathbb{C}$ minimal with respect to inclusion and such that the only algebraically closed subfield in $\mathbb{C}$ that contains the set β is the field $\mathbb{C}$.

Using the axiom of choice one can proof that a transcendence basis β exists. The cardinalities of $\mathbb{R}$, $\mathbb{C}$ and β are equal.

Every permutation of the set β induces a field automorphism of the abstract field $\mathbb{C}$. An automorphism of the field $\mathbb{C}$ is in particular a permutation of the set

β. The claim follows, since the set of permutations of the sets $\mathbb{R}$, or of $\mathbb{C}$, or of β and the power set $P(\mathbb{R})$ of subsets in $\mathbb{R}$ have equal cardinalities.

It is rare to encounter in mathematics a cardinality as big as the power set of the real numbers. In contrast, up to isomorphism of fields, the abstract field of complex numbers has a very short characterisation by rather elementary properties. This remarkable characterisation is due to Ernst Steinitz (1871–1928), a German mathematician[96].

Theorem 2.13 $\mathbb{C}$-Characterisation Theorem. *Every algebraically closed (commutative) field F of characteristic 0 and of cardinality equal to the cardinality of the power set of the natural numbers is isomorphic to the abstract field of complex numbers $\mathbb{C}$.*

Proof: Choose a transcendence basis ϕ for F and β for $\mathbb{C}$. The algebraic closure $\overline{P}$ of the prime field P in F is isomorphic to algebraic closure $\overline{Q}$ in $\mathbb{C}$ of the prime field $\mathbb{Q}$. The choice of an isomorphism $\overline{P} \to \overline{Q}$ and of a bijection $\phi \to \beta$ determines an isomorphism of fields $F \to \mathbb{C}$.

Imagine the frustration of a person who wants to buy a bike and the shop keepers tells him that he only sells e-bikes. The same frustration appears if this person asks for a construction of the abstract field $\mathbb{C}$ and only a construction of the $\mathbb{R}$-algebra $\mathbb{C}$ is offered to him or her.

Of course such a construction needs material to start with. Amazing is that such a construction is possible starting from all finite fields. The key tools for this construction arc the set theoretic devices of filter, ultrafilter and of ultraproducts. Filters and ultrafilters were invented by Henri Cartan and Jean Dieudonné (1906–1992) a French mathematician, and used by Nicolas Bourbaki in a spectacular proof of Tychonov's Theorem[13,31,32]. Seminal contributions by using ultraproducts in logic are made by the Polish mathematician Jerzy Loś (1920–1998)[62]. See the book by Hans Schoutens[92] for many other interesting applications of ultraproducts and ultrapowers.

A *filter* F on a set X is a subset $F \subset P(X)$ satisfying:

—$\emptyset \notin / F$, $X \in F$,

—if $A \in F$ and $A \subset B \subset X$ then $B \in F$,

—if $A, B \in F$ then $A \cap B \in F$.

The inclusion relation on the power set $P(X)$ induces an order relation on the set $F(X)$ of filters on X. An *ultrafilter* on X is a maximal element in $F(X)$. Ultrafilters exist by Zorn's lemma and every filter F on X is equal to the intersection of all ultrafilters on X that contain F. Ultrafilters U on X are filters with the property that for every subset A in X one of the possibilities $A \in U$ or $X \setminus A \in U$ holds.

A filter F on X is *elementary* if there exists a finite subset A in X with $A \in F$. It follows that for an elementary ultrafilter U on X a point $p \in X$ with $\{p\} \in U$ exists. On an infinite set X there do exist non-elementary ultrafilters. Indeed, let F be the Fréchet filter of all subset $A \subset X$ with finite complement $X \setminus A$. By Zorn's lemma the Fréchet filter F is the intersection of ultrafilters non of which can be elementary.

Let $P = \{2, 3, 5, \cdots\}$ be the set of prime numbers. Let U be a nonelementary ultrafilter on P. For $p \in P$ let $\overline{F}_p$ be the algebraic closure of the finite field F_p with p elements. The field $\overline{F}_p$ can be seen in a non canonical way as the union of all finite fields F_q of characteristic p. Let E be the disjoint union of all fields $\overline{F}_p$. Let $\mathbb{P}$ be the ring of all maps $s: P \to E$ such that for all $p \in P$ the value $s(p)$ belongs to $\overline{F}_p$. Addition and multiplication in $\mathbb{P}$ is point-wise: $(s+s')(p) = s(p) + s'(p)$, $(ss')(p) = s(p)s'(p)$. Let $m_U \subset \mathbb{P}$ be the ideal of all maps $s \in \mathbb{P}$ such that its set of zero's $Z_s = \{p \in P \mid s(p) = 0 \in \overline{F}_p\}$ belongs to U. The ideal m_U is maximal, so the quotient ring $\mathbb{P}/m_U$ is a field, that by the $\mathbb{C}$-Characterisation Theorem is a model for the abstract field $\mathbb{C}$.

Would the cyclist be really happy with this construction? Probally not, the group of automorphisms of the field $\mathbb{P}/m_U$ remains very well hidden! The "visible" automorphisms of $\mathbb{P}/m_U$ seem to commute since the groups $\mathrm{Aut}(\overline{F}_p)$ are isomorphic to the profinite completion $\widehat{\mathbb{Z}}$ of the commutative group $\mathbb{Z}$.

The above characterisation of the abstract field $\mathbb{C}$ allows many appearances of fields isomorphic to the field of complex numbers. Let $(X_\alpha)_{\alpha \in A}$ be a familly of commuting symbols. Assume that the indexing set A has the cardinality of the real numbers. Let F be the algebraic closure of the fraction field of the ring $\mathbb{Q}[X_\alpha]$ of polynomials with unknowns (X_α) and with rational coefficients. This field F is isomorphic to the field of complex numbers. The same holds for the algebraic closure of the fraction field of the ring $\mathbb{R}[X,Y,Z]$. Also the algebraic closure $\bar{\mathbb{Q}}_p$ of the p-adic completion $\mathbb{Q}_p$ is isomorphic to the abstract field $\mathbb{C}$.

Exercise 30: *Show the existence of a family $(F_r)_{r\in\mathbb{R}}$ of subfields in $\mathbb{C}$ such that for all $a<b$ the strict inclusion $F_a \subsetneq F_b$ holds and moreover for all a the fields F_a and $\mathbb{C}$ are isomorphic.*

Exercise 31: *Show that no proper subfield F of $\mathbb{R}$ is isomorphic to $\mathbb{R}$.*

Remember, by convention the multiplication of a field is commutative. This convention does not hold for *skew fields*.

Theorem 2.14 *No real division algebra (V,m) such that the triple $(V,+,m)$ is a field and $Dim(V) > 2$ exists.*

Proof: First we remark that no $\mathbb{R}$-division algebra (V,m) of odd dimension>1 does exist. Indeed, let $u,v \in V$ be linearly independent in V with $\mathrm{Dim}(V)$ odd and $\geqslant 3$. Consider the real line $L=\{tu+(1-t)v \mid t\in\mathbb{R}\}$.

Observe $0\notin L$. The determinant $\Delta(t)$ of the linear map

$w\in V\mapsto M_{tu+(1-t)v}(w)=m(tu+(1-t)v,w)\in V$

is a real polynomial of odd degree, hence has a root $\lambda\in\mathbb{R}$. It follows that $\lambda u+(1-\lambda)v\neq 0$ has no m-inverse, a contradiction.

Let (V,m) be a real division algebra of even dimension $n\geqslant 2$, such that $(V,+,m)$ is a field. Let $\Sigma\subset V$ be those elements $u\in V$ with $\mathrm{Det}(M_u)=1$. The set Σ is closed and bounded in V. Moreover Σ intersects each half ray in one point, so Σ is homeomorphic to the sphere of dimension $n-1$. Also the unity 1_V belongs to Σ. Also $-1_V\in\Sigma$.

Let $q:\Sigma\to\Sigma$ be the map $q(u)=u^2$. Since m is commutative, we compute the differential of q at $u\in\Sigma$ by $(Dq)_u(h)=2uh$ for $h\in T_u\Sigma=\{h\in V\mid \mathrm{Trace}M_{u^{-1}h}=0\}$. The differential of Dq is of maximal rank, so the mapping q is open by the inverse mapping theorem. Hence $q(\Sigma)$ is open in Σ. The image $q(\Sigma)$ is also closed since Σ is compact. It follows $q(\Sigma)=\Sigma$ since the sphere Σ of dimension $\geqslant 1$ is connected. Let $i\in\Sigma$ be with $q(i)=i^2=-1_V$.

The subvector space $W=\{a+bi \mid a,b\in\mathbb{R}\}$ in V spanned by 1_V and i, is a copy of the field of complex numbers. The space V is now via W also a complex vector space of complex dimension $n/2$. Assuming $n/2 > 1$, let u, v be two complex linearly independent elements in V. For $t \in W = \mathbb{C}$ let $\Delta(t)$ be the determinant of the complex linear mapping $M_{tu+(1-t)v}$. As before, now since the polynomial $\Delta(t)$ has a complex root λ, we run into a contradiction if $n/2 > 1$.

Exercise 32: *Again assume that (V, m) is a real division algebra such that $(V, +, m)$ is a field. Let Σ be as in the above proof and let $i \in \Sigma$ be with Trace $M_i = 0$. Show that $\omega_u(h) = \text{Trace } M_{u^{-1}ih}$ defines a closed 1-form on Σ. The 1-form vanishes nowhere and is exact if the sphere Σ is of dimension > 1. This yields a contradiction since the function f with $df = \omega$ has a maximum on Σ. Hint: The 1-differential form α on $V \setminus \{0\}$ with values in V and defined by $\alpha_u(h) = m(u^{-1}, h)$ is near the unity element $1 \in V$ the differential of the map $F(w) = \sum_{k=1}^{\infty} (w-1)^k/k$. Hence, α being exact near 1 is also closed near 1. The same holds for $\omega = \text{Trace}(i\alpha)$, which is a 1-differential form with real values. Deduce that the restriction of ω to Σ is closed. If the sphere is of dimension > 1, show that this restriction is exact.*

The smallest subfield in $\mathbb{C}$ is its prime field $\mathbb{Q}$ of rational numbers. A model for the algebraic closure of the field $\mathbb{Q}$ is provided by the smallest algebraic closed subfield $\overline{\mathbb{Q}}$ in $\mathbb{C}$. Number fields are subfields in $\overline{\mathbb{Q}}$ that as $\mathbb{Q}$-vector space are of finite dimension.

2.5 Coordinates and local smooth Rigidity Theorems

Smooth local rigidity Theorems provide local normal forms for smooth fields that satisfy some condition and are defined on an open subset $U \subset V$ in a vector space V. In order to express those local normal forms well adapted differentiable coordinate systems need to be constructed.

Important is following definition. Let $p \in U$ be a point in an open subset $U \subset V$ in a vector space V of finite dimension n. A *local differentiable system of coordinates* at p is a couple (U', x) where U' is an open subset in U that contains the point p and a system of differentiable functions $x = (x_1, x_2, \cdots, x_n)$ on U' such that the differentiable map $x: U' \to \mathbb{R}^n$, $q \in U' \mapsto (x_1(q), x_2(q), \cdots,$

$x_n(q)) \in \mathbb{R}^n$ maps U' bijectively with open image $x(U')$ in $\mathbb{R}^n$. Moreover, the inverse map $x^{-1}: x(U') \to U'$ is differentiable.

The following theorem provides local differential systems of coordinates and shows the importance of the concept of the differential of maps.

Theorem 2.15 Construction of local coordinates. *Let V be a vector space of dimension $n \in \mathbb{N}$. Let $U \subset V$ be an open neighborhood of $p \in V$ and let $F: U \to \mathbb{R}^n$ be a continuously differentiable map such that the differential $(DF)_p: V \to \mathbb{R}^n$ is an isomorphism of vector spaces. Denote by $x_i: U \to \mathbb{R}$ the composition of F with the ith linear coordinate function on $\mathbb{R}^n$, $i = 1, 2, \cdots, n$. Then there exists a open neighborhood $U' \subset U$ of p such that the restrictions of the functions x_i to U' build a local continuously differentiable system of coordinates at p. Denoting again by x_i these restriction, $x = (x_1, x_2, \cdots, x_n)$ is this system. If the map F is supposed to be smooth, the resulting local system of coordinates is smooth too.*

Proof: Let $(v_1, v_2, \cdots, v_n)$ be the vectors in V with $(DF)_p(v_i) = e_i$, $i = 1, 2, \cdots, n$ where e_i is the ith canonical basis vector in $\mathbb{R}^n$. We choose to work with the maximum norms $\| ? \|_V$ *and* $\| ? \|_{\mathbb{R}^n}$ in the based vector spaces V and $\mathbb{R}^n$. Observe that the differential $(DF)_p$ preserves norms. Let U' be the open ball $B(p, r)$ in V with $r > 0$ and $B(p, r) \subset U$ such that for $q \in B(p, r)$ the inequalities

$$\| (DF)_p - (DF)_q \|_{\text{OperatorNorm}} < 1/2$$

holds.

For $q \in U'$ and $v \in V$ the inequality

$$\| ((DF)_p^{-1} \circ (DF)_q) - Id_V(v) \|_V \leqslant \frac{1}{2} \| v \|_V$$

follows.

The restriction of F to U' is injective. Indeed, for $q, q' \in U'$, $q \neq q'$,

$$\| F(q') - F(q) \|_{\mathbb{R}^n} = \| \int_0^1 (DF)_{(1-t)q+tq'}(q' - q)\, dt \| \geqslant$$

$$\| (DF_p(q' - q)) \|_{\mathbb{R}^n} - \int_0^1 \| ((DF)_{(1-t)q+tq'} - (DF)_p)(q' - q) \|_{\mathbb{R}^n} dt \geqslant$$

$$\frac{1}{2} \| q' - q \|_V > 0$$

showing $F(q) \neq F(q')$.

For all $q \in U'$ the differential $(DF)_q : V \to \mathbb{R}^n$ is injective, and hence an isomorphism of vector spaces. Indeed, for $v \in V$, $v \neq 0$,

$$\| (DF)_q(v) \|_{\mathbb{R}^n} =$$
$$\| (DF)_p(v) - ((DF)_p - (DF)_q)(v) \|_{\mathbb{R}^n} \geqslant$$
$$\| v \|_V - 1/2 \| v \|_V > 0.$$

The image $F(U')$ is open in $\mathbb{R}^n$. First observe that the image $F(U')$ contains the ball $B_{\mathbb{R}^n}(F(p), r/2)$. Indeed, define for given $a \in B_{\mathbb{R}^n}(F(p), r/2)$ recursively points $p_k \in B_V(p, r)$ by $p_0 = p$ and

$$p_{k+1} = p_k - (DF)_p^{-1}(F(p_k) - a).$$

Observe, $p_1 \in B_V(p, r/2)$ and

$$p_{k+1} - p_k = p_{k+1} - p_k - (DF)_p^{-1}(F(p_{k+1}) - F(p_k))$$
$$\| p_{k+1} - p_k \|_V \leqslant 1/2 \| p_k - p_{k-1} \|_V$$

which shows that the sequence (p_k) is a Cauchy sequence with limit $q = \lim_{k \to \infty} p_k \in B_V(p, r)$. Observe

$$(DF)_p^{-1}(F(q) - a) = \lim_{k \to \infty} (DF)_p^{-1}(F(p_k) - a) \lim_{k \to \infty} p_k - p_{k+1} = 0$$

therefore $F(q) = a$ showing $B_{\mathbb{R}^n}(F(p), r/2) \subset F(U')$ as claimed. So, $F(U')$ is a neighborhood of $F(p)$.

The analogous argumentation applies for showing that for all $q \in U'$ the image $F(U')$ is a neighborhood of $F(q)$ since $(DF)_q$ is an isomorphism as seen above. So, $F(U')$, being a neighborhood of all its points, is open in $\mathbf{R}^n$.

Let the map $G : F(U') \to U'$ be the inverse of the map F. For $a, b \in F(U')$ observe

$$\| b - a \|_{\mathbb{R}^n} = \| F(G(b)) - F(G(a)) \|_{\mathbb{R}^n}$$
$$\geqslant 1/2 \| G(b) - G(a) \|_V$$

proving that G is Lipschitz continuous.

For $a, a + h \in F(U')$ put $a = F(q)$, $a + h = F(q + v)$. The maps F, G being reciprocal Lipschitz bijections with uniform Lipschitz constants 2, it follows $1/2 \leqslant \| h \|_{\mathbb{R}^n} | / | v \|_V \leqslant 2$. From the three term expansion

$$F(q + v) = F(q) + (DF)_q(v) + \mathrm{Rest}_q^F(v)$$

follows $h = (DF)_q(v) + \mathrm{Rest}_q^F(v)$. One obtains a three term expansion with the typical properties for G at the point a as follows

$$G(a+h)=G(F(q+v))=q+v=G(a)+(DF)_q^{-1}(h)-(DF)_q^{-1}(\mathrm{Rest}_q^F(v))$$

In particular the differential of G at a is given by

$$(DG)_a=(DF)_q^{-1}=(DF)_{G(a)}^{-1}$$

which proves that the map G is continuously differentiable if the map F is continuously differentiable. Also G is smooth if F is so. Composing F with the canonical linear coordinates of $\mathbb{R}^n$ yields a differentiable system of coordinates $x=(x_1,x_2,\cdots,x_n)$ on U'.

Let $U\subset V$ be an open subset in a vector space V of dimension n. Let $p\in U$ be a point. Basic examples of rigidity of fields are:

Theorem 2.16 Basic Smooth Rigidities. *Let $U\subset V$ be open in a vector space V of finite dimension.*

—a). Let $f: U\to\mathbb{R}$ be a smooth function with $(Df)_p\neq 0$, $p\in U$. Then there exist at p local smooth coordinates (U',x) with $f(q)=x_1(q)$, $q\in U'$.

—b). Let $f: U\to\mathbb{R}^k$, $1\leqslant k\leqslant n$ be smooth with $Rank((Df)_p)=k$, $p\in U$.

Then there exist at p local smooth coordinates (U',x) with $f(q)=(x_1(q),x_2(q),\cdots,x_k(q))$, $q\in U'$.

—c). Let $\omega: U\to V^*$ be a closed 1-differential form with $\omega_p\neq 0$, $p\in U$. Then there exist at p local smooth coordinates (U',x) with $\omega=dx_1$ on U'.

—d). Let $X_1,X_2,\cdots,X_n: U\to V$ be smooth vector fields such that at $p\in U$ the fields are linearly independent and the Lie brackets $[X_i,X_j]_{Lie}$, $1\leqslant i<j\leqslant n$, vanish on U. Then there exist at p local smooth coordinates (U',x) with on $X_i=\frac{\partial}{\partial x_i}$, $i=1,2,\cdots,n$ on U'.

—e). Let $X: U\to V$ be a smooth vector field with $X_p\neq 0$, $p\in U$. Then there exist at p local smooth coordinates (U',x) with $X_q=\frac{\partial}{\partial x_1}$, $q\in U'$.

Proof: —a)

Choose a basis $v_1,v_2,\cdots,v_n$ for V such that $(Df)_p(v_1)=1$. Let $(y_1,y_2,\cdots,y_n)$ be the linear function on V with $y_i(v_j)=\delta_i^j$. Let $F: U\to\mathbb{R}^n$ be defined by $F(q)=(f(q),y_2(q),\cdots,y_n(q))\in\mathbb{R}^n$. Now apply to F the Theorem Constructing Local Coordinates and get local coordinates (U',x) at p. Clearly $f=x_1$ on U'.

—b). Choose a basis $v_1, v_2, \cdots, v_n$ for V such that $(Df)_p(v_i) = e_i$, $i = 1,2,\cdots,k$. Define $F: U \to \mathbb{R}^n$ by $F(q) = (f(q), y_{k+1}, \cdots, y_n) \in \mathbb{R}^k \times \mathbb{R}^{n-k} = \mathbb{R}^n$. Apply to F the Theorem Constructing Local Coordinates and get local coordinates (U', x) at p with $f = (x_1, x_2, \cdots, x_k)$ on U'.

—c). Choose $U' \subset U$ to be an open star shaped neighborhood of p. Let $f: U' \to \mathbb{R}$ be with $df = \omega$. Apply -a) and get local coordinates (U'', x) with $\omega = dx_1$ on U''.

—d). Choose a star shaped open neighborhood $U' \subset U$ of p such that at $q \in U'$ the vector fields are linearly independent. Define differential 1-forms ω_i on U' by $\omega_i(X_j) = \delta_i^j$. The forms are closed. Let $f_i: U' \to \mathbb{R}$ be with $df_i = \omega_i$. Apply the Theorem Constructing Local Coordinates to $F = (f_1, f_2, \cdots, f_n)$ and get local coordinates (U'', x). Observe $x_i = f_i$. Hence, $X_i = \dfrac{\partial}{\partial x_i}, i = 1,2,\cdots,n$ on U''.

—e) Choose a basis $v_1, v_2, \cdots, v_n$ for V with $v_1 = X_p$. Let $B_\epsilon(\mathbb{R}^n)$ be the "box". $\{h \in \mathbb{R}^n \mid |x_i(h)| < \epsilon, i = 1,2,\cdots,n\}$ Define the map $\beta: B_\epsilon(\mathbb{R}^n) \to V$ by $h \mapsto p + \sum_{i=2}^{n} x_i(h) v_i$. Let $\epsilon_0 > 0$ be such that for all $h \in B_{\epsilon_0}(\mathbb{R}^n)$ the solution curve $t \in]-\epsilon_0, \epsilon_0[\mapsto \phi_X(\beta(h), t) \in U$ of the differential equation corresponding to the vector field X with initial condition $\beta(h)$ exists. Define the map $G: B_{\epsilon_0}(\mathbb{R}^n) \to V$ by $h \mapsto \phi_X(\beta(h), x_1(h))$. The map G is continuously differentiable and $(DG)_p(e_i) = v_i$. So, the main part of the proof of the Construction of Local Coordinates applies, hence G maps injectively a smaller box $B_\epsilon(\mathbb{R}^n)$ onto an open neighborhood U' of p and $F = G^{-1}$ is continuously differentiable too. The composition of F with the canonical coordinate functions of $\mathbb{R}^n$ provides a local coordinate system (U', x) such that $X = \dfrac{\partial}{\partial x_i}$ on U' holds.

Point-e) of previous theorem affirms that the solution curves of the differential equation corresponding to a smooth vector field X near a point p with $X_p \neq 0$ are segments. More precisely, expressed using the local coordinates (U', x) the segments with x_1 running in $]-\epsilon, \epsilon[$ and the other coordinates fixed. In particular a solution curve leaves the flow box after at most every 2ϵ-time interval. The coordinates (U', x) are called *local flow box coordinates* for the vector field X.

The local rigidity of smooth non-vanishing vector fields leads to a global result for vector fields on the plane.

Theorem 2. 17 Poincar'e-Bendixon Theorem. *Let* X: $\mathbb{R}^2 \to \mathbb{R}^2$ *be a smooth vector field. Assume that the forward solution* $t \in [0, +\infty[\mapsto \phi_X(p, t)$ *exists and is a bounded planar curve. Let* K *be the closure of* $\{\phi_X(p, t) \mid t \in [0, +\infty]\}$ *in* $\mathbb{R}^2$. *Assume that* $X_q \neq 0$, $q \in K$, *holds. Then there exist a periodic solution* γ: $\mathbb{R} \to \mathbb{R}^2$ *with image in* K *of the differential equation corresponding to* X, *see figure 7.*

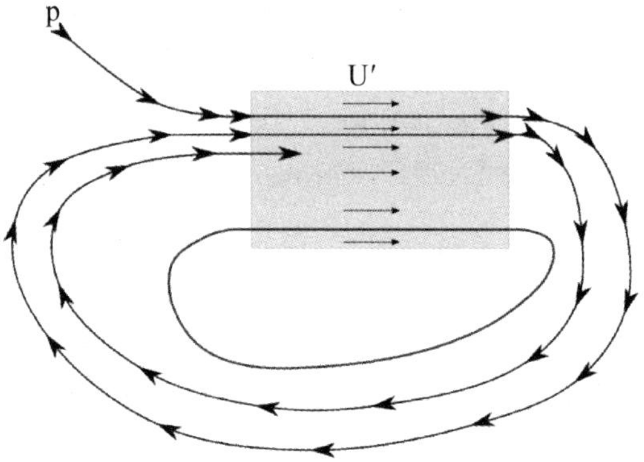

Figure 7　The red limiting periodic trajectory

Proof: The closure K is compact. Cover K with finitely many flow boxes. The solution $t \in [0, +\infty[\mapsto \phi_X(p, t)$ leaves each flow box after a time interval of positive length that is from below uniformly bounded from below. Hence one flow box (U', x) is run through infinitely many times by the trajectory $t \in [0, +\infty[\mapsto \varphi_X(p, t)$. If the trace of that trajectory on U' has finitely many connected components, the trajectory $t \in [0, +\infty[\mapsto \phi_X(p, t)$ is periodic. If there are infinitely many connected components, those components accumulate in $U' \cap K$ to the trace on U' of a periodic trajectory . This limiting trajectory is part of a periodic solution.

Exercise 33: *Let* X *be a smooth vector field on* $\mathbb{R}^2$ *for which there exists a bounded forward solution* $t \in [0, +\infty[\mapsto \phi_X(p, t)$. *Show that* X *vanishes at a point* $q \in \mathbb{R}^2$.

2.6 Differentiation in Banach spaces

A *Banach space* is a vector space E together with a norm $\| ? \|_E : V \rightarrow \mathbb{R}$ such that E is *complete*, i.e. such that every Cauchy sequence in E converges to a limit belonging to E. Clearly, a finite dimensional normed vector space $(V, \| ? \|_V)$ is a Banach space. A typical example of an infinite dimensional Banach space is the space $C^0([0,1], \mathbb{R})$ of all continuous functions $f: [0,1] \rightarrow \mathbb{R}$ equipped with the supremum norm $\| f \|_{C^0} = \sup_{t \in [0,1]} | f(t) |$. The choice of norm is important, for instance $C^0([0,1], \mathbb{R})$ equipped with the L^1-norm $\| f \|_{L^1} = \int_0^1 |f(t)| dt$ is not a Banach space. The same remark holds for the L^2-norm $\| f \|_{L^2} = \left(\int_0^1 |f(t)|^2 dt \right)^{\frac{1}{2}}$. Both the L^1 and L^2-norm compare only on one side with the C^0-norm. In fact they compare from below as follows:

$\| f \|_{L^2} \leqslant \| f \|_{L^1} \leqslant \| f \|_{C^0}$.

An important result, due to Baire-Banach-Schauder that we will study in a later section concerns two norms $\| ? \|_1$ and $\| ? \|_2$ on a vector space E such that the first compares from below or from above to the second. If E equipped with the norm $\| ? \|_1$ and E equipped with the norm $\| ? \|_2$ are both Banach spaces, then the norms compare, i.e. there exists a constant $C > 1$ such that $1/C \| f \|_1 \leqslant \| f \|_2 \leqslant C \| f \|_1$, $f \in E$, holds. In particular the topologies on E provided by the norms $(E, \| ? \|_1)$ and $(E, \| ? \|_2)$ coincide. This result is elementary for Banach spaces of finite dimension, and not at all elementary in general.

Let $(E, \| ? \|_E)$ and $(F, \| ? \|_F)$ be normed spaces and let $A: E \rightarrow F$ a linear map. In the case of finite dimensional spaces a linear map is continuous. This is no longer true in general. The following theorem characterises the continuous maps among the linear ones.

Theorem 2.18 *Let $A: E \rightarrow F$ be a linear map between normed spaces $(E, \| ? \|_E)$ and $(F, \| ? \|_F)$. The following are equivalent:*

—A is continuous,

—A is continuous at $0 \in E$,

—there exists a constant $C \geqslant 0$ such that the inequality

$$\| A(u) \|_F \leqslant C \| u \|_E, u \in E,$$

holds.

The proof follows immediately from the definitions.

Let $(E, \| ? \|_E)$ and $(F, \| ? \|_F)$ be normed spaces. Let $U \subset E$ be open in E and let $f: U \to F$ be a map. Let $p \in U$ be a point. The map is *differentiable* at p if there exists a three term expansion with the typical properties

$$f(p+h) = f(p) + L(h) + \text{Rest}(h), \quad h \in E, a+h \in U$$

such that moreover the linear map $L: E \to F$ is continuous.

The Theorem Construction of local Coordinates uses as input a continuously differentiable map $F: U \to \mathbb{R}^n$ defined on an open set in a vector space V of finite dimension n and moreover at a point $p \in U$ the differential $(DF)_p: V \to \mathbb{R}^n$ was assumed to be an isomorphism of vector spaces. A first step in the proof was the construction of Cauchy sequences in V and using the fact that in a finite dimensional vector space every Cauchy sequence converges in V. It followed the existence of an open neighborhood U' of p in U such that the image $F(U')$ is open in $\mathbb{R}^n$ together with the construction of a continuously differentiable map $G: F(U') \to U'$ such that G and the restriction of F to U' are reciprocal bijections. This part of the proof works in the more general setting of Banach spaces and proves:

Theorem 2.19 Inverse Mapping Theorem. *Let $U \subset E$ be open in a Banach space E. Let $p \in U$ be a point. Let $f: U \to F$ be a differentiable map with values in a normed space F, such that the differential $(Df)_p: E \to F$ is bijective, continuous with continuous reciprocal $((Df)_p)^{-1}: F \to E$ map. Then there exists an open neighborhood $U' \subset U$ of p such that f maps bijectively U' to an open neighborhood $f(U')$ of $f(p)$ in F. Moreover the reciprocal map $g: f(U') \to U'$ is differentiable.*

The differential at a point of a function with vectors as arguments and as values was introduced in the more general context of Banach and Fréchet spaces by Maurice Fréchet, see the books of Henri Cartan[23,24] and Jean Dieudonné[31,32].

2.7 Sard's Theorem

Let $f:]a,b[\to \mathbb{R}$ be a differentiable function. Moreover we assume that the derivative $f':]a,b[\to \mathbb{R}$ is continuous. Remember $f'(t) \stackrel{\text{def}}{=} (Df)_t(1)$. At a point $t \in]a,b[$ with $f'(t) \neq 0$ we can say something about the local behaviour at t of f, namely in a neighborhood $]t-\epsilon, t+\epsilon[\cap]a,b[$ the function f is strictly monotone. At a point $t \in]a,b[$ with $f'(t)=0$ we cannot say much about the local behaviour of f, except if moreover f'' is continuous and $f''(t) \neq 0$ holds. In this case f has at t a local maximum or minimum and is near t strictly convex or concave.

A point t with $f'(t)=0$ is called a critical point of f. Critical since a statement, without making further assumptions, about the local behaviour at t of f is not possible. A point t with $f'(t)=0$ and $f''(t) \neq 0$ is called a good critical point.

A function can have many critical points. Take for example a constant function.

A critical value of f is the value $f(t)$ at a critical point t of f. Can a function have many critical values? For instance a constant function has many critical points but only one critical value.

In order to state a first result of Arthur Sard[91] we need the following definition. Arthur Sard (1909–1980) was an American mathematician. A subset X in $\mathbb{R}$ is *Jordan small* if for every $\epsilon > 0$ there exist finitely many intervals $[a_i, b_i]$, $1 \leqslant i \leqslant N$, that cover X and of total lengths $\sum_{i=1}^{N}(b_i - a_i) < \epsilon$.

Marie Ennemond Camille Jordan (1838–1922) was a French mathematician.

Theorem 2.20 Sard in dimension 1. *Let $f: [a,b] \to \mathbb{R}$ be continuously differentiable. Then the set of critical values of f is Jordan small.*

Proof: Given $\epsilon > 0$, let $m\left(f', \frac{\epsilon}{b-a}\right) > 0$ be a continuity modulus for f' and

$\frac{\epsilon}{b-a}$, i. e. for $t,s \in [a,b]$ with $|t-s| < m\left(f', \frac{\epsilon}{b-a}\right)$ the inequality $|f'(t) - f'(s)| < \frac{\epsilon}{b-a}$ holds. For $N \in \mathbb{N}$ with $\frac{b-a}{N} < m\left(f', \frac{\epsilon}{b-a}\right)$ we subdivide the interval $[a,b]$ into N intervals of length $\frac{b-a}{N}$. Let C_i, $1 \leqslant i \leqslant K$, be the list of intervals in this subdivision that contain a critical point of f. We have $K \leqslant N$. We also have

$$\text{Length}\,(f(C_i)) \leqslant \int_{C_i} |f'(t)|\,\mathrm{d}t \leqslant \frac{b-a}{N}\frac{\epsilon}{b-a} = \frac{\epsilon}{N}.$$

The finitely many intervals $f(C_i)$, $1 \leqslant i \leqslant K$, cover the set of critical values of f and have total length less ϵ.

Theorem 2.21 *Let f: $[a,b] \to \mathbb{R}$ be twice continuously differentiable. Let L: $\mathbb{R} \to \mathbb{R}$, $L(t) = \lambda t$ be linear with λ not a critical value of f'. The function $g \overset{def}{=} f - L$: $[a,b] \to \mathbb{R}$ has finitely many critical points, all being good.*

Proof: Let t be a critical point of g, i.e. $g'(t) = f'(t) - \lambda = 0$. Since λ is not a critical value of f', we conclude $f''(t) \neq 0$, hence $g''(t) = f''(t) - L''(t) = f''(t) \neq 0$ and the critical point t of g is good. At an accumulation point s of critical points of g we would have $g'(s) = 0$ by the continuity of g' and also $g''(s) = 0$ by the theorem of Rolle together with the continuity of g''. This is impossible since s would be a non good critical point of g. An infinity of critical points of g is excluded, since otherwise by the compactness of $[a,b]$ an accumulation of critical points of g would follow.

As consequence we see that for a continuously twice differentiable function f: $[a,b] \to \mathbb{R}$ many linear functions L : $\mathbb{R} \to \mathbb{R}$ exist such that $f - L$ has only good critical points. In particular we can choose $L(t) = \lambda t$ with λ arbitrarily small. Moreover we can choose L such that $f - L$ has different values at different critical points or boundary points a, b.

It follows that the counting function

$$s \in \mathbb{R} \mapsto \#\{t \in [a,b] \mid f(t) - L(t) = s\} \in \mathbb{N}$$

changes by ± 2 or ± 1 for $s_{\pm} \overset{def}{=} s \pm \epsilon$ if s is a critical value or if s is a boundary value.

Let Graph$(f) \subset \mathbb{R} \times \mathbb{R}$ be the graph of the function f in the Cartesian plane with X and Y axes. We can change the X-axis to a new X'-axis with $X' \overset{def}{=}$

Graph(L) and remark that the graph Graph(f) of f with respect to the axes X, Y is also the graph of $f - L$ with respect to the axes X', Y.

Changing the system of axes from X, Y to X', Y amounts to changing the coordinate functions x, y to the functions $x, y - L(x)$. We have learned from the above that a function $y = f(x)$ with continuous second derivative cannot be made responsible for having a "bad graph". It is rather due to the choice of coordinates.

Here we think that a graph is "good" if we see only finitely many critical points, all maxima and minima with strictly concave or convex local behaviour. This kind of graphs have been studied at high school. We did not know at high school that every graph of a C^2-function becomes "good" by turning a little the X-axis. This applies for instance to the function

$$y = f(x) \stackrel{\text{def}}{=} (1 - \cos(x^2))\sin\left(\frac{1}{x}\right).$$

Does the above remains true for mappings defined on an open subset U in a real vector space V of finite dimension and with values in a real vector space W of the same dimension? The answer is very short: yes. In order to formulate it we need to adapt some definitions.

Let $g: U \to W$ be a continuously differentiable mapping. If the differential $(Dg)_p: V \to W$ is an isomorphism, we understand the local behaviour of g at p by the Theorem of local inversion. More generally, if the differential $(Dg)_p: V \to W$ is injective or surjective the local behaviour at p of the mapping g is equal to the local behaviour of the linear map $(Dg)_p: V \to W$. So, a point p is called a critical point if the differential $(Dg)_p$ is not of maximal rank, i.e. not an isomorphism, not injective or not surjective. Let $f: U \to \mathbb{R}$ be a continuously differentiable function. If $(Df)_p \neq 0$ at a point $p \in U$ we understand the local behaviour of f at p by the implicit function theorem. So p is a critical point of f if $(Df)_p = 0$. Remember, each time a main tool for the local study of functions/mappings fails, we have a critical situation.

Let W be equipped with a basis $e_1, e_2, \cdots, e_n$. The basic cube in W is the subset $B \stackrel{\text{def}}{=} \{t_1e_1 + t_2e_2 + \cdots + t_ne_n \mid 0 \leqslant t_i \leqslant 1\}$. An affine cube C in W is the image $C \stackrel{\text{def}}{=} \phi(B)$ under an affine map $w \in W \mapsto A(w) + w_0 \in W$, $w_0 \in W$, $A \in \operatorname{Hom}(W, W)$. We declare the volume of $C \stackrel{\text{def}}{=} \phi(B)$ to be the absolute value of the determinant of A . A subset X of W is *Jordan small* if for every $\epsilon > 0$ there exists a finite family $C_1, C_2, \cdots, C_N$ of affine cubes in W , that cover X and with total volume less ϵ. The high dimensional, both range and target, Sard's Theorem[91] is:

Theorem 2.22 Arthur Sard. *Let V and W be real vector spaces of finite dimensions n and m and let U be open in V. Let $g: U \to W$ be k-times continuously differentiable, $k \geqslant \max\{n-m+1, 1\}$. Let $C \subset U$ be an affine cube. Then the set of critical values of the restriction $g_{|C}$ to C is Jordan small in W.*

For the proof in case $n \neq m$ see the book[69] of John Milnor.

Proof: We consider only the case $n = m$. We choose in V a basis such that C is a translation of the basic cube. Also we work in V with the maximum norm $\| \ \|_V$ relative to this basis. In W we will work with a norm that derives from a scalar product. For $p \in U$ we denote by $\|(dg)_p\|_{\text{Operator}}$ the norm of $(dg)_p$: $V \to W$. Let b be an upper bound for $\|(dg)_p\|_{\text{Operator}}, p \in C$. Given $\epsilon > 0$, let $m(df, \epsilon) > 0$ be a continuity modulus for the restriction of dg to C , i.e. for $p, q \in C$ with $\|p - q\|_V < m(dg, \epsilon)$ the inequality $\|(dg)_p - (dg)_q\|_{Operator} < \epsilon$ holds. For $N \in \mathbb{N}$ with $\dfrac{1}{N} < m(dg, \epsilon)$ we subdivide the cube C in $N^{\text{Dim}(V)}$ in sub-cubes by cutting C along hyperplanes parallel to the faces of C in such a way that the sub-cubes are congruent pairwise by translations. Let C_i, $1 \leqslant i \leqslant K$, be the list of sub-cubes that contain a critical point p_i of g . We have $K \leqslant N^{\text{Dim}(V)}$. We wish to cover $g(C_i)$ by finitely many affine cubes of W and control the total volume. We use for $p_i + h \in C_i$ the three term expansion for g at the point p_i .

$$g(p_i + h) = g(p_i) + (Dg)_{p_i}(h) + \int_0^1((Dg)_{p_i+th} - (Dg)_{p_i})(h)\,dt.$$

Since $\|h\|_V \leqslant \dfrac{1}{N} < m(dg, \epsilon)$ we have

$$\left\| \int_0^1((Dg)_{p_i+th} - (Dg)_{p_i})(h)\,dt \right\|_W \leqslant \frac{\epsilon}{N}.$$

We see that the image $g(C_i)$ is contained in the ϵ/N-tubular neighborhood of $g(p_i) + (Dg)_{p_i}(C_i)$. The cube C_i has $2\text{Dim}(V)$ faces F_{ij}, $1 \leqslant j \leqslant 2\text{Dim}(V)$. Since $(Dg)_{p_i}$ is not injective the image $(Dg)_{p_i}(C_i)$ is covered by the $g(p_i)$ translates of the images $(Dg)_{p_i}(F_{ij})$ which are cubes of dimension $\mathrm{Dim}(W)-1$ in W. The spanning vectors of such a cube $(Dg)_{p_i}(F_{ij})$ have $\|\ \|_W$ norm less than $\frac{b}{N}$. Hence, since we work in W with norm and volume deriving from a scalar product, its ϵ/N-tubular neighborhood is contained in an affine cube of volume less than

$$\left(\frac{b}{N}+\frac{2\epsilon}{N}\right)^{\mathrm{Dim}(W)-1}\frac{2\epsilon}{N}$$

by the Hadamard inequality. We conclude that $g(C_i)$ is covered by $2\mathrm{Dim}(V)$ affine cubes of total volume

$$2\mathrm{Dim}(V)\left(\frac{b}{N}+\frac{2\epsilon}{N}\right)^{\mathrm{Dim}(W)-1}\frac{2\epsilon}{N}.$$

The image $g(\cup C_i)$ contains the critical values of the restriction of g to C and is covered in W by less than $2\mathrm{Dim}(V)N^{\mathrm{Dim}(V)}$ affine cubes of total volume less

$$2N^{\mathrm{Dim}(V)}\mathrm{Dim}(V)\left(\frac{b}{N}+\frac{2\epsilon}{N}\right)^{\mathrm{Dim}(W)-1}\frac{2\epsilon}{N}.$$

It suffices to work with $0<\epsilon\leqslant 1$. Our total volume estimate simplifies then to

$$4\mathrm{Dim}(V)\,(b+2)^{\mathrm{Dim}(W)-1}\epsilon$$

which can be made arbitrarily small.

Theorem 2.23 *Notations U, V, C as above. Let $f\colon U\to\mathbb{R}$ be twice continuously differentiable. Let $L\colon V\to\mathbb{R}$ be linear with $L\in V^*$ not being a critical value of $df\colon C\to V^*$. Then the function $g\overset{def}{=}f-L\colon U\to\mathbb{R}$ has finitely many critical points $p\in C$, all such that $(D(df))_p\colon V\to V^*$ is an isomorphism.*

Proof: Let $p\in C$ be a critical point of g, i.e. $(Dg)=(Df)_p-L=0$. Since L is not a critical value of df, we conclude that $(D(df))_p\colon V\to V^*$ is an isomorphism, hence $(D(dg))_p=(D(df))_p-(D(dL))_p=(D(df))_p$ is also an isomorphism. The remaining part will be proved in the next section.

Exercise 34: *Let f be the differentiable function on $\mathbb{R}$ defined by the formula $x^4\sin(\frac{1}{x})$. For which $a\in\mathbb{R}$ does $x^4\sin(\frac{1}{x})+ax$ have only good critical points?*

2.8 Morse Lemma, Morse functions

Let $f:]-1,+1[\to \mathbb{R}$ be a twice continuously differentiable function with $f'(0)=0, f''(0)\neq 0$. Assume $f''(t)>0$ on $]-\epsilon,+\epsilon[$. Define the function $y:]-\epsilon,+\epsilon[\to \mathbb{R}$ by $y(t) \overset{\text{def}}{=} \sqrt{f(t)-f(0)}, t \geq 0$ and $y(t) \overset{\text{def}}{=} \sqrt{f(t)-f(0)}, t < 0$. The function y will be twice differentiable with $f_{l]-\epsilon,+\epsilon[} = f(0) + y^2$. If $f''(t) < 0$, put $y(t) \overset{\text{def}}{=} \sqrt{f(t)-f(0)}, t \geq 0$ and $y(t) \overset{\text{def}}{=} -\sqrt{f(t)-f(0)}$, $t < 0$.

We then have $f_{|]-\epsilon,+\epsilon[} = f(0) - y^2$. In the first case f has at 0 a local minimum, in second a local maximum. The following is a generalisation due to Harold Calvin Marston Morse (1892–1977), an American mathematician, for functions on open sets in vector spaces[73].

Theorem 2.24 Morse Lemma. *Let $f: U \to \mathbb{R}$ be a twice continuously differentiable function defined on an open subset U in a real vector space V of finite dimension n. We assume f is critical at $p \in U$ and that $(D(df))_p: V \to V^*$ is an isomorphism. Then there exists an open subset $U' \subset U$ with $p \in U'$, twice differentiable functions $y_1, y_2, \cdots, y_n: U' \to \mathbb{R}$ with $y_i(p)=0$, which are on U' a system of differential coordinates, and with*

$$f_{|U'} = f(p) \pm y_1^2 \pm y_2^2 \pm \cdots \pm y_n^2.$$

A twice continuously differentiable function $f: U \to \mathbb{R}$, $U \subset V$, such that at every critical point p the second differential $(D(df))_p: V \to V^*$ is an isomorphism, which is called a *Morse function*. From the Morse Lemma it follows that critical points of Morse functions do not accumulate. This observation finishes the proof of the last Theorem of the previous section.

The Morse Lemma is followed by induction from its stronger version.

Theorem 2.25 Strong Morse Lemma. *Let $f: U \to \mathbb{R}$ be a twice continuously differentiable function defined on an open subset U in a real vector space V of finite dimension n. We assume f is critical at $p \in U$ and that $(D(df))_p \neq 0$. Then there exists an open subset $U' \subset U$ with $p \in U'$, twice differentiable functions $y_1, x_2, \cdots, x_n: U' \to \mathbb{R}$ with $y_i(p)=0$, which are on U' a system of differential coordinates,* *and a function* $g:\mathbb{R}^{n-1}\rightarrow\mathbb{R}$ *with*

$$f_{|U'}=f(p)\pm y_1^2+g(x_2,x_3,\cdots,x_n).$$

Proof: of the Morse Lemma. If $(D(df))_p$ is an isomorphism, $(D(df))_p\neq 0$ and the Strong Morse Lemma applies. The Hessian of f at p now splits as a direct sum of the Hessian of $\pm y_1^2$ at p and the Hessian of g at $0\in\mathbb{R}^{n-1}$. So, if $n>1$, the Strong Morse Lemma applies again for the critical point $0\in\mathbb{R}^{n-1}$ of g. Repeating $n-1$ times we get the Morse Lemma.

Proof: of the Strong Morse Lemma. The Hessian $(D(df))_p$ is symmetric and by assumption not 0. Let $e_1, e_2,\cdots,e_n$ be a basis of V such that $(D(df))_p(e_1)(e_1)\neq 0$. Let $z_1,x_2,\cdots,x_n$ be linear coordinates with $z_1(p)=0$, $dz_1(e_1)=1, dz_1(e_i)=0$, $x_i(p)=0$, $i=2,3,\cdots$, and $dx_i(e_j)=\delta_i^j$, $i,j=2,3,\cdots$. The function f restricted to the curve $C_0\overset{\text{def}}{=}\{q\in V\mid x_2(q)=x_3(q)=\cdots=x_n(q)=0\}$ is near p strictly convex or concave with its extremum at p. Think the curve C_0 locally near p as z_1-axis and moreover parametrized by $s\in\,]a,b[\,\mapsto\gamma(t)\in C_0$ with $\gamma(0)=p$ and $\frac{\mathrm{d}}{\mathrm{d}s}z_1(\gamma(t))\equiv 1$. The composed function $f\circ\gamma$ will be convex or concave near $0\in\,]a,b[$. We may assume

$$\frac{\partial^2 f}{\partial^2_{z_1}}(p)=((D(df))_p(e_1))(e_1)>0$$

and $f_{|C_0}$ will be strictly convex with a minimum at p.

Let $T\overset{\text{def}}{=}\{t\in V\mid z_1(t)=0\}$ be the $x_2, x_3,\cdots,x_n$ coordinate hyperplane through p. For $t\in T$ and t near p let C_t be the curve $C_t\overset{\text{def}}{=}\{q\in V\mid x_i(q)=x_i(t)\}$. The restriction $f_{|C_t}$ is strictly convex near a point $q_t\in C_t$. Let $k(z_1,x_2,\cdots,x_n)=f$ be the local expression of f in the coordinates $z_1,x_2,\cdots,x_n$. Let $m(x_2(t), x_3(t),\cdots,x_n(t))$ be the z_1 coordinate value of q_t. The number $m(x_2(t),x_3(t),\cdots,x_n(t))$ is implicitly defined by the equation $\frac{\partial k}{\partial z_1}(m(x_2(t),\cdots,x_n(t)),x_2(t),x_3(t),\cdots,x_n(t))=0$. The implicit function theorem applies since $\frac{\partial^2 f}{\partial z_1^2}(p)\neq 0$. We make a first coordinate change, only changing the first coordinate function: $z_1\overset{\text{def}}{=}z_1-m(x_2,x_3,\cdots,x_n)$, $x_2\overset{\text{def}}{=}x_2,\cdots,x_n\overset{\text{def}}{=}x_n$. In the new coordinate z_1 the minimum of f restricted to C_t is achieved at the point q_t with z_1

$(q_t) = 0$.

We make a second coordinate change by changing again only the new coordinate function z_1. For $q \in C_t$ we put $y_1(q) \overset{\text{def}}{=} \text{Sign}(z_1(q))\sqrt{f(q) - f(q_t)}$.

We have for $q \in V$ locally at p

$f(q) = y_1(q)^2 + k(m(x_2(q), x_3(q), \cdots, x_n(q)), x_2(q), \cdots, x_n(q))$.

Finally, putting $g(x_2, \cdots, x_n) \overset{\text{def}}{=} k(m(x_2, x_3, \cdots, x_n), x_2, \cdots, x_n)$ we get

$$f = f(p) + y_1^2 + g(x_2, \cdots, x_n)$$

as required.

Applying r-times the Strong Morse lemma, the co-rank $n - r$ Morse lemma follows. The Morse lemma is in fact the special case $r = n$.

Theorem 2.26 Co-rank Morse Lemma. *Let $f: U \to \mathbb{R}$ be a twice continuously differentiable function defined on an open subset U in a real vector space V of finite dimension n. We assume f is critical at $p \in U$ and that the Hessian $(D(df))_p: V \to V^*$ has rank $r \geqslant 1$. Then there exists an open subset $U' \subset U$ with $p \in U'$, twice differentiable functions $y_1, y_2, \cdots, y_r, x_{n-r}, \cdots, x_n: U' \to \mathbb{R}$ with $y_i(p) = 0$, which are on U' a system of differential coordinates, and a function $g: \mathbb{R}^{n-1} \to \mathbb{R}$ with*

$$f_{|U'} = f(p) \pm y_1^2 \pm \cdots \pm y_r^2 + g(x_{n-r}, x_{n-r+1}, \cdots, x_n)$$

Exercise 35: *Study the 17 critical points of $f = xy(x^2+y^2-1)(x^2+y^2-1/4)$ on $\mathbb{R}^2$. Take figure 8 as an example.*

Exercise 36: *Two Morse functions $a, b: M \to \mathbb{R}$ are called family equivalent if there exists a smooth function $c: M \times [0,1] \to \mathbb{R}, (p,t) \mapsto c_t(p) \in \mathbb{R}$ such that the functions $c_t: M \to \mathbb{R}, t \in [0,1]$, are Morse functions with $a = c_0$, $b = c_1$. A maximal set of family equivalent functions is called a Morse family. Count the families of Morse functions on $\mathbb{R}$ with 5 critical points. A Morse function is called general if the number of critical points equals the number of critical values. Count the number of families of general Morse functions with 5 critical points. Count also those families for $n \in \mathbb{N}$ critical points and values.*

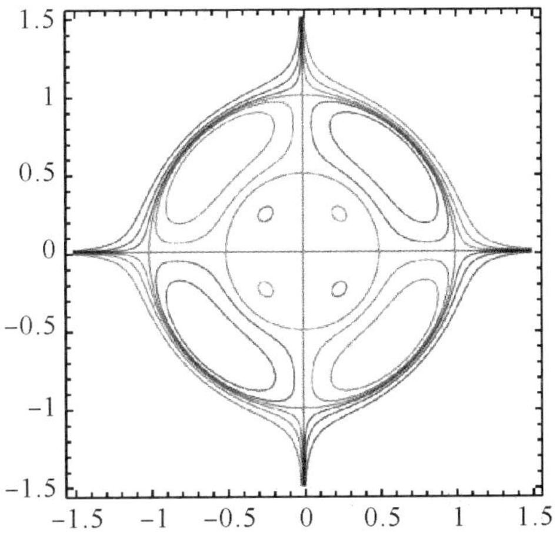

Figure 8 $-0.05, -0.02, -0.0065, 0, +0.0065, +0.02, +0.05$-**levels of** $f = -xy(x^2 + y^2 - 1)(x^2 + y^2 - 1/4)$.

Exercise 37: *A Morse function is called exceptional if it has two critical values. How many families of exceptional Morse functions on* $\mathbb{R}$ *exist? Do such families have polynomial members? Are those polynomials famous?*

Exercise 38: *How many families of exceptional Morse functions on the one and two dimensional spheres* S^1 *and* S^2 *exist?*

3 Geometry of Manifolds

3.1 Differential manifolds

We wish to paste together open subsets in vector spaces in order to get more general spaces on which fields and their operations are defined. We proceed in four or five steps.

1. Let A be a set. Let $(U_\alpha)_{\alpha \in A}$ be a family indexed by A of open subsets of a real vector space V of finite dimension. Let X be the disjoint union $X \stackrel{\text{def}}{=} \dot{\bigcup}_{\alpha \in A} U_\alpha$ with its topology.

2. Let $\sim$ be an equivalence relation on X. Let Y be the quotient topological space $Y \stackrel{\text{def}}{=} X/\sim$.

On X we wish to do all the constructions concerning fields of the first section. In the next steps 3 and 4 we impose on the equivalence relation $\sim$ properties, which will insure the possibility of executing all the constructions of the first section on Y.

3. For each couple $(\alpha, \beta) \in A \times A$ there exist (possibly empty) open subsets $U_{\alpha\beta} \subset U_\beta$ and $U_{\beta\alpha} \subset U_\alpha$ together with a differentiable map $\phi_{\alpha\beta}: U_{\alpha\beta} \to U_{\beta\alpha}$ such that the composition $\phi_{\beta\alpha} \circ \phi_{\alpha\beta}$ is the identity map of $U_{\alpha\beta}$. For a couple $(\alpha, \beta) \in A \times A$ with $\alpha = \beta$ the equality $U_{\alpha\alpha} = U_\alpha$ holds and the differential map $\phi_{\alpha\alpha}$ is the identity of $U_{\alpha\alpha}$. The equivalence relation $\sim$ is generated by $p \in U_{\alpha\beta} \sim \phi_{\alpha\beta}(p) \in U_{\beta\alpha}$.

4. For each triple $(\alpha, \beta, \gamma) \in A \times A \times A$ the restrictions to $U_{\alpha\gamma} \cap U_{\beta\gamma}$ of the composition $\phi_{\alpha\beta} \circ \phi_{\beta\gamma}$ and of $\phi_{\alpha\gamma}$ are equal maps into $U_{\gamma\alpha} \cap U_{\beta\alpha}$.

Let $\pi : X \to Y$ be the quotient map. It follows from the properties 3,4 that the map $\pi : X \to Y$ is open, and that the restrictions π_α of π to each U_α are injective. So, the family of images $\pi(U_\alpha) \subset Y$ is an open cover of Y. The family of pairs $(\pi(U_\alpha), \phi_\alpha)$ where $\phi_\alpha : \pi(U_\alpha) \to U_\alpha$ is the right inverse to the restriction of π to U_α are an atlas with differentiable transition maps for the space Y.

If we wish to have the Hausdorff separation property for the space Y we impose on the equivalence relation $\sim$ moreover:

5. For $p \in U_\alpha$ and $q \in U_\beta$ with $\pi(p) \neq \pi(q)$ there exist open subsets $U_\alpha' \subset U_\alpha$ and $U_\beta' \subset U_\beta$ with $p \in U_\alpha', q \in U_\beta'$ and $\pi(U_\alpha') \cap \pi(U_\beta') = \emptyset$.

In this text a manifold M is the data of families $(U_\alpha)_{\alpha \in A}$ and $(\phi_{\alpha\beta} : U_{\alpha\beta} \to U_{\beta\alpha})_{(\alpha,\beta) \in A \times A}$ as above with the properties from the steps 3,4,5.

Let M be a manifold. The dimension of M is by definition the dimension of the vector space V in which lie the open sets $(U_\alpha)_{\alpha \in A}$ of the first family. The topological space Y of step 2 is the underlying topological space of M. We say that a manifold M has a topological property if its underlying topological space has the property in question. Examples of topological properties are to be connected, simply connected, compact, homeomorphic to some topological space T, homotopic to some homotopy type H, ….

The family $(\pi_\alpha(U_\alpha))_{\alpha \in A}$ together with the family $(\phi_\alpha)_{\alpha \in A}$ of right inverses of the maps π_α is called the family of *charts* of M or is *atlas* for M, see figure 9.

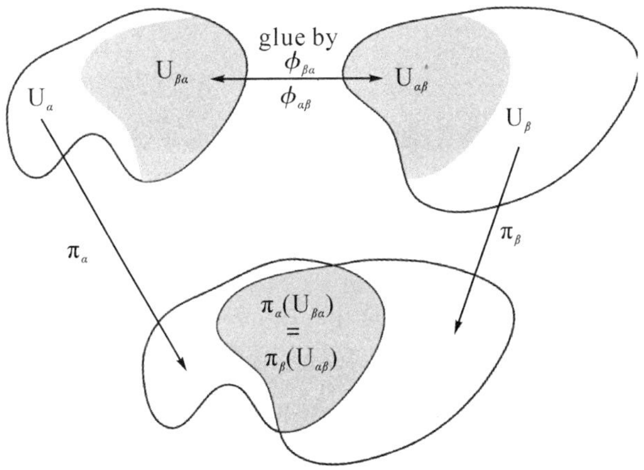

Figure 9 Gluing makes manifold. $\pi_{\alpha} |_{U_{\beta\alpha}} = \pi_\beta |_{U_{\alpha\beta}} \circ \phi_{\beta\alpha}$

Imaging that the underlying topological space is the surface of some planet Y. Different institutions, academies, armies organise expeditions and explore Y locally, Institution $\alpha \in A$ explores a region $\pi(U_\alpha)$ of Y. Important for building the appropriate theoretical language is that the expeditions take also place in the imagination of humans. The result of the efforts of Institution α is a paper map $U_\alpha \subset \mathbb{R}^2$ of the region $\pi(U_\alpha)$. The other Institutions, other expeditions, explore other regions $\pi(U_\beta)$, $\pi(U_\gamma)$, $\cdots$ of planet Y. Finally, the explored regions $\pi(U_\alpha)$, $\pi(U_\beta)$, $\pi(U_\gamma)$, $\cdots$ cover the planet Y and a lot of money has been spent. All paper maps are stored by an Academy in their library. A critical voice suddenly proposes to compare the results of the different expeditions. Regions $\pi(U_\alpha)$ and $\pi(U_\beta)$ of the planet sometimes overlap, so in the library of an important Academy one can draw subsets $U_{\beta\alpha} \overset{\text{def}}{=} (\pi_\alpha)^{-1}(\pi(U_\alpha) \cap \pi(U_\beta)) \subset U_\alpha$ and $U_{\alpha\beta} \overset{\text{def}}{=} (\pi_\beta)^{-1}(\pi(U_\alpha) \cap \pi(U_\beta)) \subset U_\beta$, and while deploring the waste of research resources, discover maps $(\phi_{\alpha\beta} : U_{\alpha\beta} \to U_{\beta\alpha})_{(\alpha,\beta) \in A \times A}$ that compare the paper maps drawn by the Institutions. Many years later in a newspaper appears the headline (see figure 10.):

The planet Y is a differentiable manifold.

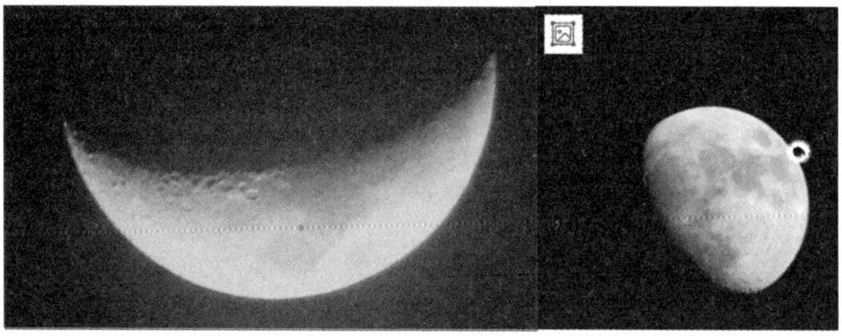

Figure 10 **Our moon, seen, November** 2017, **from ICTS Bangalore and December** 2019, **from BHU Varanasi**

Today humanity tries to describe the universe, but also our brain, music or the space of all DNA configurations as a manifold.

Let M be a differentiable manifold given by families $(U_\alpha)_{\alpha \in A}$ and $(\phi_{\alpha\beta} : U_{\alpha\beta} \to U_{\beta\alpha})_{(\alpha,\beta) \in A \times A}$. Let U_σ be a chart and assume that the underlying topological space Y is already covered by the family $\pi(U_\alpha)$, $\alpha \neq \sigma$. Strictly speaking, we have now two manifolds, M and also M' given by the families $(U_\alpha)_{\alpha \in A'}$

and $(\phi_{\alpha\beta}:U_{\alpha\beta}\rightarrow U_{\beta\alpha})_{(\alpha,\beta)\in A'\times A'}$ with $A'\stackrel{def}{=}A\setminus\{\sigma\}$. We declare that the manifolds *M and M'* are equivalent. More generally we declare that two manifolds N and M are equivalent if one can go from N to M by adding or deleting charts to the atlas keeping the underlying topological space fixed. Logically speaking, a manifold is an equivalence class of manifolds given by families $(U_\alpha)_{\alpha\in A}$ and $(\phi_{\alpha\beta}:U_{\alpha\beta}\rightarrow U_{\beta\alpha})_{(\alpha,\beta)\in A\times A}$ that satisfy the above properties 1,2,3,4 and maybe the property 5.

A manifold M is called *orientable* or is *oriented* if M admits a presentation or is presented with families$(U_\alpha)_{\alpha\in A}$ and $(\phi_{\alpha\beta}:U_{\alpha\beta}\rightarrow U_{\beta\alpha})_{(\alpha,\beta)\in A\times A}$ such that for all α,β, $p\in U_{\alpha\beta}$, the determinant of the differentials $(D\phi_{\alpha\beta})_p:V\rightarrow V$ is >0.

The real projective plane $P^2(\mathbb{R})$ is an example of a non orientable manifold. The real projective space $P^3(\mathbb{R})$ is an orientable manifold.

Examples:

1. Let $Y\subset\mathbb{R}^N$ be a subset in N-dimensional numerical space. We suppose the existence a differentiable proper map $F:\mathbb{R}^N\rightarrow\mathbb{R}^k$ having $0\in\mathbb{R}^k$ as regular value with $Y=F^{-1}(0)$. Then using the implicit function theorem, one can find an atlas with differentiable transition maps for the space Y.

2. Let $Y\subset\mathbb{R}^N$ be a subset in N-dimensional numerical space. We suppose the existence of a family$(S_\alpha)_{\alpha\in A}$ of open subsets in $\mathbb{R}^N$ covering Y and a family of proper above 0 regular differentiable maps $(F_\alpha:S_\alpha\rightarrow\mathbb{R}^k)_{\alpha\in A}$ with $Y\cap S_\alpha=F_\alpha^{-1}(0)$. Then again using the implicit function theorem, one can find an atlas with differentiable transition maps for the space Y.

3. Let M be a manifold given by families $(U_\alpha\subset V)_{\alpha\in A}$ and $(\phi_{\alpha\beta}:U_{\alpha\beta}\rightarrow U_{\beta\alpha})_{(\alpha,\beta)\in A\times A}$. We define the manifold TM by families $(U_\alpha\times V\subset V\times V)_{\alpha\in A}$ and $(T\phi_{\alpha\beta}:U_{\alpha\beta}\times V\rightarrow U_{\beta\alpha}\times V)_{(\alpha,\beta)\in A\times A}$, where $T\phi_{\alpha\beta}$ is the map

$$(p,u)\in U_{\alpha\beta}\times V\mapsto(\phi_{\alpha\beta}(p),(D\phi_{\alpha\beta})_p(u))\in U_{\beta\alpha}\times V.$$

The manifold TM is called the tangent space of M. It comes with a differentiable map $\pi:TM\rightarrow M$ which is induced by the projection maps $\pi_\alpha:U_\alpha\times V\rightarrow U_\alpha$. For each point $p\in M$ the fibre $\pi^{-1}(p)$ is a vector space isomorphic to V. The isomorphism of $\pi^{-1}(p)$ to V is not canonical, but depends on the chosen chart $p\in U_\alpha$.

4. We define the manifold T^*M by families $(U_\alpha\times V^*\subset V\times V^*)_{\alpha\in A}$ and $(T^*\phi_{\alpha\beta}:U_{\alpha\beta}\times V^*\rightarrow U_{\beta\alpha}\times V^*)_{(\alpha,\beta)\in A\times A}$, where $T^*\phi_{\alpha\beta}$ is the map

$$(p,L) \in U_{\alpha\beta} \times V^* \mapsto (\phi_{\alpha\beta}(p), L \circ (D\phi_{\beta\alpha})_p^{-1}) \in U_{\beta\alpha} \times V^*$$

The manifold T^*M is called the co-tangent space of M. Observe that the linear part of the transition map at $p \in U_{\alpha\beta}$ is the transpose of the inverse of $(D\phi_{\alpha\beta})_p$.

Manifolds of the examples 1 and 2 are sub-manifolds of the numerical space $\mathbb{R}^N$. Every manifold with a countable atlas of dimension n is diffeomorphic to a sub-manifold in $\mathbb{R}^{2n+1}$.

Please consider the following exercises:

Exercise 1: *Describe the real projective plane $P^2(\mathbb{R})$ as a sub-manifold in $\mathbb{R}^5$.*

Exercise 2: *Let $F: \mathbb{C}^2 \to \mathbb{C}$ be the complex function $F \stackrel{def}{=} z_1 z_2$. Show that the manifolds $L \stackrel{def}{=} F^{-1}(1)$, $\mathbb{C} \setminus \{0\}$ and $S^1 \times \mathbb{R}$ are diffeomorphic.*

Exercise 3: *The value 1 is a regular value of the determinant function on square matrices with real or complex entries. Conclude that the spaces of $n\times n$ matrices $Sl(n,\mathbb{R})$ and $Sl(n,\mathbb{C})$ of determinant 1 are manifolds.*

The group operation of multiplication $(A,B)\mapsto AB$ and the inverse map $A \mapsto A^{-1}$ are smooth.

Exercise 4: *Show that the manifolds $S^1\times \mathbb{R}^2$, $SL(2,\mathbb{R})$ and $PSL(2,\mathbb{R})$ are diffeomorphic.*

Exercise 5: *Show that the manifolds $S^3\times\mathbb{R}^3$ and $SL(2,\mathbb{C})$ are diffeomorphic.*

Exercise 6: *Show that the manifolds $SL(2,\mathbb{C})$ and $PSL(2,\mathbb{C})$ are not diffeomorphic.*

Exercise 7: *Let $ac, vel \subset \mathbb{R}^2$ be the planar subsets*

$$ac \stackrel{\text{def}}{=} \{p \in \mathbb{R}^2 \mid x(p) \geqslant 0 \wedge y(p) \geqslant 0\}$$

$$vel \stackrel{\text{def}}{=} \{p \in \mathbb{R}^2 \mid x(p) \geqslant 0 \vee y(p) > 0\}.$$

The logical symbol "$\wedge$" indicates the logical conjunction and the symbol "$\vee$" indicate the logical inclusive disjunction, see firure 11. Does there exist a homeomorphism $\phi:\mathbb{R}^2\to\mathbb{R}^2$ with $\phi(ac)=vel$? Does there exist a diffeomorphism $\phi: \mathbb{R}^2\to\mathbb{R}^2$ with $\phi(ac)=vel$?

Let the manifold M be given by families $(U_\alpha \subset V)_{\alpha\in A}$ and $(\phi_{\alpha\beta}: U_{\alpha\beta} \to U_{\beta\alpha})_{(\alpha,\beta)\in A\times A}$. We assume M to be compact and wish to realize M explicitly as a sub-manifold in a finite dimensional real vector space W. First we equip V with

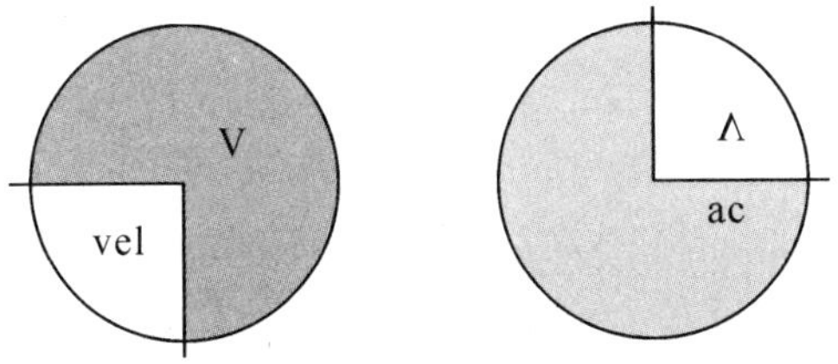

Figure 11 Intersection of the planar regions *ac* **and** *vel* **with the unit disc**

a scalar product and work with the induced norm $\| \ \|_V$ on V. For every point $p \in M$ choose in a chart U_α and an open ball $B(p, r_p) \subset U_\alpha$. The open balls $B(p, r_p/2)$ cover M, so let finitely many among them with centers $p_1, p_2, \cdots, p_k$ already cover M. We define mappings $\phi_i: M \to V \times \mathbb{R}$ as follows. For $q = p_i + h \in B(p_i, r_{p_i}/2) \subset U_{\alpha i} \subset V$ put $\phi_i(q) = (q, 0)$, for $q = p_i + h \in B(p_i, r_{p_i}) \backslash B(p_i, r_{p_i}/2)$ put $\phi_i(q) = [q - \chi(\|h\|_V]/r_{p_i}) h, \chi(\|h\|_V)/r_{pi}))$. Finally for $q / \in B(p_i, r_{pi})$ put $\phi_i(q) = (p_i, 1)$. Here χ is a C^∞-function, with $\chi(t) = 0$, $t < 1/2$, $\chi(t) = 1$, $t > 1$, χ positive and strictly monotone on $[1/2, 1]$. The image $\phi_i(M)$ is a topological sphere of Dim(M) = Dim(V) in V× $\mathbb{R}$.

Let ϕ $M \to (V \times \mathbb{R})^k$ be the product mapping

$$p \in M \mapsto \phi(p) = (\phi_1(p), \phi_2(p), \cdots, \phi_k(p)) \in (V \times \mathbb{R})^k.$$

The mapping ϕ is injective and its differential at every point is of rank Dim(M). So it is an embedding of M into a finite dimensional vector space $W = (V \times \mathbb{R})^k$.

Theorem 3. 1 *Let M be a manifold given by a countable family $(U_\alpha \subset V)_{\alpha \in A}$. Then there exists a Morse function $f: M \to \mathbb{R}$.*

The following proof uses an embedding of the manifold into a vector space of finite dimension, so still needs to be completed for non-compact manifolds.

Proof: First embed M by ϕ: $M \to W$ in a vector space W as above. For each cube $C \subset U_\alpha$, the set of all $L \in W^*$ such that the restriction to $\phi(C)$ is a Morse function is of full Lebesgue measure in W^*. Since M is covered by countably many cubes, the set of $L \in W^*$ such that the restriction to $\phi(M)$ is a Morse function is of full Lebesgue measure in W^*.

Exercise 8: *Let $p_0, p_1, \cdots, p_n$ be $(n+1)$ points in $\mathbb{R}^2$, $n > 1$. We assume p_0 and p_n at fixed position with $x(p_0) = y(p_0) = 0 = y(p_n)$ and $x(p_n) = n - \frac{1}{2}$.*

Further we assume that the points $p_i, 1 \leqslant i \leqslant n-1$, *can move in the plane, only constrained by* $(x(p_i)-x(p_{i-1}))^2+(y(p_i)-y(p_{i-1}))^2=1$, $1 \leqslant i \leqslant n$. *Let P the space of all possible positions of the points* p_i. *Show that P is a manifold.*

Exercise 9: *Continuation. Let* $f: P \to \mathbb{R}$ *be the function defined by* $\sum_{i=n}^{n} = (x(p_i)-x(p_{i+1}))(y(p_i)+y(p_{i+1}))$. *Show that f is a Morse function with two critical points. Prove that P is diffeomorphic to the sphere of dimension* $n-2$.

Exercise 10: *Show that the function Trace* : $Sl(2, \mathbb{R}) \to \mathbb{R}$ *is a Morse function with two critical points. Study the Morse index at the critical points.*

Exercise 11: *Show that the function Trace* : $Sl(2, \mathbb{C}) \to \mathbb{C}$ *is a complex Morse function with two critical points. Study the Morse index at the critical points of* $A \mapsto Re(Trace(A))$.

3.2 Fields on manifolds

Let M be a manifold given by a family $(U_\alpha \subset V)_{\alpha \in A}$ of open subsets in a fixed finite dimensional vectorspace V and a family of gluing maps $(\phi_{\alpha\beta}: U_{\alpha\beta} \to U_{\beta\alpha})_{(\alpha,\beta) \in A \times A}$. A family $(X_\alpha: U_\alpha \to V)_{\alpha \in A}$ of vector fields on each U_α defines a vector field on M if for all $(\alpha,\beta) \in A \times A$ the restriction of X_α to $U_{\beta\alpha}$ by the differential of $\phi_{\beta\alpha}$ is transformed to the restriction of X_β to $U_{\alpha\beta}$. If so, the family (X_α) defines a section of $\pi: TM \to M$. We call a map $X: M \to TM$ a *section* of the tangent bundle $\pi: TM \to M$, or also in short a section of TM, if $\pi \circ X$ is the identity map of M.

Sections of TM are called vector fields on M. Sections ω of T^*M are called 1-differential forms on M.

We have as before the insertion of a vector field in a 1-differential form ω. We have to check, that the value of the function $i_X\omega$ at a point $p \in M$ is independent of the chosen chart U_α containing p. We also check that the differential of a function f on M defines a 1-differential form df on M. The same is true for the Lie bracket of vector fields on M.

Our first definition of $d\omega$ uses the linear structure on U_α which is not preserved by the maps $\phi_{\beta\alpha}$. Hence it is not immediately clear that the exterior differential is well defined on a manifold. The alternative definition from exercise 12 helps out and the exterior differential is also well defined on manifolds. Indeed, we can work with the three terms definition:

$$d\omega(X,Y) \overset{def}{=} X\omega(Y) - Y\omega(X) - \omega([X,Y]_{\mathrm{Lie}}).$$

A new difficulty appears: why does $(d\omega(X,Y))_p$ only depend on the values X_p, Y_p of the vector fields X, Y at the point p ?

To see why we have a positive answer to this question, let X' be an other vector field with $X_p = X'_p$. Then the difference vector field $X - X'$ in the chart U_α equals the linear combination $Z = X - X' = a_1 E_1 + a_2 E_2 + \cdots + a_n E_n$ of coordinate vector fields E_i, where the coefficients are functions $a_1, a_2, \cdots, a_n$ having at p as a common zero. Hence

$$(d\omega(X,Y))_p - (d\omega(X',Y))_p = (d\omega(X - X',Y))_p = \sum_i (d\omega(a_i E_{i,Y}))_p$$

The three terms of the above definition are $\mathbb{R}$-linear in the arguments X and Y. Only one term satisfies a stronger linearity property: namely, for an expression $T(X,Y)$, the property $T(fX,Y) = fT(X,Y)$ where f is not a number, but a smooth real valued function. Clearly, the first term satisfies this stronger linearity property. The two others don't, but there sum does! Indeed, by using $[fX,Y] = f[X,Y] - (Yf)X$ and $\omega(gX) = g\omega(X)$,

$$
\begin{gathered}
d\omega(fX,Y) = \\
fX\omega(Y) - Y\omega(fx) - \omega([fX,Y]) = \\
fX\omega(Y) - Y(f\omega(X)) - \omega(f[X,Y] - (Yf)X) = \\
fX\omega(Y) - fY\omega(X) - (Yf)\omega(X) - f\omega([X,Y]) + (Yf)\omega(X) = \\
fd\omega(X,Y)
\end{gathered}
$$

In particular at the point p it follows that

$$(\mathrm{d}\omega(a_i E_i, Y))_p = a_i(p)(\mathrm{d}\omega(E_i, Y))_p = 0$$

So, $(d\omega(X,Y))_p - (d\omega(X',Y))_p = 0$. In conclusion, $d\omega$ is indeed a 2 differential form.

We give more examples of fields on manifolds. Let M be a manifold given by families $(U_\alpha \subset V)_{\alpha \in A}$ and $(\phi_{\alpha\beta}: U_{\alpha\beta} \to U_{\beta\alpha})_{(\alpha,\beta) \in A \times A}$.

A k-differential form η will be a field given by a family

$$\eta_\alpha : U_\alpha \to \Lambda^k(V)$$

such that the restriction of η_α to $U_{\alpha\beta}$ transforms by $\Lambda^k(\phi_{\alpha\beta})$ to the restriction of η_β

to $U_{\beta\alpha}$. Here $\Lambda^k(V)$ is the vector space of all bilinear alternating maps with k arguments from V^k to $\mathbb{R}$. The space of k -differential forms on M is denoted by $\Omega^k(M)$. The *exterior differential* is a map

$$d:\Omega^k(M) \to \Omega^{k+1}(M)$$

difined by $$d\omega(X_0,X_1,\cdots,X_k) \overset{def}{=} \sum_{0\leq i\leq k} (-1)^i X_i\omega(X_0,\cdots \hat{X}_i,\cdots,X_k) + \sum_{0\leq i<j\leq k} \omega([X_i,X_j],X_0,\cdots,\hat{X}_i,\cdots,\hat{X}_j,\cdots,X_k).$$

Exercise 12: *Please check $d\omega \in \Omega^{k+1}(M)$. Find a more geometric definition in charts using the linear structure and integration of k-forms over faces of a hyper-cube.*

An almost complex structure J on a manifold M with charts $U_\alpha \subset V$ is a family of fields $J_\alpha : U_\alpha \to J(V)$ such that the restriction of J_α to $U_{\alpha\beta}$ transforms by $J \mapsto \phi_{\alpha\beta}{}_*^* J$ to the restriction of J_β to $U_{\beta\alpha}$. What is $J(V)$? What is $\phi_{\alpha\beta}{}_*^*$? $J(V)$ is the space of all linear maps $J: V \to V$ with $J^2 = -Id_V$. The transformation $J \mapsto \phi_{\alpha\beta}{}_*^* J$ has to be the only natural one we can think off: for $p \in U_\alpha$ the value $J_{\alpha,p}$ of J_α at p transforms by $(D\phi_{\alpha\beta})_p \circ J_{\alpha,p} \circ (D\phi_{\alpha\beta})_q^{-1}$ to the value $J_{\beta,q}$ at $q = \phi_{\alpha\beta}(p)$ of J_β. We denote by $J(TM)$ the space $J(TM) = \cup_{p\in M} J(T_pM)$. The space $J(TM)$ comes with a natural projection $\pi : J(TM) \to M$. Above a chart U_α observe $\pi^{-1}(U_\alpha) = U_\alpha \times J(V)$. The gluings organize π as a locally trivial bundle map with typical fiber $J(V)$. So, J -fields on M are sections of the bundle $\pi : J(TM) \to M$.

New operations between fields appear. For instance, an almost complex structure J makes out of a 1-differential form ω a new 1-differential form ω^J by defining $(\omega^J)_p \overset{\text{def}}{=} \omega_p \circ J_p$. For a function f we can formulate in the presence of a J field a new condition, namely $dd^Jf = 0$, where $d^Jf \overset{\text{def}}{=} (df)^J = (df) \circ J$. This leads to the very interesting and useful class of J -harmonic functions satisfying $dd^Jf = 0$. A closely related class of functions with complex values are the J -holomorphic functions satisfying: $(Df)_p(Jh) = i(Df)_p(h)$,$i \overset{\text{def}}{=} \sqrt{-1}$.

Of special importance is the case of surfaces S with J -field J . The operator $f \mapsto \Delta_J = d(df \circ J)$ is called the J -Laplace operator and maps functions to 2-differential forms. See the section: Analysis of Laplace operators.

A *Riemannian metric* on M is a family of fields $SP_\alpha : U_\alpha \to SP(V)$, naturally compatible with the family of transitions between charts $(\phi_{\alpha\beta} : U_{\alpha\beta} \to U_{\beta\alpha})_{(\alpha,\beta)\in A\times A}$. Here $SP(V)$ is the space of scalar products on V.

Explain the natural transition between charts for a Riemannian metric.

Please take care of the following exercises.

Exercise 13: *$J(V)$ is empty for an odd dimensional real vector space V. If Dim $(V) = 2n$ then $J(V)$ is a manifold of dimension $(2n)^2 - 2n^2$.*

Exercise 14: *Let X, Y, A, B be four 2-dimensional sub-vector spaces in a 4-dimensional real vector space V. We assume that the subspaces intersect two-by-two only in the origin. Construct out of the quadruple X, Y, A, B an automorphism of X. Show that two systems X, Y, A, B and X', Y', A', B' are linearly equivalent if and only if the corresponding automorphisms of X and X' are conjugate.*

Exercise 15: *Characterize those quadruples X, Y, A, B of two dimensional sub-vector spaces in general position in a real 4-dimensional vector space V that are fixed by some $J \in J(V)$. Is this set X of quadruples a submanifold in $Grass_2(V)^4$? Of which dimension? Equivalently, characterize those quadruples X, Y, A, B for which there exists an $\mathbb{R}$-linear map ϕ: $V \to \mathbb{C}^2$ such that the images $\phi(X)$, $\phi(Y)$, $\phi(A)$, $\phi(B)$ are $\mathbb{C}$-sub-vector spaces in $\mathbb{C}^2$. Same questions, but now for quintuples X, Y, A, B, C?*

Exercise 16: *Let J be the constant field on $\mathbb{R}^2$ with $J_p = \begin{pmatrix} 0 & 1 \\ -1 & 0 \end{pmatrix}$. Use standard coordinate functions x, y and write the operator $dd^J f$ explicitly.*

Exercise 17: *Put on the space $Grass_k(n)$ of all k-dimensional subspaces in $\mathbb{R}^n$ a differentiable system of charts.*

3.3 Integrability condition of Frobenius

Let V, B be vectorspaces of finite dimension. Suppose that at every point $p = (q, b) \in V \times B$ is given a vector space $G_p \subset T_p(V \times B) \cong T_q V \times T_b B \cong V \times B$ satisfying

-Dim(G_p) = Dim(B),

– $G_p \cap V\times\{0\}=\{0\}$.

Observe that for every $p\in V\times B$ the direct sum decomposition $T_p(V\times B)=V\oplus G_p$ holds.

A field $G: p\in V\times B \mapsto G_p \subset V\times B$ as above is called a *distribution supplementary to the factor* V.

Let $\pi_p^G: T_p(V\times B)\to T_bV\cong V$ be the linear projection with kernel G_p. Think of π^G as a 1-differential form on $V\times B$ with values in V.

The following global and local questions, which are versions of the so called *Pfaff Problem*, need answers. Answers were give by Jacobi, Clebsch, Deahna and Frobenius [28,90].

Global question: Given $p=(q,b_0)\in V\times B$, does there exist a smooth map $f:B\to V$ such that $f(b_0)=q$ and $\mathrm{Graph}((Df)_b)=G_{(f(b),b)}, b\in B$?

Local question: Given $p=(q,b_0)\in V\times B$, does there exist an open neighborhood U of b in B and a smooth map $f:U\to V$ such that $f(b_0)=q$ and $\mathrm{Graph}((Df)_b)=G_{(f(b),b)}, b\in B$?

Global question: Given $p=(q,b_0)\in V\times B$, does there exist a smooth map $F:V\times B\to V$ such that $F(p)=q$ and $\ker(dF)=\ker(\pi^G)=G$?

Local question: Given $p=(q,b_0)\in V\times B$, does there exist an open neighborhood U of p in $V\times B$ and a map $F: U\to V$ such that $F(p)=q$ and $\ker(dF)=\ker(\pi^G)=G$ hold?

For the first global and local questions, the desired map f appears in the condition $\mathrm{Graph}((Df)_b)=G_{(b,f(b))}, b\in B$, on both sides of the equality. This question is the most difficult one.

In the last two questions the desired map F appears only on one side. The local sufficient and necessary condition for the existence of $F: U\to V$ on a neighborhood of p is the condition $(d\pi^G)_q(u,v)=0$ for $u,v\in\ker(\pi_q^G)$ The condition does not ask for π^G to be a closed 1-form, but asks that the restriction of $d\pi^G$ to the kernel of π^G vanishes.

Interesting is a reformulation, as done in the next Theorem, of this condition in terms of vector fields with values in the distribution G.

Theorem 3.2 Jacobi-Clebsch-Deahna-Frobenius Integrability Theorem. *For finite dimensional vector spaces V,B, let G be a smooth distribution supplementary to* *the factor V on V ×B. Assume the following condition: Lie brackets* $[X,Y]_{Lie}$ *of vector fields X, Y on an open subset* $U \subset V\times B$*, both with values in G, take values in G. Then for every* $p_0 = (q_0, b_0) \in U$ *there exist an open neighborhood U′ of* p_0 *in U and a smooth map* $F: U' \to V$ *with* $ker(dF) = ker(\pi^G) = G$ *and* $F(p_0) = q_0$*.*

Proof: Let $v_0, v_1, \cdots, v_m$ be a basis for V and $e_1, e_2, \cdots, e_n$ a basis for B. Let z_0, $z_1, \cdots, z_m, x_1, x_2, \cdots, x_n$ be the corresponding linear coordinate functions on $V \times B$.

Denote by $X_i = \frac{\partial}{\partial x_i}$ and $Z_k = \frac{\partial}{\partial z_k}$ the corresponding coordinate vector fields on $V \times B$. Denote by $a_{i,k}: V \times B \to \mathbb{R}$ the well-defined smooth functions such that the vector field $X_i^G = X_i + \sum_k a_{i,k} Z_k$ takes values in G.

For a piece-wise smooth curve $\gamma: [0,1] \to B$, a G-lift along V is a smooth curve $\gamma^G: [0,1] \to V \times B$, $t \mapsto \gamma^G(t) = (\lambda^G(t), \gamma(t)) \in V \times B$ with $\lambda^G(t) \in V$ and speed $\dot{\gamma}^G(t) = (\dot{\lambda}^G(t), \dot{\gamma}(t)) \in G$. For every $q \in V$, there exist a unique

G-lift $\gamma_q^G = (\lambda_q^G, \gamma)$ along V with $\lambda_q^G(0) = q$.

The following key property relating G-lifts and Lie brackets of the G-lifted coordinate vector fields $[X_i^G, X_j^G]_{Lie}$ should be compared with the definition in an earlier section of the exterior derivative of a differential 1-form.

For $p = (q,b) \in V \times B, s \in \mathbb{R}, s > 0$, define $\gamma_{s,i,j,b}: [0,4] \to B$ to be the closed path that bounds the s-scaled square $P(b, b+se_i, b+se_i+se_j, b+se_j)$. Let $\gamma_{s,i,j,q,b}^G$ be the G-lift of $\gamma_{s,i,j,b}$ with $\gamma_{s,i,j,q,b}^G(0) = (q,b) \in V \times B$. Then $\gamma_{s,i,j,q,b}^G(4) = (q(s), b) \in V \times B$. The following holds:

$$([X_i^G, X_j^G]_{Lie})_{(q,b)} = \lim_{s \to 0} \frac{q(s) - q}{s^2}.$$

The coordinate value $z_k(q(s) - q)$ is computed as a sum of 4 path integrals along $\gamma_{s,i,j,q,b}^G$ of functions $a_{i,k}$. We spell out:

$$z_k(q(s) - q) = \int_0^1 sa_{i,k}(\gamma_{s,i,j,q,b}^G(t))\,dt + \int_1^2 sa_{j,k}(\gamma_{s,i,j,q,b}^G(t))\,dt +$$

$$\int_2^3 sa_{i,k}(\gamma_{s,i,j,q,b}^G(t))\,dt + \int_3^4 sa_{j,k}(\gamma_{s,i,j,q,b}^G(t))\,dt =$$

$$s\int_0^1 a_{j,k}(\gamma_{s,i,j,q,b}^G(t)) - a_{i,k}(\gamma_{s,i,j,q,b}^G(3-t))\,dt +$$

$$s\int_1^2 a_{j,k}(\gamma_{s,i,j,q,b}^G(t)) - a_{j,k}(\gamma_{s,i,j,q,b}^G(5-t))\,dt.$$

In particular, if at $p=(q,b)$ the Lie bracket $([X_i^G, X_j^G]_{\text{Lie}})_{(q,b)}$ vanishes, then there exists a constant A such that for $0<s\leqslant 1$, $k=1,2,\cdots,m$, the estimate

$$|z_k(q(s)-q)|\leqslant As^3$$

holds. The constant is controlled by second order derivatives of the functions $a_{i,k}$. The constant A can be chosen uniformly over compact subsets.

Work with the norm $\|b\|_\Sigma=\sum_i|x_i(b)|$ on B. A zigzag path in B is a path $\gamma:[0,L]\to B$ that is continuous, piece-wise differentiable, with speed vectors belonging to $\{\pm e_1,\pm e_2,\cdots,\pm e_n\}$ and of length $\|\gamma(0)-\gamma(L)\|_\Sigma=L$.

For given $b\in B$ let $\gamma_b:[0,\|b-b_0\|_\Sigma]\to B$ be the unique continuous path from b_0 to b with norm-speed 1, piece-wise smooth, with constant speed vector $\pm e_1$ on first piece, $\pm e_2$ on second piece, $\cdots$, $\pm e_n$ on last piece. Let $\gamma_b^{G,q}$ be its G-lift along V with $\gamma_b^{G,q}(0)=(q,b_0)$.

Define maps $\lambda^q: B\to V\times B$ by

$$b\in B\mapsto\lambda(b)=\gamma_b^{G,q}(\|b\|_\Sigma)\in V.$$

The definition of γ_b and of λ^q depend on the order of the coordinates $x_1,x_2,\cdots,x_n$. Let $\lambda^{\phi,q}$ be the map obtained after permuting the coordinates by a permutation ϕ. So, $\lambda^{\phi,q}(b)$ is obtained by G-lifting along V the unique continuous path γ_b^ϕ from b_0 to b with norm-speed 1, piece-wise smooth, with constant speed vector $\pm e_{\phi(1)}$ on the first piece, $\pm e_{\phi(2)}$ on thc second piece, $\cdots$, $\pm e_{\phi(n)}$ on the last piece to the path $\gamma_b^{G,\phi,q}$ with $\gamma_b^{G,\phi,q}(0)=(q,b_0)$.

For $\epsilon>0$ define $U'=U_\epsilon=\{(q,b)\in V\times B\,\|\,z_K(q-q_0)|<\epsilon,\|b\|_\Sigma<\epsilon\}$.

Fix $\epsilon>0$ such that for all $(q,b)\in U_\epsilon$ all G-lifts γ^G with $\gamma^G(0)=q$ of zigzag paths γ_b from b_0 to b of length $\|b-b_0\|_\Sigma$ stay in U. If $U=V\times B$ then the choice $U'=V\times B$ is admissible.

Claim 1: The map $\lambda: B\to V$ is differentiable.

Indeed, one can construction f by solving the differential equation of the vector fields X_i^G. Solutions depend smoothly on the initial data, so the claim.

Claim 2: For fixed $(q,b_0)\in U'$, the restrictions to $U'\cap B$ of the maps $\lambda^{\phi,q}$ coincide.

Indeed, G-lifts in U' of a closed path that bound a coordinate rectangle R of size ρ are closed too. Such a rectangle can be decomposed in N^2 coordinate rectangles, all equal up to translation and of size $\leqslant \frac{\rho}{N}$. So, since all Lie brackets vanish, there exists a constant A such that the above boundary path integral around a rectangle of the subdivision fails to close up to $\frac{A\rho}{N^3}$. It follows that the boundary path integral over the boundary of R fails to close up to a translation of size $N^2 \frac{A\rho}{N^3}$ $= \frac{A\rho}{N}$. This estimate holds for all N. In conclusion, the G-lift of the boundary path is a closed path too.

Every permutation ϕ is a product of transpositions, so $\lambda^{\phi,q}$ does not depend upon ϕ.

For $(q, b_0) \in U'$ define Λ_q to be the graph of λ^q. For $p = (q, b) \in U'$ define $F(p) \in V \cap U'$ implicitly such that $p \in \Lambda^{F(p)}$.

Claim 4: The map F is smooth of maximal rank.

The value $F(p)$, $p = (q, b) \in U'$, can be computed by G-lifting the path γ_b to $\gamma_b{}^G$ with $\gamma_b{}^G(\| b \|_\Sigma) = p$. Then $F(p) = \gamma_b{}^G(0) = p$.

Claim 5: Kernel$(DF)_p = G_p$, $p \in U'$.

Levels sets of $\{p \in U' \mid F(p) = q\}$ are the graphs Λ^q of $\lambda^{\phi,q}$, any permutation ϕ. At $p \in U'$ $(D\lambda^{\phi,q})_p((X^G_{\phi(n)})_p) = 0$. Hence,

$$Kernel((DF)_p) = T_p\Lambda^{F(p)} = Span\{(X^G_{\phi(n)})_p\} = G.$$

Let M be a differentiable manifold of dimension n. A k-distribution G on M is a map $p \in M \mapsto G_p \subset T_pM$ where G_p is a linear subspace of dimension k in the tangent space T_pM. A k-distribution G is smooth if locally there exist k smooth vector fields such that point-wise G is the span of the values of the vector fields.

Exercise 18: *Let G be a smooth k-distribution on a manifold M of dimension $n > k$. Show for every point $p \in M$ the existence of an open neighborhood U of p and a system $\alpha = (\alpha_1, \cdots, \alpha_{n-k})$ of smooth 1-differential forms on U such that at $q \in U$ the subspace G_q is the intersection of the kernels of the forms $(\alpha_i)_q, i = 1, n-k$.*

The system of 1-forms α of the previous exercise can be considered as a

1-form on $U \subset M$ with values in $\mathbb{R}^{n-k}$ by posing $\alpha_p(u) = [(\alpha_{1,p}(u), \cdots, \alpha_{n-k,p}(u)] \in \mathbb{R}^{n-k}$ and $\alpha_p : T_pM \to \mathbb{R}^{n-k}$ is a linear map. The kernel of α_p is the intersection of the kernels of $\alpha_{i,p}$.

Exercise 19: *Let G be a smooth k-distribution on an n-manifold M. Show the equivalence of the two conditions of integrability:*

–Lie brackets of vector fields on M with values in G are vector fields with values in G,

–For $p \in M$, let the distribution G be defined on an open neighborhood U of p as kernel of the 1-form $\Omega^1(U, \mathbb{R}^{n-k})$. Then $d\alpha \in \Omega^2(U, \mathbb{R}^{n-k})$ vanishes on $G_{|U} =$ Kernel(α).

Any smooth k -distribution G on an n -manifold is locally transversal to an $n-k$ -dimensional submanifold. More precisely, for $p \in M$ the exists a chart $\phi_\alpha : U_\alpha \to \mathbb{R}^n$ with $p \in U_\alpha$ and the distribution $\varphi_{\alpha \cdot *} G$ being transverse to $\mathbb{R}^{n-k} \times \{0\} \subset \mathbb{R}^n$.

As a consequence, the above Theorem holds for smooth k -distributions on n-manifolds.

Ferdinand Georg Frobenius (26 October 1849–3 August 1917) was a German mathematician[36].

3.4 Foliations on manifolds

Let E be a topological space. A natural equivalence relation $\sim_{\text{path}}$ on E is generated by its topology as follows. Declare $p, q \in E$ to be equivalent for the relation $\sim_{\text{path}}$ if and only if there exists a continuous path $\gamma : [0,1] \to E$ with values $\gamma(0) = p$ and $\gamma(1) = q$. Please show that this declaration defines indeed an equivalence relation.

If additionally to its topology E carries another structure, one can possibly impose extra conditions on the paths that generate an equivalence relation. As an example let E be a differentiable n -manifold M equipped with a smooth k -distribution G. Declare $p, q \in M$ to be equivalent for $\sim_G$ if and only if there exists a piece-wise smooth path $\gamma : [0,1] \to M$ with speed vectors $\dot{\gamma}(t)$ in G and $\gamma(0) = p$, $\gamma(1) = q$.

Please show that this declaration also defines an equivalence relation. A piece-wise smooth path γ with speed vectors in G is called *G-horizontal*. The equivalence relation $\sim_G$ is called the *horizontal equivalence relation* of the distribution G.

The following are main examples. Let G_1 be the 2-distribution on $\mathbb{R}^3$ given by the kernels of the 1-form dz and G_2 the 2-distribution on $\mathbb{R}^3$ given by the kernels of $dz + xdy$. The equivalence relations $\sim_{G_1}$ and $\sim_{G_2}$ are very different. The distribution G_1 is integrable, the distribution G_2 is not integrable.

Indeed, the G_1-horizontal paths are the paths such that the composition $t \mapsto z(\gamma(t))$ is constant. Hence, the equivalence classes of $\sim_{G_1}$ are the levels of the function z, i.e. the planes parallel to the X, Y-coordinate plane.

In contrast, the entire $\mathbb{R}^3$ is the only equivalence class for the relation $\sim_{G_2}$! Indeed, $p = (a, b, c) \in \mathbb{R}^3$ is $\sim_{G_2}$-equivalent to $p' = (1, b, c)$ by the linear segment $[p, p']$, the point p' is equivalent to $p'' = (1, b-c, 0)$ by $[p', p'']$ and finally p'' is equivalent to $c = (1, 0, 0)$ by $[p'', c]$.

Exercise 20: *Consider the space $E_{G,g} = \mathbb{R}^3$ equipped with the 2-distribution $G = G_2$ and the standard Riemannian metric $g(u, v) = x(u)x(v) + y(u)y(v) + z(u)z(v)$. Define a distance function $D_{G,g}$ on E by the infimum*

$$D_{G,g}(p, q) = \mathrm{Inf}_\gamma \, \mathrm{Length}_g(\gamma)$$

taken over all G-horizontal paths γ from p to q. Draw the $D_{G,g}$-ball of radius 4 and center $(0, 0, 0)$. Study the topology of the metric $D_{G,g}$.

Exercise 21: *Allow distance functions to take the value $+\infty$. Study the metric on $E_{G_1,g}$. Study the topology of the metric $D_{G_1,g}$.*

A *k-foliation* F on an n-manifold M is the partition of M by the equivalence classes of the horizontal relation $\sim_G$ of an integrable k-distribution G on M. The equivalence classes of $\sim_G$ are $(n-k)$-dimensional submanifolds of M and are the *leafs* of the foliation F. Through each point $p \in M$ runs a leaf Λ_p.

Be aware, the converse is not true. Consider in $\mathbb{R}^2$ the submanifolds R_θ and L_h: for $\theta \in \,]0, \pi[$ define $R_\theta = \{(e^t \sin(\theta), e^t \cos(\theta)) \mid t \in \mathbb{R}\}$ and for $h \in \mathbb{R}$, $h \leqslant 0$, define $L_h = \{p \in \mathbb{R}^2 \mid y(p) = h\}$. Then $\mathbb{R}^2$ is the disjoint union of the submanifolds R_θ and L_h. This partition is not a foliation. The manifold $\mathbb{R}^3$ is the disjoint union of the spheres $S_r = \{p \in \mathbb{R}^3 \mid x(p)^2 + y(p)^2 + z(p)^2 =$

$r\}, r > 1$, and the discs $D_c = \{p \in \mathbb{R}^2 \mid z(p) = c, x(p)^2 + y(p)^2 < 1 - c^2\}$, $-1 < c < 1$,. This partition of $\mathbb{R}^3$ by smooth 2-manifolds is not a 2-foliation.

The property for a k-distribution G on an n-manifold M of being integrable is local. The Integrability Theorem affirms for $p \in M$ the existence of an open neighborhood U of p and a map $F: U \to \mathbb{R}^{n-k}$ such that $G_{|U}$ coincides with the kernels of the differential of F. A more care-full choice of the neighborhood U and map F allows to assume that the image $F(U)$ is an open ball in $\mathbb{R}^{n-k}$ and that the preimages $F^{-1}(v)$, $v \in F(U)$, are diffeomorphic to open balls in $\mathbb{R}^k$. Such a choice (U, F) is called a *pile box* for the foliation. A preimage is called a *plate* of the pile box (U, F). If one wishes to remember the local map F we use the term F-plate. For $p \in U$ one has the inclusion of F-plate in leaf: $F^{-1}(F(p)) \subset \Lambda_p$. Two points a, b in the same F-plate are clearly in the same leaf. Be aware: the converse is not true, as is shown in the following example. On $M = \mathbb{R}^2 \setminus \{0\}$ with Euclidean norm define the 1-distribution G to be the kernels of the 1-form $\alpha = (y - f)\,dx - (x + f)\,dy$ for $f(p) = 0$, $\|p\| \leqslant 1$, and $f(p) = e^{\frac{-1}{\|p\| - 1}}$, $\|p\| > 1$. The leafs of the foliation induced by $\sim_G$ are circles C_r with center $0 \in \mathbb{R}^2$ and radius $0 < r \leqslant 1$ and lines L that spiral to the circle C_1. No choice of a pile box (U, F) is possible for $p \in C_1$ such that two points $a, b \in U$ belonging to the same leaf, also belong to the same F-plate. The intersection of a spiralling leaf L and U is an infinite union of plates. For all points $p \notin C_1$ such a choice is possible.

Exercise 22: *Construct on the 3-torus T^3 a 2-foliation such that every leaf is dense in T^3. Every leaf intersects every pile box along infinitely many plates.*

The multiplicative group $T = \{z \in \mathbb{C} \mid |z| = 1\}$ acts on the sphere $S^3 = \{(u, v) \in \mathbb{C}^2 \mid u\bar{u} + v\bar{v} = 1\}$ by $(\lambda, (u, v)) \mapsto (\lambda^2 u, \lambda^3 v)$. The orbit partition of S^3 is a 1-foliation for which all points $p = (u, v)$ admit a pile box (U, F) such that the intersection, if non-empty, of a leaf Λ with U consists of one, two or three plates.

The local structure of a k-foliation on an n-manifold is rigid and is described by typical pile box. The more global structure of a foliation is reflected in how pile boxes and leafs intersect each other.

3.5 Topology of connected, compact surfaces

In this section a surface is defined as a differentiable manifold of dimension two. In particular, we do not study surfaces with boundary. See the treatise of André Gramain[40] for a more general topological study of surfaces. Let S be a compact connected surface. How do we get control on the topology of S ? One possibility the method of slicing: let $f: S \to \mathbb{R}$ be a function. Study the levels $L_t \overset{def}{=} f^{-1}(t)$, $t \in \mathbb{R}$, and study how the levels change by varying $t \in \mathbb{R}$. This method will work particularly well if we already understand locally the function f. Examples of such functions are the Morse functions.

So, let $f: S \to \mathbb{R}$ be a Morse function. We assume that different critical points of f have different critical values and call such a Morse function *elementary*. Since S is assumed to be connected and compact, the set of values of f is an interval $[m, M]$. The set of critical values is finite, which we number in monotone increasing way: $m = c_1 < c_2 < \cdots < c_k = M$. Let $p_1, p_2, \cdots, p_k$ be the critical points with $f(p_i) = c_i$. For $t \in \mathbb{R}, t < c_1$, the level $L_t = \phi$. For $t = c_1$ the level L_t is the one point set $\{p_1\}$ where f takes its minimal value. According to the Morse Lemma locally near p_1 on a neighborhood U_1 of p_1 there exist differentiable coordinates x_1, y_1 with $x_1(p_1) = y_1(p_1) = 0$ and $f_{|U_1} = m + x_1^2 + y_1^2$. It follows that all levels $L_t, t \in]m, c_2[$, are diffeomorphic to a circle. What happens at $t = c_2$? Again by Morse Lemma, locally near the unique critical point p_2 with $f(p_2) = c_2$, on a neighborhood U_2 there exist differentiable coordinates x_2, y_2 , with $x_2(p_2) = y_2(p_2) = 0$ and $f_{|U_1} = c_2 + x_2^2 + y_2^2$. Up to permuting the names of the coordinates x_2, y_2 , we have three three possibilities.

1. $f_{|U_1} = c_2 - x_2^2 - y_2^2$. In this case, $c_2 = M$ and the surface is diffeomorphic to the sphere S^2.

2. $f_{|U_1} = c_2 - x_2^2 + y_2^2$. In this case the level L_{c_2} looks like the writing of the cipher "eight", as used in most countries. This writing produces a closed planar curve with one double point where locally to branches cross with transversal tangents. The circle L_t, $t < c_2$, pinch as t converges to c_2 . The levels L_t, $c_2 < t <$

c_3, are diffeomorphic to the disjoint union of two circles.

3. $f_{|U_1} = c_2 + x_2^2 + y_2^2$. In this case the L_{c_2} looks like the disjoint union of a circle and a 1-point set. At p_2 the function f has a local minimum. The levels L_t, $c_2 < t < c_3$, are diffeomorphic to the disjoint union of two circles.

In cases 2. or 3. the slicing continues: at c_3 one of the circles will be pinched like in case 2. at c_2 or will be stopped by a local maximum like in case 1. at c_2 or the two circles will merge to one circle if the critical point p_3 with $f(p_3) = c_3$ is connected in $S_{c_3} \overset{def}{=} \{ p \in S \mid f(p) \leqslant c_3 \}$ by a path to p_2 and also by another path to p_1.

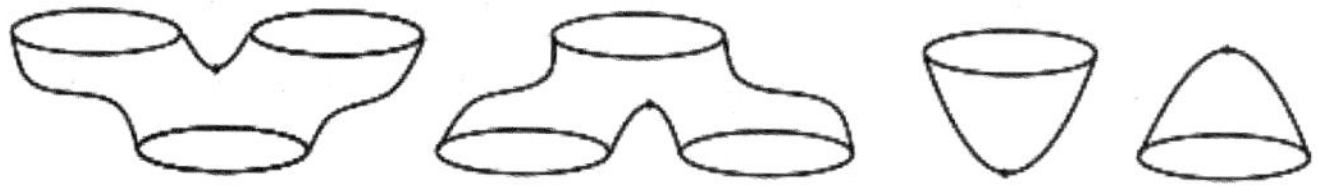

Figure 12 **Morse transitions up-down**

Using an elementary Morse function $f: S \to \mathbb{R}$ with $k \geqslant 2$ critical points and values we decompose the surface S into three types of standard pieces, see figure 12. Let $r_1, r_2, \cdots, r_{k-1}$ be regular values with $c_i < r_i < c_{i+1}$, $i = 1, 2, \cdots, k-1$. The connected components of the complement of the union of the levels L_{r_i} are open surfaces in S and their closures are closed surfaces "with boundary"... We call a closure of a connected component a piece. Such a pieces can be a cylinder, a disc or a pair of pants, see figure 13. We can reduce the number of pieces in the following way. If a disc and a cylinder meet along a common boundary circle, we replace thc disc and the cylinder by their union, which is again a disc. So we have one piece less. If a disc and a pair of pants have a common boundary circle, we replace the disc and the pair of pants by their union, which is a new cylinder. So again one piece less. If two cylinders have a common boundary we replace them by their union, which is again a cylinder. So again one piece less. If a cylinder and a pair of pants have one common boundary component, we replace by the union of the cylinder and the pair of pants, which is again a pair of pants. Again one piece less.

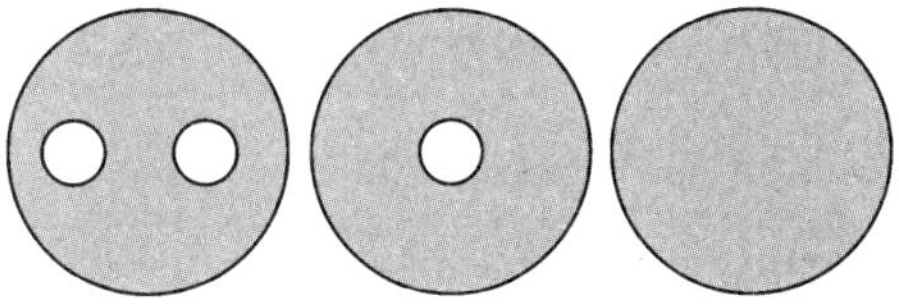

Figure 13 **Pairs of pants, cylinder, disc**

This process will stop. We have four possibilities:

1. We have one disc, which touches its boundary from both sides. In this case the surface is the real projective plane $P^2(\mathbb{R})$ obtained by identifying the points on the boundary circle of the disc by $\theta \sim -\theta$.

2. We have two discs with common boundary. In this case the surface S is obtained by gluing the boundary point θ of the first disc to the boundary point θ of the second disc. The surface S is diffeomorphic to the two sphere S^2.

3. We have one cylinder, the two boundaries coincide. In this case the surface S is diffeomorphic to the torus $T \overset{def}{=} S^1 \times S^1$ or to the Klein K bottle $\mathrm{K} \overset{def}{=} [-1,+1] \times S^1/\sim$, where $\sim$ is generated by $(-1,\theta) \sim (+1,\bar{\theta})$

4. We have an even number $e = 2(g-1)$, $g \geqslant 2$, of pairs of pants with $3e = 6(g-1)$ boundary components, glued two-by-two such that the resulting surface is connected. Up to diffeomorphism we have two possibilities for the resulting surface S: the orientable surface $S_g = S_g^+$ of genus g and the nonorientable surface S_g^-.

With the use of a Morse function one can cut a surface into discs, cylinders and pairs of pants. This can be seen as the beginning of a triangulation of the surface: first introduce two vertices on each of the boundary circles that appear in the decomposition. Each circle gets decomposed into two edges. Introduce in the cylinders 4 more edges and in the pairs of pants 9 more edges without introducing extra vertices. Introduce in the interior of each disc a vertex and two edges. The surface is now triangulated with vertices, edges and triangles. Leonard Euler introduced the number

$$e(S) = -\#\text{vertices} + \#\text{edges} - \#\text{triangles}$$

Leonhard Euler (1707–1783), born in Basel, was a Swiss, Russian, Prussian mathematician, physicist, astronomer, logician and engineer. The number $e(S)$ is independent of the chosen triangulation, so $e(S)$ is a topological invariant of the surface S. It follows that the genus $g(S) = \frac{1}{2}e(S) + 1$ is also a topological invariant. Nowadays one works with the opposite sign convention and defines the Euler characteristic $\chi(S)$ of a surface to be the number $-e(S)$.

The Euler Characteristic $\chi(S)$ is very powerful for the problem of classifying surfaces. It is known for which values of e a connected, oriented, compact surface S with Euler Characteristic $\chi(S) = e$ exists. Moreover two such surfaces with equal Euler characteristic are diffeomorphic. One says that the Euler characteristic with values in $\{2, 0, -2, -4, \cdots\}$ is a complete invariant of classification up to homeomorphism or diffeomorphism for connected, oriented, compact surfaces (again without boundary).

For a connected, oriented compact surfaces S the natural number $g(S) = \frac{1}{2}(2 - \chi(S))$ is called the *genus* of the surface.

Theorem 3.3 *For every even integer $e \leqslant 2$ or natural number $g = 0, 1, 2, \cdots$ there exists a connected, oriented, compact surface S with Euler characteristic e or with genus g. Two connected, oriented, compact surfaces with equal Euler characteristic or genus are diffeomorphic.*

The greek word γένος was introduced 23 centuries ago by Aristoteles. As concept, it emphasis a property that different objects may have in common. See the recent book *What is the Genus?* by Patrick Popescu-Pampu[83]. For further study of topology enjoy[30].

Exercise 23: *Construct a Morse function with 3 critical values on the torus T^2, the two sphere S^2 and on the surface S_g of genus $g \geqslant 2$.*

Exercise 24: *Let P be a regular polygonal region in the plane. We assume that P has 10 sides. Let c be a two-by-two pairing of the sides of P. We glue the sides two-by-two by isometries according the pairing c. How many topological types of surfaces do we get?*

Exercise 25: *Assume that there exists an embedding of the real projective space $P^2(\mathbb{R})$ into $\mathbb{R}^3$. Let F be the image of such embedding. Construct a compact 1-dimensional manifold C in $\mathbb{R}^3$ that intersects F transversally in one point. For $v \in \mathbb{R}^3$, $v \neq 0$, let $(C_t)_{t \in \mathbb{R}}$ be the family $C_t = C + tv$ of translates of C. Show that there ex-*

ists a vector v, $v \neq 0$, *such that all intersections* $C_t \cap F, t \in \mathbb{R}$, *are transversal or with tangencies of order* 1. *Conclude that* $\#C_0 \cap F - \#C_T \cap F$, T *large*, *is an even integer equal to* 1. *So*, *the assumption has to be rejected. The real projective plane admits no embedding in* $\mathbb{R}^3$.

Exercise 26: *Find an embedding of* $P^2(\mathbb{R})$ *in the 4-dimensional sphere.*

Exercise 27: *Let* M *be the set of subsets in* S^1 *having two or one element. Declare on* M *a topology such that* M *is homeomorphic to a differentiable surface with boundary.*

4 Hyperbolic Geometry

4.1 Hyperbolic plane $\mathbb{H} = \mathbb{H}_I$

A set can be defined by its elements. In my opinion a richer way is a definition which gives to those elements, also called points, a personality with culture and interactions with other personalities from the same set or from other sets.

Let us start out with the ring of polynomials in one indeterminate X and with real coefficients. A common notation for this ring is $\mathbb{R}[X]$. It is endowed with an addition and multiplication of polynomials. The triple $(\mathbb{R}[X], +, .)$ satisfies the axioms of a commutative ring with unit element. It is not a field, non-zero polynomials of degree $\geqslant 1$ are not invertible. A natural question is how to compare the ring $\mathbb{R}[X]$ with fields. More precisely, we study all surjective ring homomorphism from $\mathbb{R}[X]$ to a field F. So here a personality is a surjective ring homomorphism $p: \mathbb{R}[X] \to F$ where F is any field. We call two such ring homomorphisms $p: \mathbb{R}[X] \to F$ and $p': \mathbb{R}[X] \to F'$ equivalent if there exists a field isomorphism $f: F \to F'$ with $p' = f \circ p$. Let us also assume that for some reason surjective ring homomorphisms up to equivalence from $\mathbb{R}[X]$ to fields are interesting for our civilisation. Observe that the similar map 上海-Rank: {University} → {Number} seems nowadays to be of interest.

Let us start the study of $\mathbb{R}[X]$. The first step will be to declare A to be the set of all surjective ring homomorphisms up to equivalence from $\mathbb{R}[X]$ to some field. It turns out that such a ring homomorphism $p: \mathbb{R}[X] \to F$ up to equivalence is characterized by the kernel of p, which is the ideal

$$I_p \stackrel{\text{def}}{=} \{ P(X) \in \mathbb{R}[X] \mid p(P(X)) = 0 \}$$

in the ring $\mathbb{R}[X]$. Not every ideal in $\mathbb{R}[X]$ is kernel of a surjective ring homomorphism $p: \mathbb{R}[X] \to F$ to a field. Those kernels are precisely the the ideal equal to the whole ring $I = \mathbb{R}[X]$ or maximal proper ideals, i.e. ideals I that are maximal with respect to inclusion and satisfy $I \neq \mathbb{R}[X]$. Further it turns out that every ideal I in $\mathbb{R}[X]$ is generated as an ideal by one polynomial $P(X)$. The ideal $(P(X)) \subset \mathbb{R}[X]$ generated by $P(X)$ is the set of all its multiples

$$(P(X)) \stackrel{def}{=} \{ Q(X)P(X) \mid Q(X) \in \mathbb{R}[X] \}.$$

If $1 \in I = \mathbb{R}[X]$ the ring homomorphism takes its values in the field F_1 with only one element. Usually a field is assumed to have at least two elements 0, 1, $0 \neq 1$. The study of the field F_1 was initiated by Jacques Tits, a BelgianGerman-French mathematician, in 1956[97]. If $1 \notin I = (P(X))$ the degree of $P(X)$ exceeds 0. If the degree of $P(X)$ equals $d > 0$, we may replace $P(X) = a_d X^d + a_{d-1} x^{d-1} + \cdots + a_0$ by the monic polynomial $\frac{P(X)}{a_d}$ without changing the ideal generated by $P(X)$. The monic generator of an ideal I in $\mathbb{R}[X]$ is uniquely defined. The ideal $I = (P(X))$ will be maximal and proper if the polynomial $P(X)$ is of degree > 0 and $P(X)$ is not the product of two polynomials of lower degree > 0. Now we see that for $P(X)$ monic and generating a maximal ideal not containing $1 \in \mathbb{R}[X]$ there are only two possibilities.

1. The polynomial $P(X)$ is of degree 1: $P(X) = X - a$, $a \in \mathbb{R}$.

2. The polynomial $P(X)$ is of degree 2 and without real zeros: $P(X) = X^2 + bX + c$, $b, c \in \mathbb{R}$, $b^2 - 4c < 0$.

We redefine the set A as the set of maximal ideals, proper or not proper, in the ring $\mathbb{R}[X]$. We can also define the set A as the set of monic polynomials $P(X)$ such that the ideal $(P(X))$ is maximal. We see, using the second redefinition, that the set A is the disjoint union of three sets:

$$A_0 = \{(1)\}, \quad A_1 \stackrel{def}{=} \{ (X - a) \mid a \in \mathbb{R} \},$$

$$A_2 \stackrel{def}{=} \{ (X^2 + bX + c) \mid b, c \in \mathbb{R}, b^2 - 4c < 0 \}.$$

More intrinsically, it turns out that for a surjective ring homomorphism $p: \mathbb{R}[X] \to F$ to a field F the field F can only be isomorphic to the field with only one element F_1, the field of real numbers $\mathbb{R}$ or the field of complex numbers $\mathbb{C}$.

Points in A_1 correspond to surjections to the field of the real numbers, as points in A_2 correspond to surjections to a field isomorphic to the field of complex numbers. The unique point in A_0 is denoted by the symbol ∞.

We will make a beginning of the study of personalities and cultures in A_1 and A_2.

We have a lot of symmetries. Substituting in place of the indeterminate X the indeterminate $X-t, t \in \mathbb{R}$, defines a map $P(X)=X-a \mapsto Q(X)=X-(a+t)$. We see that the additive group $\mathbb{R}$ of the real numbers acts by

$$(t,(P(X))) \in \mathbb{R} \times A_1 \mapsto (P(X-t)) \in A_1$$

transitively on A_1. The multiplicative group $\mathbb{R}^*$ of real numbers ($\neq 0$) acts also by substituting for the indeterminate X the indeterminate λX as

$$(\lambda,(P(X)))=(\lambda,(X-a)) \mapsto (Q(X))=\left(X-\frac{a}{\lambda}\right).$$

The first action suggests that the notion of "distance": $d((X-a),(X-b)) \stackrel{def}{=} |a-b|$ is invariant under the natural symmetries of A_1. The second action shows that this notion of distance is not invariant, hence not natural.

Is there some other *structure* = *culture* in A_1? The answer is "yes"! We can define the symmetry invariant 3-point function of Michel Chasles (1793–1880), a French mathematician,

$$CH: A_1 \times A_1 \times A_1 \setminus \text{first diagonal} \to \mathbb{R}.$$

Let $(P(X)),(Q(X)),(R(X))$ be three different points in A_1. We assume that the three ideals are given by monic generators $P(X)=X-a, Q(X)=X-b$, $R(X)=X-c$. We define

$$CH(P(X)),(Q,(X)),(R(X)) \stackrel{def}{=} \frac{c-a}{b-a}.$$

The three point function CH is natural, i.e. the function CH is invariant by the above actions of the additive and multiplicative groups of real numbers on $A_1 \times A_1 \times A_1 \setminus$ first diagonal.

Exercise 1: *Let A_1 be equipped with the coarsest topology such that the map CH is continuous. Is A_1 homeomorphic to $\mathbb{R}$? What other natural structures has A_1? Structure of differential manifold? Hint: A_1 is called the real affine line $\mathbb{A}^1(\mathbb{R})$.*

Exercise 2: *Determine the group of all bijections ϕ: $A_1 \to A_1$ that preserve the* *structure given by CH.*

The union $A_0 \cup A_1 = \mathbb{R} \cup \{\infty\}$ is a model for the real projective line $\mathbb{P}^1(\mathbb{R})$. Indeed, let V be a real vector space of dimension 2, let L be a line in V not passing through the origin. The line L is a model for the real affine line and can be identified with $A_1 = L$. Let l_∞ be the one dimensional sub-vector space in V that does not intersect L. The map $\lambda : \mathbb{P}(V) \to A_0 \cup A_1$ given by $l \in \mathbb{P}(V) \mapsto \lambda(l) \in A_0 \cup A_1$, $\{\lambda(l)\} = l \cap L$ if $l \neq l_\infty$ and $\lambda(l_\infty) = \infty$ realizes the claimed identification. The group $PGL(2, \mathbb{R})$ is the group of projective automorphisms of $\mathbb{P}^1(\mathbb{R})$. This group acts simply transitive on triples (p, q, r) of distinct points in $\mathbb{P}^1(\mathbb{R})$, hence has no triple point invariant like CH on the real affine line $\mathbb{A}^1(\mathbb{R})$.

What about A_2? Again substitutions of $X - t$ for X, $t \in \mathbb{R}$, give symmetries. At High School we have learned that $(P(X)) \in A_2$, $P(X) = X^2 + bX + c$ transforms to $(Q(X))$ with the substitution $t = \frac{-b}{2}$ to $Q(X) = X^2 + (\frac{b^2}{4} + c)$.

The substitution of λX for X with $\lambda = \sqrt{\frac{b^2}{4} + c}$ will transform the ideal $(Q(X))$ to the ideal $(X^2 + 1)$. This shows that the space A_2 is homogeneous. Moreover the point $(X^2 + 1) \in A_2$ is the unique fixed point of the composition σ of the substitution $\frac{-1}{X}$ for X followed by multiplication by X^2.

The composition σ is an involution that transform $(X^2 + bX + c) \in A_2$ to

$$(cX^2 - bX + 1) = \left(X^2 - \frac{b}{\sqrt{c}}X + \frac{1}{c}\right).$$

Do we have more natural structure? Natural means invariant by the above symmetries. The following shows, that there exists a natural two point function:

$$CR : A_2 \times A_2 \to \mathbb{R}.$$

For $((P(X)), (Q(X))) \in A_2 \times A_2$ given by monic polynomials $P(X) \neq Q(X)$ let $I_{P(X),Q(X)}$ be the set $\{ t \in \mathbb{R} \mid tP(s) + (1-t)Q(s) > 0, s \in \mathbb{R} \}$. The set $I_{P(X),Q(X)}$ is an interval $I_{P(X),Q(X)} =]t^-, t^+[$. Possibly we have $t^- = -\infty$, $t^+ = +\infty$. We define

$$CR((P(X)),(Q(X))) \stackrel{def}{=} cr(t^{-},0,1,t^{+}) \stackrel{def}{=} \frac{(1-t^{-})(t^{+}-0)}{(0-t^{-})(t^{+}-1)},$$

where the following expression cr(a,b,c,d) is used that involves four distinct numbers $a,b,c,d \in \mathbb{R} \cup \{\infty\}$ and applies the rules $\frac{\infty}{\infty}=1$ and $\pm\infty \pm t=\infty$, $t \in \mathbb{R}$,

$$cr(a,b,c,d) = \frac{(c-a)(d-b)}{(b-a)(d-c)}.$$

This expression is well know in geometry and was already used by Pappus of Alexandria, a Greek mathematician, more then 2300 years ago. It can also be written as a ratio of ratio's: $\dfrac{\frac{c-a}{b-a}}{\frac{d-c}{d-b}}$, and is called the *cross-ratio* , bi-rapport, 交比, Doppelverhältnis or 非和比 of a,b,c,d. The cross-ratio plays a central role in geometry, vision, image recognition, finance, sociology and many other activities. In fact, the function cr defines a 4-point function on the real projective line $\mathbb{R} \cup \{\infty\} = \mathbb{P}^1(\mathbb{R})$.

The structure on A_2 that comes from the map CR is very rich. We first change the name of the set A_2 to $\mathbb{H}_I$. Remember $\mathbb{H}$ is for hyperbolic, and I for ideal. In short we set $\mathbb{H}=\mathbb{H}_I$. The set $\mathbb{H}$ with all the structure that we will discover soon is a model for the *hyperbolic plane* .

Theorem 4.1 Hyperbolic Distance in $\mathbb{H}=\mathbb{H}_I$. *The two point function $d_{\mathbb{H}}: \mathbb{H} \times \mathbb{H} \to \mathbb{R}$*

$$d_{\mathbb{H}}((P(X)),(Q(X))) \stackrel{def}{=} \frac{1}{2}\log(CR((P(X),Q(X))))$$

is a distance function on $\mathbb{H}$.

For points $p=(P(X)), q=(Q(X))$ in $\mathbb{H}$, $(P(X)) \neq (Q(X))$ given by monic polynomials $P(X), Q(X)$ we define the *hyperbolic line* $L_{pq} = L_{P(X),Q(X)} \subset \mathbb{H}$ through $p=(P(X)), q=(Q(X))$ as the subset

$$L_{pq} = L_{P(X)Q(X)} \stackrel{def}{=} \{t(P(X)+(1-t)Q(X)) \in \mathbb{H} \mid t \in I_{P(X),Q(X)}\}.$$

The *hyperbolic segment* $[(P(X)),(Q(X))]_{\mathbb{H}}$ is the subset

$$[(P(X)),(Q(X))]_{\mathbb{H}} \stackrel{def}{=} \{t[P(X)+(1-t)Q(X)] \in \mathbb{H} \mid t \in [0,1]\}.$$

For hyperbolic lines $L_{pq} = L_{P(X)Q(X)}$ with $P(X) = X^2 + bX + c, Q(X) = X^2 + b'X + c'$ and $b \neq b'$ here exist $i_{pq}, i_{qp} \in \mathbb{R}$ such that $L_{pq} = \{(t(X - i_{pq})^2 + (1-t)(X - i_{qp})^2) \mid t \in]0,1[\}$. Indeed put $i_{pq}, i_{qp} \in \mathbb{R}$ to be the numbers s.t. $(X - i_{pq})^2 = t_-(p,q)P(X) + (1 - t_-(p,q))Q(X)$ and $(X - i_{qp})^2 = t_+(p,q)P(X) + (1 - t_+(p,q))Q(X)$. Putting $L_{i_{qp}i_{qp}} = \{(t(X - i_{pq})^2 + (1-t)(X - i_{qp})^2) \mid t \in]0, 1[\}$ we have $L_{i_{qp}i_{qp}} = L_{pq}$.

If instead of $b \neq b'$ one has $b = b'$ and $c < c'$ put $i_{pq} = \frac{b}{2}$ and $i_{qp} = \infty$ with

$L_{i_{pq}\infty} = L_{i_{qp}i_{qp}} = \{(t(X - i_{pq})^2 + (1-t)(0X - 1)^2) \mid t \in]0,1[\}$.

Again $L_{i_{qp}i_{qp}} = L_{pq}$ holds. The points $i_{pq}, i_{qp} \in A_1 \cup \{\infty\}$ are the *ideal extremities* of the line L_{pq}.

Observe that for any pair of distinct points p, q in $A_2 \cup A_1 \cup \{\infty\}$ there exists a unique line L_{pq} in $A_2 = \mathbb{H}_I$ passing through or having as ideal extremity the points p and q.

The following is surprising, we re-discover a new geometry, the Hyperbolic Geometry, that is very young compared to the Euclidean Geometry. Nikolai Ivanovich Lobachevsky (1792 – 1856), a Russian mathematician, and János Bolyai (1802–1860), a Hungarian mathematician are the creators of hyperbolic geometry.

Theorem 4.2 $\mathbb{H}_I$ as model for the Hyperbolic Plane. *The geometry on $\mathbb{H}_I$ defined by the hyperbolic lines and by the metric $d_{\mathbb{H}}$ satisfies the axioms* Ⅰ, Ⅱ, Ⅲ, Ⅳ *of Euclid and the axiom V': given a line $L \subset \mathbb{H}$ and a point $p \in \mathbb{H}$, $p \notin L$, there exist more then one line in $\mathbb{H}$ through p that does not intersect the line L.*

In the Euclidean plane, a figure consisting of a triple of lines A, B, C with $A \neq B$, $A \cap B \neq \emptyset$, $A \cap C = B \cap C = \emptyset$ does not exist, but in the hyperbolic plane $\mathbb{H}$ this can occur.

Proof: From the forthcoming study of triangles and trigonometry in $\mathbb{H}$ will follow that the axioms Ⅰ, Ⅱ, Ⅲ, Ⅳ hold in $\mathbb{H}$. The symmetries, see below, of $\mathbb{H}_I$ provide the needed motions.

For a triple of pairwise distinct points $p, q, r \in \mathbb{H}$ with $r \notin L_{pq}$ the two distinct lines $L_{ri_{pq}}, L_{ri_{qp}}$ pass through r, and are disjoint from L_{pq}. Hence V' holds.

On $\mathbb{H} = \mathbb{H}_I$ we define a coordinate function $z: \mathbb{H} \to \mathbb{C}$ by

$$(P(X)) = (X^2 + bX + c) \mapsto z((P(X))) = \frac{-b + i\sqrt{-b^2 + 4c}}{2}.$$

The value of z on an ideal $I \in \mathbb{H}$ is the only zero in the upper half plane $\mathbb{C}_+$ of the ideal I. Observe: $\operatorname{Re} z((p(X))) = \frac{-b}{2}$. Take figure 14 as an example.

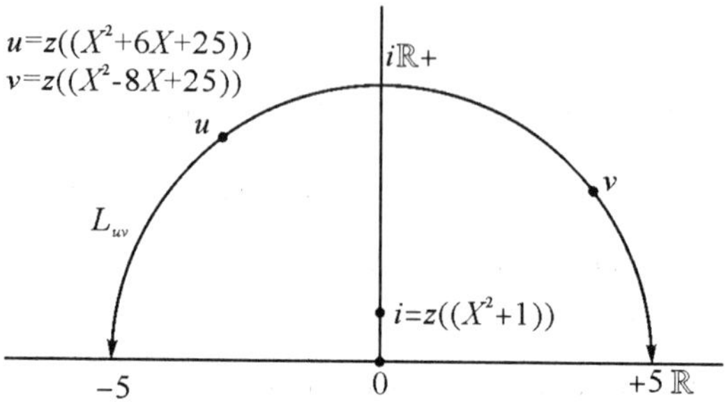

Figure 14 The hyperbolic line L_{uv} in the upper half plane $\mathbb{C}_+$ through $u = z((X^2 - 6X + 25))$ and $v = z((X^2 - 8X + 25))$

Theorem 4.3 *The function z is a bijection from $\mathbb{H}$ to the upper half plane $\mathbb{C}_+ \overset{def}{=} \{u \in \mathbb{C} \mid Im(u) > 0\}$. Images of most lines in $\mathbb{H}$ by z are intersections of the upper half plane with circles $\{u \in \mathbb{C} \mid |u-a| = r,\ a \in \mathbb{R},\ r > 0\}$. Images by the coordinate z of lines $L_{P(X)Q(X)}$ with $P(X) - Q(X) \in \mathbb{R}$ are real half rays perpendicular to the real line in $\mathbb{C}_+$.*

Proof: If $P(X) - Q(X) \neq 0$ is of degree 0 the polynomials differ by a real constant, so $P(X) = X^2 + bX + c$ and $Q(X) = X^2 + bX + c + d$. Without loss of generality, assume $-c < d < 0$. Then $t^+(P(X), Q(X)) = +\infty$ and $t^-(P(X), Q(X)) = \frac{b^2 - 4c - 4d}{4d} < 0$. For $t \in [t^-, t^+]$ the root $z_t \in \mathbb{C}_+$ of the polynomial $P_t(X) = t(P(X)) + (1-t)Q(X) = X^2 + bX + tc + (1-t)(c+d)$ runs through the half line in $\mathbb{C}_+$ with $\operatorname{Re}(z_t) = -b/2$.

If $P(X) - Q(X) \neq 0$ is of degree 1 let $S \in \mathbb{R}$ be with $P(S) = Q(S)$.

Observe that $t \in [t^-, t^+] \mapsto |z(P_t(X)) - S|^2$ is constant. It follows that the z-image of the line $L_{P(X)Q(X)}$ is a half circle with center at $S \in \mathbb{R}$.

Let $\Pi: \mathbb{C}_+ \to \mathbb{H}$ be the reciprocal bijection:

$$u \in \mathbb{C}_+ \mapsto \Pi(u) = [(X-u)(X-\bar{u})] \in \mathbb{H}$$

We wish to understand natural symmetries of $\mathbb{H}$. For instance the substitution

$X-t$ for X, $t\in\mathbb{R}$ corresponds via z to the translation $u\mapsto u+t$ on $\mathbb{C}_+$. The substitution $\frac{X}{\lambda}$ for X, $\lambda>0$, corresponds via z to the stretching $u\mapsto\lambda u$ on $\mathbb{C}_+$.

The following is a hidden symmetry, hidden if one only thinks in terms of polynomials. It is the symmetry $(P(X))\mapsto(X^2P(-1/X))$ of $\mathbb{H}$ which fixes the ideal $(X^2+1)\in\mathbb{H}$. This symmetry corresponds via the coordinate z to the holomorphic symmetry $u\mapsto\frac{-1}{u}$ of $\mathbb{C}_+$ which is an involution and fixes $i\in\mathbb{C}_+$

The coefficient "b" of $P(X)=X^2+bX+c$ equals the derivative $P'(0)$ evaluated at 0. The map $P(X)\mapsto P(X)-2P'(0)X$ is a symmetry of the 2point function CR on $\mathbb{H}$, which fixes point wise the line $\{(X^2+c)\mid c>0\}\subset\mathbb{H}$. This symmetry corresponds via the coordinate z to the anti-holomorphic involution $u\mapsto-\bar{u}$. This symmetry does not preserve any orientation of $\mathbb{H}$.

Theorem 4.4 *The symmetries: substitution $X-t$ for $X, t\in\mathbb{R}$, $\frac{X}{\lambda}$ for $X, \lambda\in\mathbb{R}^*$, symmetries $(P(X))\mapsto(X^2P(-1/X))$ and $(P(X))\mapsto((X)-2P'(0)X)$ as above, generate the group of symmetries of the map $CR:\mathbb{H}\times\mathbb{H}\to\mathbb{R}$.*

We call symmetries of the map $CR:\mathbb{H}\times\mathbb{H}\to\mathbb{R}$ symmetries of the geometric space $\mathbb{H}$, which are precisely the isometries of the metric $d_{\mathbb{H}}$.

Theorem 4.5 *The group of orientation preserving automorphisms of $\mathbb{H}$ is isomorphic to the group $PSL(2,\mathbb{R})$. Its action on $\mathbb{H}$ corresponds via the coordinate z: $\mathbb{H}\to\mathbb{C}_+$ to the modular action $u\mapsto\frac{au+b}{cu+d}$ on $\mathbb{C}_+$.*

A point $p\in A_2=\mathbb{H}_I$ defines an involution θ_p of $A_0\cup A_1=\mathbb{P}^1(\mathbb{R})$ in the following way: for $l\in A_0\cup A_1$ define $\theta_p(l)\in A_0\cup A_1$ by requiring that $l\neq\theta_p(l)$ and that the hyperbolic line in A_2 with end points $l,\theta_p(l)$ passes through p. This construction, as explained to me by Jacques Tits, leads to the following model $\mathbb{H}_\theta$ of the hyperbolic plane: The hyperbolic plane is the space of all involutions $\theta:\mathbb{P}^1(\mathbb{R})\to\mathbb{P}^1(\mathbb{R})$ of the real projective line $\mathbb{P}^1(\mathbb{R})$ that preserve the cross-ratio cr, i.e. the 4-point function, and that act fixed point free. Clearly it follows that the groups of automorphisms of the hyperbolic planes $\mathbb{H}=\mathbb{H}_I=\mathbb{H}_\theta$ are all isomorphic to the group of automorphisms $PGL(2,\mathbb{R})$ of the real projective line $\mathbb{P}^1(\mathbb{R})$.

The structure of $\mathbb{H}$ is really very rich, for instance:

Theorem 4.6 *Let $Hess_p$ be the Hessian at p of the function $q \in \mathbb{H} \mapsto d_{\mathbb{H}}^2(p,q)$. The field $p \mapsto \frac{1}{2}Hess_p$ defines a Riemannian metric $\rho = \rho_{\mathbb{H}}$ on $\mathbb{H}$. The Riemannian metric ρ is isotropically homogeneous.*

Proof: The coordinate $z: \mathbb{H} \to \mathbb{C}_+$ is a bijection. The transported Riemannian metric $z_*\rho$ on the upper half plane $\mathbb{C}_+$ evaluates at $q \in \mathbb{C}_+$ and tangent vectors $u, v \in T_q C_+ = C$ to $_{\rho C_+}(u,v) = \frac{\mathrm{Re}(u\bar{v})}{im^2(q)}$. The modular action is isotropically homogeneous by isometries, so also the action of $PSL(2,\mathbb{R})$ on $\mathbb{H}$. The group $PSL(2,\mathbb{R})$ realizes by the modular action the group of conformal automorphisms of $\mathbb{C}_+$, so is isomorphic via the isometry z to the group of orientation preserving isometries of $\mathbb{H}$.

The coordinate $z: \mathbb{H} \to \mathbb{C}_+$ transports the Riemannian metric $\rho_{\mathbb{H}}$ to the metric $\rho\,\mathbb{C}_+$ which is conformal to the Euclidean metric of the Gaussian plane $\mathbb{C}$. The length $\| h \|$ of a tangent vector $h \in T_p$ H is given by $\| h \| = \frac{|(dz)_p(h)|}{\mathrm{Im}z((p))}$.

By integration one can get a closed formula for the distance between points $p, q \in \mathbb{H}$. The proof of the following theorem is not by integration.

Theorem 4.7

$$d_{\mathbb{H}}(p,q) = arc\ \mathrm{Cosh}\left(1 + \frac{|z(p) - z(q)|^2}{2\mathrm{Im}(z(p))\mathrm{Im}(z(q))}\right).$$

Proof: The following proof uses the group of isometries of $(\mathbb{H}, d_{\mathbb{H}})$. Both sides are invariant by the above four basic symmetries of $\mathbb{H} = \mathbb{H}_I$. Moreover we claim that the formula holds for $p = (X^2 + 1)$ and $q_t = (t(X-1)^2 + (1-t)(X+1)^2), t \in [\frac{1}{2}, 1[$. Notice that $t \in]0,1[\mapsto q_t \in \mathbb{H}_I$ is a line, moreover $p = q_{\frac{1}{2}}, q_0, q_1 \notin \mathbb{H}$and

$$z(p) = i,\ z(q) = (-1+2t) + i\sqrt{1-(1-2t)^2}.$$

So by equivariance and isotropical transitivity the formula will be proved. For the claim observe

$$LHS = d_{\mathbb{H}}(p, q_t) = \frac{1}{2}\log\left(cr\left(0, \frac{1}{2}, t, 1\right)\right) = \frac{1}{2}\log\left(\frac{t}{1-t}\right) \quad \text{and}$$

$$RHS = arcCosh\left(1 + \frac{1 - \sqrt{1 - (1 - 2t)^2}}{\sqrt{1 - (1 - 2t)^2}}\right) - arcCosh\left(\frac{1}{\sqrt{1 - (1 - 2t)^2}}\right)$$

Further observe

$$\cosh^2(LHS) = \frac{1}{4t(1 - t)}, \cosh^2(RSH) = \frac{1}{1 - (1 - 2t)^2} = \frac{1}{4t(1 - t)}$$

Hence $\cosh^2(LHS) = \cosh^2(RHS)$, which finishes the proof since cosh is a strictly monotone positive function on the positive reals.

Theorem 4. 8 *Let $J^{\pm}$ be the continuous fields on $\mathbb{H}$ of turning by $\pm\pi/2$ corresponding to the Riemannian metric ρ of the previous theorem. These fields correspond via the coordinate z: $\mathbb{H} \to \mathbb{C}$ to the constant J-fields $m_{\pm i}: h \mapsto \pm ih$ on $\mathbb{C}_+$.*

So, the m_i -field that we have in $\mathbb{C}_+$ corresponds via the coordinate z to a natural J -field on $\mathbb{H}$. We say that the coordinate z is holomorphic. The same holds for a variant of the coordinate z. The coordinate

$$w: \mathbb{H} \to \mathbb{D}, w = \frac{z - i}{z + i}$$

maps $\mathbb{H}$ to the open unit disc $\mathbb{D} = \{ v \in \mathbb{C} \mid |v| < 0 \}$, which in this role is called the Poincaré disc. Most lines L in $\mathbb{H}$ are mapped by the coordinate w to intersection of the circles

$$C_c = \{ v \in \mathbb{C} \mid |v - c| = r, r^2 = (|c|-1)(|c|+1), |c| > 1\}$$

with $\mathbb{D}$. Here, exceptions are the lines in $\mathbb{H}$ through $(X^2 + 1)$ which are mapped by w to straight diameters of the disc $\mathbb{D}$. The circles C_c have their center c outside the closure of $\mathbb{D}$ and meet orthogonally the boundary of the closure of $\mathbb{D}$. Circles with "centers" at ∞ correspond to the exceptions. From the coordinate w on $\mathbb{D}$ we can retrieve the coordinate z on $\mathbb{H}$ by

$$z = -i\frac{w + 1}{w - 1}.$$

The spaces $A_0 \cup A_1 = \mathbb{P}^1(\mathbb{R})$ and $A_2 = \mathbb{H}_I = \mathbb{H}_\theta$ carry natural topologies. The following properties define a topology T on the union $\overline{\mathbb{H}} = A_0 \cup A_1 \cup A_2$. The first property requires that $A_0 \cup A_1$ is a closed subspace in $(\overline{\mathbb{H}}, T)$ and that the induced topology is the natural topology of $\mathbb{P}^1(\mathbb{R})$. The second property requires that A_2 is open in $(\overline{\mathbb{H}}, T)$ and that the induced topology is the topology of $\mathbb{H}_I$.

The third property requires that the only sequences in $(p_n)_{n\in\mathbb{N}} \in \mathbb{H}_l$ with limit $l \in A_0 \cup A_2$ are those sequences that do not have accumulation points in $\mathbb{H}_l$. Moreover it is required that there exits a sequence of lines $(L_n)_{n\in\mathbb{N}}$ with $p_n \in L_n$ and with endpoints $a_n, b_n \in A_1 \subset \mathbb{P}^1(\mathbb{R})$ such that $\lim_{n\to\infty} a_n = l$, $\lim_{n\to\infty} b_n = l$.

The coordinate $w: A_2 = \mathbb{R}_l \to \mathbb{D}$ extends to a homeomorphism $\bar{w}: \overline{\mathbb{H}} \to \overline{\mathbb{D}}$. Here $\overline{\mathbb{D}}$ is the closure of the open unit disc $\mathbb{D}$ in $\mathbb{C}$. It follows that the space $\overline{\mathbb{H}} = (A_0 \cup A_1 \cup A_2, T)$ is a compactification of the space $\mathbb{H}$.

The closed disc $\overline{\mathbb{D}}$ is a compact, convex subspace with non empty interior in $\mathbb{C}$. Its interior $\mathbb{D}$ inherits a metric by the following construction.

Let $K \subset \mathbb{R}^n$ be a compact convex set with non empty interior K°. The Hilbert metric d_K on K° is the two point function defined for $p, q \in K^\circ$, $p \neq q$, by

$$d_K(p,q) = \frac{1}{2}\log(cr(P,p,q,Q))$$

where $CR(P,p,q,Q)$ is the cross-ratio of the four points P,p,q,Q on the line $L(p,q)$ through p and q, where P,Q are the boundary points of the interval $L(p,q) \cap K$ with p in between P,q.

The space $\mathbb{D}$ with its Hilbert metric $d_{\mathbb{D}}$ is isometric to the hyperbolic plane $\mathbb{H}$ and hence provides a further model for the hyperbolic plane which is due to Felix Klein. The homeomorphism is made visible in figure. Interestingly, the lines in this Kleinian model are just the straight chords. The price for this adventage is that the measure of angles differs from the Euclidean measure of angles, which is in contrast to the Poincaré model $\mathbb{D}$.

Exercise 3: *Show that d_K defines a metric on K°, see figure* 15.

Exercise 4: *Re-prove the Perron-Frobenious Theorem, see a previous exercise, by showing that the self map $\bar{A}$ on the simplex K that is spanned by the standard basis of $\mathbb{R}^n$ is contracting with respect to the Hilbert metric on K°.*

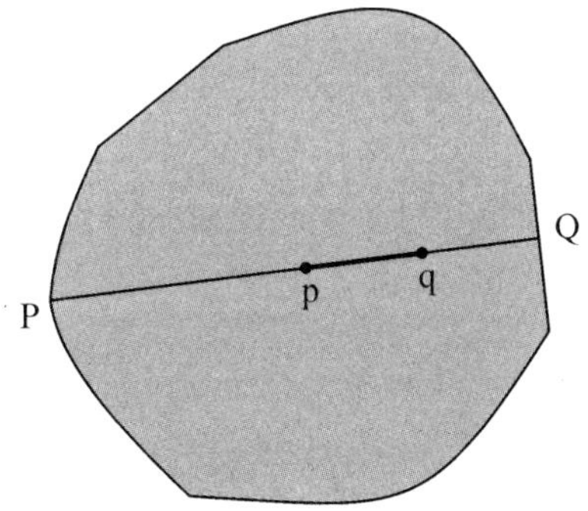

Figure 15 **Hilbert metric** $d_K(p,q) = \frac{1}{2}\log\frac{(q-P)(Q-p)}{(p-P)(Q-q)}$ **on** K°

The Hilbert metric

$$d^I_{Hilbert}(a,b) = \frac{1}{2}\left|\log\frac{(b-t^-)(t^+-a)}{(a-t^-)(t^+-b)}\right|, a,b \in]t^-,t^+[$$

on the interior I° of an interval $I = [t^-, t^+]$ defines an isometric parametrisation of I° by the real line $\mathbb{R}$ such that translations of the parameter become d_I -isometries:

Theorem 4.9 *The lines in* $\mathbb{H}_I$ *are precisely the geodesics for the metric* ρ *on* $\mathbb{H}_I$. *Moreover, the parametrisation*

$$t \in]t^-,t^+[\mapsto (tP(X)+(1-t)Q(X))$$

of the line $L_{P(X)Q(X)}$ *is geodesic if one uses on the interval* $]t^-,t^+[$ *its Hilbert metric* $d^{t^-t^+}_{Hilbert}(a,b)$.

The distance in $\mathbb{H}_I$ between $(P(X))$ and $(Q(X))$ can be computed as follows. First compute the lower and upper boundary points t^-, t^+ of the interval $I_{(P(X)),(Q(X))}$. Then

$$d_{\mathbb{H}}((P(X)),(Q(X))) = \frac{1}{2}\log\left(\frac{(1-t^-)t^+}{t^-(1-t^+)}\right).$$

The coordinate functions z and w are holomorphic, which allows us to measure angles of sectors bounded by lines in the upper half plane $\mathbb{C}_+$ or in the Poincar'e disc $\mathbb{D}$.

We compute a few examples. Consider $(1+h)i, i \in \mathbb{C}_+, h \in]-1,\infty[$. We have, remember $\Pi(z) = ((X-z)(X-\bar{z}))$,

$$d_{C_+}((1+h)i,i)=d_{\mathbb{H}}(\Pi((1+h)i),\Pi(i))$$
$$=d_{\mathbb{H}}((X^2+(1+h)^2),(X^2+1)).$$

We have, if $h>0, t^-=\dfrac{-1}{(1+h)^2-1}, t^+=+\infty$. Hence

$$d_{\mathbb{C}_+}((1+h)i,i)=\frac{1}{2}\log\left(\frac{1+\dfrac{1}{(1+h)^2-1}}{\dfrac{1}{(1+h)^2-1}}\right)=\log(1+h).$$

If $h\in]-1,0]$ the values of $t^\pm$ become, $t^+=\dfrac{-1}{(1+h)^2-1}, t^-=-\infty$, and

$$d_{\mathbb{C}_+}((1+h)i,i)=\frac{1}{2}\log\left(\frac{\dfrac{-1}{(1+h)^2-1}}{\dfrac{-1}{(1+h)^2-1}}\right)=-\log(1+h).$$

For $i+h, i\in\mathbb{C}_+, h\in\mathbb{R}$, we find

$$d_{\mathbb{C}_+}(i+h,i)=d_{\mathbb{H}}\left(\prod\left(i+h,\prod(i)\right)\right)=$$
$$d_{\mathbb{H}}((X^2-2hX+h^2+1),(X^2+1))$$
$$t^\pm=\frac{1}{2}\pm\sqrt{\frac{1}{4}+\frac{1}{h^2}}$$

hence,

$$d_{\mathbb{C}_+}(i+h,i)=\frac{1}{2}\log\left(\frac{\left(\dfrac{1}{2}+\sqrt{\dfrac{1}{4}+\dfrac{1}{h^2}}\right)\left(\dfrac{1}{2}+\sqrt{\dfrac{1}{4}+\dfrac{1}{h^2}}\right)}{\left(-\dfrac{1}{2}+\sqrt{\dfrac{1}{4}+\dfrac{1}{h^2}}\right)\left(-\dfrac{1}{2}+\sqrt{\dfrac{1}{4}+\dfrac{1}{h^2}}\right)}\right)=$$
$$\log\left(1+\sqrt{h^2+\frac{h^4}{4}}+h^2\right).$$

For $0,h\in\mathbb{D}$, $h\in]-1,1[\subset\mathbb{D}$, we compute

$$z(h)=i\frac{1+h}{1-h}, z(0)=i\in\mathbb{C}_+$$

and conclude

$$d_{\mathbb{D}}(0,h)=d_{\mathbb{C}_+}(z(h),z(0))=\log\left(\frac{1+|h|}{1-|h|}\right)$$

by the previous computation. Rotations of $\mathbb{D}$ with center 0 are automorphism of $\mathbb{D}$ as model for the hyperbolic plane. It follows that for $u \in \mathbb{D}$ the hyperbolic distance from u to 0 is given by

$$d_{\mathbb{D}}(0,u) = \log\left(\frac{1+|u|}{1-|u|}\right).$$

One way of computing the distance $d_{\mathbb{H}}((P(X)),(Q(X)))$ is to bring the point $(P(X))$ to (X^2+1) by a symmetry ϕ of $\mathbb{H}$ and next compute $d_{\mathbb{H}}((X^2+1),\phi((Q(X))))$ using the coordinate z and a previous formula. By applying a rotation ρ with center (X^2+1) one can achieve that $\phi(Q(X))$ transforms to $(X^2+\lambda^2),\lambda \geqslant 1$, so finally $d_{\mathbb{H}}((P(X)),(Q(X))) = \log(\lambda)$.

For a further study and history of the hyperbolic plane[1,11,88,89].

4.2 Intermezzo: Higher Cross Ratios

The automorphism group G of a k-vector space V of finite dimension acts on various spaces that are attached to the vector space V. A *figure* or also a *configuration of labelled points* in V is a map $A:[1,2,\cdots,n]\to V$. The number n is called the number of points of the configuration A. For instance a triangle in V is a map from the labelled three elements set $[1,2,3]$ to V. We denote by $P(n,V)$ the space of configurations of points in V, that have n points. The group G acts on each of the spaces $P(n,V)$.

Two configuation $A,B \in P(n,V)$ are called G-congruent if there exists a $\gamma \in G$ with $B_i = \gamma(A_i)$, $i=1,2,\cdots,n$.

Up to G-congruence there exist only two configurations in $P(1,V)$, assuming that V is of dimension $\geqslant 1$, namely a configuration A with $A_1=0$ or with $A_1 \neq 0$.

The list of possibilities for configurations up to G-congruence in $P(2,V)$ is longer even infinite if the field k has infinitely many elements. Assuming now that the dimension of V is $\geqslant 2$, the first three possibilities are $A_1 = A_2 = 0$, $A_1 = 0$, $A_2 \neq 0$ and $A_1 \neq 0$, $A_2 = 0$. Moreover for every $\lambda \in K$, $\lambda \neq 0$, there is the possibility $A_1 \neq 0$, $A_2 = \lambda A_1$. The last possibility is the case that A_1 and A_2 are linearly independent. So if the field has q elements, the number of possibilities up to G-congruence, i.e. the number of G-orbits in $P(2,V)$ equals $q+3$.

Exercise 5: *Assuming that the field k has q elements, and that the dimension of V is $\geqslant 3$, count the number of G-orbits on $P(3,V)$. Count $\#P(n,V)/G$.*

A figure or a configuration of labelled lines in V is a map $L:[1,2,\cdots,n]\to P^1V$. A configuration of labelled lines in V is a labelled configuration of points in the projective space P^1V of all sub-vector spaces of dimension 1 in V. We denote by $L(n,V)$ the space of labelled configurations of lines in V, consisting of n lines. The group G acts on the spaces $L(n,V)$. Two configurations $L,L'\in L(n,V)$ are called congruent if there exists $\gamma\in G$ such that $L_i'=\gamma(L_i)$, $i=1,2,\cdots,n$.

Assuming that the dimension of V exceeds 1, up to G-congruence the spaces $L(n,V)$, $n\leqslant 3$, have only finitely many elements. The first cases where up to G-congruence infinitely many labelled line configurations may exist start from configurations with 4 lines in a vectorspace of dimension 2.

The cross-ratio, which is the theme of this section, associates to 4 distinct labelled lines $A=(L_1,L_2,L_3,L_4)$ in a k-vector space V of dimension 2 a scalar $CR(L_1,L_2,L_3,L_4)\in k\setminus\{0,1\}$, such that two labelled configurations A,B are G-congruent if and only if $CR(A)=CR(B)$.

The definition of the number $CR(A)$ for a $A\in L(4,V)$ is as follows. Consider $X=L_1$ and $Y=L_2$ as cartesian coordinate axes on V. Consider L_3 as the graph of a linear map $\phi: X\to Y$. Consider L_4 as the graph of a linear map $\psi: Y\to X$. The composition $\psi\circ\phi: X\to X$ is a linear endomorphism of a k-vector space X of dimension 1. The maps ϕ, ψ are invertible and $\phi\neq\psi^{-1}$ since $L_3\neq L_4$, so the composition is invertible too and is given by the stretching $u\in X\mapsto\psi(\phi(u))=\lambda u\in X$, $\lambda\neq 0,1$. The stretching factor $\lambda\in k\setminus\{0,1\}$ is the scalar $CR(A)$.

Theorem 4.10 *The scalar CR detects in the above "if and only if" sense G-congruence of distinct labelled 4-line configurations in a two dimensional k-vector space.*

Exercise 6: *Let a be a non-labelled configuration of 4 distinct lines in a two dimensional vector space V. There are 24 different labellings $\pi\in S_4$ for a. Let*

$\lambda(a,\pi)$ *be the cross-ratio of* $A=(a,\pi)$. *Study the map* $\pi\in S_4\to\lambda(a,\pi)\in k\backslash\{0,1\}$.

The above cross-ratio construction can be used in many different situation. Here an example. Let $Gr_{2,4}(\mathbb{R})$ be the Grassmannian of two-dimensional sub-vector spaces in a four dimensional real vector space. Let $P(4,Gr_{2,4}(\mathbb{R}))$ be the space of labelled configurations of 4 two dimensional sub-vector spaces in a four dimensional real vector space. For such a *generic* configuration of 4 labelled planes $A=(P_1,P_2,P_3,P_4)$ in a real vector space V of dimension 4 the cross-ratio $CR_{2,4}(A)$ is defined analogously to the case of 4-line configurations and is an endomorphism of the two dimensional vector space P_1. The term generic means in the present context, that the planes P_i intersect two by two only in the origin. The endomorphism $CR_{2,4}(A)$ is invertible and moreover $CR_{2,4}(A)-\mathrm{Id}_{P_1}$ is invertible too.

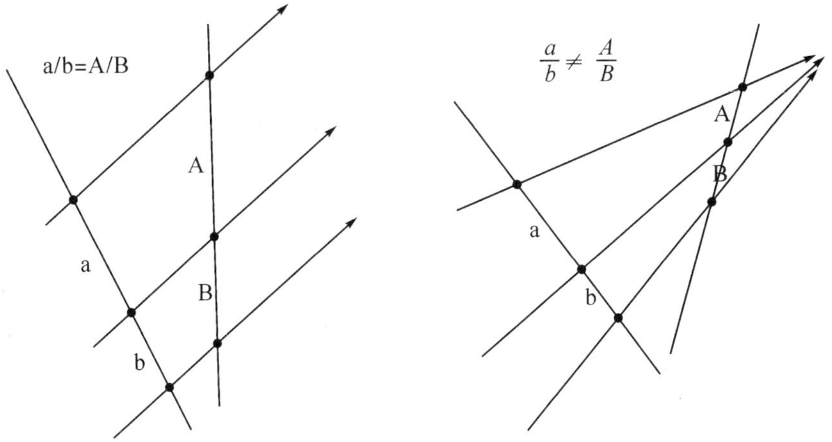

Figure 16 Affine invariance of ratio, projective non-invariance of ratio

A labelled configuration C of four distinct 1-dimensional complex subvector spaces in a 2-dimensional complex vector space provides examples of generic labelled configurations $A\in P(4,Gr_{2,4}(\mathbb{R}))$ by considering the involved vectors spaces as real vector spaces . So the configuration A is obtained by forgetting the structure of a complex vector space on the various spaces, and remembering only the structure of real vector spaces, as shown in figure 16.

The cross-ratio $CR_{2,4}(A)$ gives an answer to the following question. Which generic $A \in P(4, Gr_{2,4}(\mathbb{R}))$ are obtained by forgetting a complex structure? More precisely, let $A = (P_1, P_2, P_3, P_4)$ a generic labelled configuration of planes in a real 4-dimensional vector space V. Under which condition on A does there exist a complex structure $J: V \to V$ on V such that the planes satisfy $J(P_j) = P_j$, $j = 1,2,3,4$?

Remember, a $\mathbb{R}$-linear map $J: V \to V$ endows the real vector space V with the structure of a complex vector space if J satisfies $J^2 = -\mathrm{Id}_V$ by declaring as multiplication

$$(a + bi)u = au + bJ(u), a, b \in \mathbb{R}, u \in V.$$

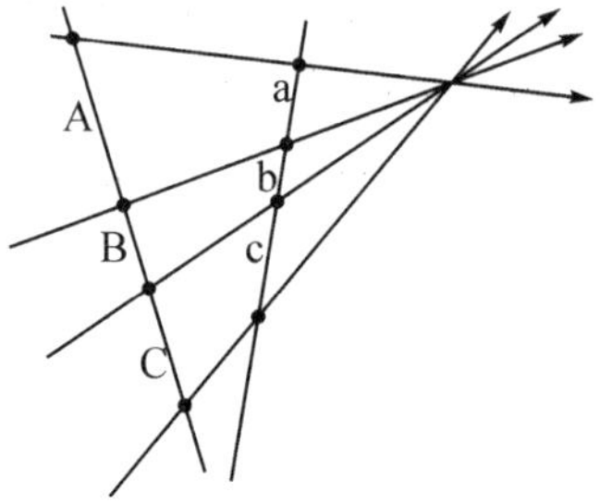

$$\frac{(a+b)(b+c)}{ac} = \frac{(A+B)(B+C)}{AC}$$

Figure 17 Projective invariance of cross ratio

So very concretely the problem is to find for a given configuration A a linear map $J: V \to V$ satisfying $J^2 = -\mathrm{Id}_V, J(P_j) = P_j$. This is a non-linear but quadratic problem with 16 unknowns. The input of the configuration involves 32 parameters, see figure 17.

A similar more basic problem is solved by:

Theorem 4. 11 *Let $\phi: V \to V$ be an endomorphism of a real vector space V of dimension two. There exists a complex structure $J: V \to V$ that commutes with ϕ if and only if*

$$Trace(\phi)^2 < 4Det(\phi).$$

Or if ϕ is a multiple of the identity Id_V.

Proof: Let J be a complex structure on V. The maps ϕ and J commute if and only if ϕ is a complex linear endomorphism of (V, J). Let λ be the eigenvalue of ϕ on (V, J), so that λ, $\bar{\lambda}$ are the eigenvalues of ϕ acting on real space V.

The inequality

$$\mathrm{Trace}(\phi)^2 = (\lambda + \bar{\lambda})^2 \leqslant 4\lambda\bar{\lambda} = 4Det(\phi)$$

will follow if and only if a complex structure$J$ commuting with ϕ exists. In case of equality one remarks that ϕ is moreover diagonisable over $\mathbb{R}$.

Remark. In case of strict inequality only two complex structures $\pm J$ commuting with ϕ exist. For the other case, the space of solutions with its geometry turns out to be the union of two anti-oriented copies of the hyperbolic plane. See a later section.

Theorem 4. 12 Four Complex Lines Theorem. *Let $A = (P_1, P_2, P_3, P_4)$ be a generic labelled configuration of planes in a real 4-dimensional vector space V. There exists a complex structure $J : V \to V$ with $J(P_j) = P_j$ if and only if*

$$Trace(CR_{2,4}(A))^2 < 4Det(CR_{2,4}(A))$$

or if $CR_{2,4}(A)$ is a multiple $\lambda Id_{P1}, \lambda \neq 1$, of the identity Id_{P_1}.

Proof: Such a complex structure J exists if and only J preserves P_1 and $CR_{2,4}(A)$ commutes with the restriction of J to P_1 .

A similar theorem concerning the opposite inequality, holds in the symplectic setting. A bilinear anti-symetric non-degenerate map $\omega : V \times V \to \mathbb{R}$ on a vector space V is called a linear symplectic form on V. Assume V is of dimension four. A two dimensional linear subspace L in V is called a linear Lagrangian subspace if $\omega(u, v) = 0$ holds for all $u, v \in L$.

Theorem 4. 13 Four Langrangian Theorem. *Let $A = (P_1, P_2, P_3, P_4)$ be a generic labelled configuration of planes in a real 4-dimensional vector space V. There exists a linear symplectic structure ω on V such that the planes P_i are ω-Lagrangian if and only if*

$$Trace(CR_{2,4}(A))^2 > 4Det(CR_{2,4}(A))$$

or if $CR_{2,4}(A)$ is a multiple λId_{P1}, $\lambda \neq 1$, of the identity Id_{P_1}.

Proof: Assume that a linear symplectic structure ω exists for which the planes P_i become Lagrangian. Then ω allows to identify P_4 with the dual space P_1^*. Hence, P_2 and P_3 can be interpreted as maps α , $\beta: \mathrm{P}_1 \to \mathrm{P}_1^*$,and therefor as 1-differential forms on P_1 . The forms α, β are closed since the graphs P_2 , P_3 are Lagrangians. It follows that the maps α, β are symmetric, hence, define on P_1 non-degenerate quadratic forms. The Main Axes Theorem applies, hence there exists a linear diagonalisable map $\Lambda : P_1 \to P_1$ with real eigenspaces and with $\alpha = \beta \circ \Lambda$. *It follows that* $CR_{2,4}(A) : P_1 \to P_1$ is diagonalisable over the reals, hence the inequality. This argument can be reversed step by step.

The cross-ratio $CR_{n,2n}$ construction associates an endomorphism $CR_{n,2n}(A)$ of the first subspace to a labelled configuration $A \in P(4, Gr_{n,2n})$ of 4 n dimensional subspaces in a $2n$-dimensional vector space.

Exercise 7: *Given a configuration $A \in P(4, Gr_{n,2n})$ work out the condition on $CR_{n,2n}(A)$ that is equivalent to the existence of a linear complex structure or a linear symplectic structure that complexifies or symplectifies the configuration as in the above Theorems.*

The cross-ratio $CR_{n,2n}$ can be useful in the following problem. Given a generic $A \in P(N, Gr_{n,2n})$ determine the group G_A of linear maps $g \in \mathrm{GL}(2n, \mathbb{R})$ satisfying $g(A_k) = A_k$, $k = 1, 2, \cdots, N$. For $N = 1$ the group G_A is isomorphic to the subgroup in the matrix group $\mathrm{GL}(2n, \mathbb{R})$ consisting of the block matrices M with $M_{ij} = 0$ for $i > n$ and $j \leqslant n$. For $N = 2$ the group G_A is isomorphic to $\mathrm{GL}(n, \mathbb{R})^2$, for $N = 3$ to $\mathrm{GL}(n, \mathbb{R})$. For $N = 4$ G_A is isomorphic to the group of matrices in $\mathrm{GL}(n, \mathbb{R})$ that commute with $CR_{n,2n}(A)$. For $N > 5$ the group is mostly reduced to the sub-group of multiples of the identity in $\mathrm{GL}(n, \mathbb{R})$.

Exercise 8: *Given generic $A \in P(4, Gr_{n,2n})$ study the group P_A of all linear transformation g with $g(\cup A_j) = \cup A_j$. Study P_A/G_A. The word generic has a meaning that can vary depending on context! "More generic" in present context would be the case if moreover $P_A = G_A$ holds.*

Exercise 9: *Study all more generic $A \in P(4, Gr_{1,2})$ and $A \in P(4, Gr_{2,4})$.*

The following question leads to a tri-ratio. In a 3-dimensional vector space V let C and C' be two given configurations of 3 pairwise distinct subspaces H_1, H_2, H_3 of dimension 2 and 3 subspaces L_1, L_2, L_3 of dimension 1 such that $L_i \subset H_i$ and $L_i \not\subset H_j$, $i, j \in \{1, 2, 3\}$, $i \neq j$. The problem is to construct a computable criterion that decides if there exists an automorphism of V sending the configuration C to C' respecting labels.

Consider L_2 as graph of a linear map M_2 from $H_2 \cap H_1$ to $H_2 \cap H_3$, see figure 18. Accordingly, M_1 with graph L_1 maps $H_1 \cap H_3$ to $H_1 \cap H_2$ and M_3 with graph L_3 maps $H_3 \cap H_2$ to $H_3 \cap H_1$. The composition $M = M_1 \circ M_3 \circ M_2$ is an endomorphism of the 1-dimensional space $H_2 \cap H_1$. Define the tri-ratio $TR(H_1, H_2, H_3, L_1, L_2, L_3)$ of the given configuration $C = (H_1, H_2, H_3, L_1, L_2, L_3)$ of subspaces in V as the stretch factor of M. The configuration C corresponds to three labelled complete flags in generic position in the space V of dimension 3. The stretch factor $TR(C)$ is an invertible element in the ground field.

One has the following answer to the above question.

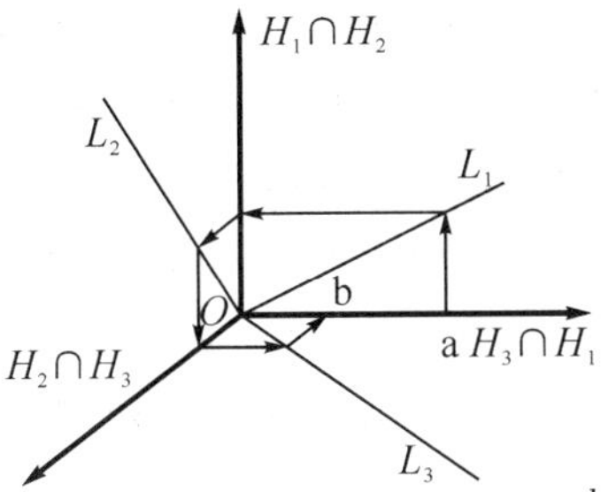

Figure 18　$\tilde{E}_6$ **tri-ratio invariant** $\dfrac{b}{a}$

Theorem 4. 14 *Two labelled generic configurations C and C' of flags in a 3-dimensional vector space are linearly equivalent if and only if $TR(C) = TR(C')$ holds.*

A flag $L \subset H \subset V$ corresponds to an incidence $p \in \Lambda$ of a point p and a line Λ in the projective plane $P(V)$. A configuration C as above corresponds to a labelled triple of point-line incidences $p_i \in \Lambda_i$, $i = 1, 2, 3$, in $P(V)$. The tri-ratio $TR(C)$ corresponds to a tri-ratio for a generic triple of point-line incidences $TR(\Lambda_1, \Lambda_2, \Lambda_3, p_1, p_2, p_3)$. Two labelled triples of pointline incidences can be transformed into each other by a projective motion of $P(V)$ if and only if their tri-ratio's agree.

Exercise 10: *Let C be a generic configuration $C = (H_1, H_2, H_3, L_1, L_2, L_3)$ of subspaces in V with $L_i \subset H_i$ of real dimensions 6 for V, 4 for H_i and 2 for L_i. Formulate a computable condition P such that P holds if and only if there exists a complex structure J on V with $J(H_i) = H_i$ and $J(L_i) = L_i$.*

4.3 Hyperbolic trigonometry

We will consider the elements in $\mathbb{H}$ as *points*. A *triangle* is a triple of points (A, B, C) in $\mathbb{H}$ that are not elements of a common line. We will denote by $a, b, c \in \mathbb{R}$ the distances $a = d_{\mathbb{H}}(B, C)$, $b = d_{\mathbb{H}}(C, A)$, $c = d_{\mathbb{H}}(A, B)$. The numbers a, b, c are called the side lengths of the triangle. The angle at A of the triangle (A, B, C) between the lines through A, B and A, C is denoted by $\alpha \in]0, \pi[$. Accordingly, the angles at B and C are denoted by β and γ.

Two triangles (A, B, C) and (A', B', C') are called congruent if there exists an isometry of $(\mathrm{H}, d_{\mathrm{H}})$ mapping A to A', B to B' and C to C'

A first result claims the existence of triangles, unique up congruence.

Theorem 4.15 *Let $(a, b, c) \in \mathbb{R}$ be three numbers, satisfying the inequalities:*

$$0<a<b+c, 0<b<a+c, 0<c<a+b.$$

Then there exists a triangle (A, B, C) in the hyperbolic plane $\mathbb{H}$ having side lengths a, b, c. Moreover, if (A', B', C') is a triangle with side lengths a, b, c, then there exists a unique isometry of $\mathbb{H}$ mapping A to A', B to B' and C to C'.

Proof: Start with three points A, C, B on a line in that order such that the distances AC and CB are equal to b and a. Further assume $a \leqslant b$. In that position the distance AB is equal to $a + b = c$. By varying the angle $\sphericalangle ABC$ from π to 0, and keeping the points B and C fixed, the point A moves in between C and B and the distance AB varies continuously from $a + b$ to $-a + b < c$. (Use the Hyperbolic Cosine Law Theorem, that will be treated later in this section.) By the intermediate value theorem there exist an angle $\sphericalangle ACB$ such that the distance AB equals c.

Theorem 4.16 *Let $(\alpha, \beta, \gamma) \in]0, \pi[$ be three numbers, satisfying the inequality:*

$$\alpha+\beta+\gamma < \pi.$$

Then there exists a triangle (A, B, C) in the hyperbolic plane $\mathbb{H}$ having angles α, β, γ. Moreover, if (A', B', C') is a triangle with angles α, β, γ, then there *exists a unique isometry of* $\mathbb{H}$ *mapping* A *to* A', B *to* B' *and* C *to* C'.

Proof: Again use the intermediate value theorem. Start with three oriented lines L, K and H through a point A such that the angles of the three sectors are $\sphericalangle HK = \alpha$, $\sphericalangle KL = \beta$, $\sphericalangle HL = \alpha + \beta$. Now move continuously the line L while keeping the angle with K equal to β and such that the intersection $L \cap H$ is non-empty. The angles of the triangles bordered by the lines H, K, L are α, β and a third angle that varies continuously from $\pi - \alpha - \beta$ to 0. So there exists a position L' for the moving line L with third angle equal to γ, see figure 19.

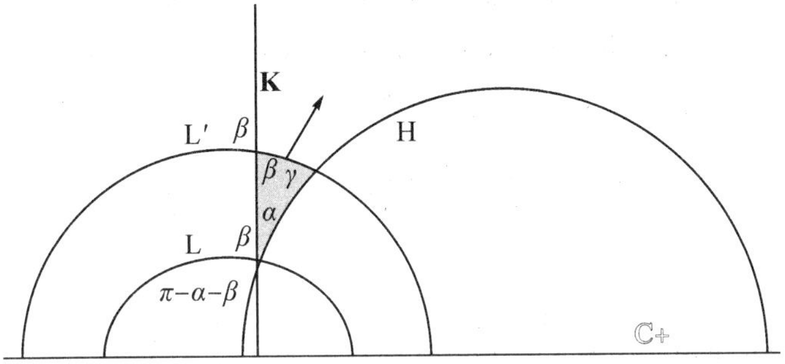

Figure 19 **Construction of triangle from** α, β, γ

The Hyperbolic Cosine Law Theorem permits to compute the side lengths from the angles. Unicity follows from the previous Theorem.

The first theorem also holds also in the Euclidean plane. The second does not. This striking difference was directly, but also indirectly used to question about the existence of the hyperbolic plane. The existence of a planar geometry satisfying the modified fifth postulate V' was already questioned by Euclid (circa 330–275, B.C.), and has remained a hot topic of mathematical research for at least 2000 years, see the book of Roberto Bonola[11] with its supplements by the inventors of hyperbolic geometry Nicholas Lobachevski and Jǎnos Bolyai.

Both theorems together have as consequence, that the side lengths of a triangle in $\mathbb{H}$ determine the angles, and conversely, that the angles of a triangle in $\mathbb{H}$ determine the side lengths, which is rather unexpected if educated in an Euclidean school.

In hyperbolic trigonometric the following theorem for right-angled triangles is as central as the Pythagoras theorem in Euclidean geometry:

Theorem 4.17 Pythagoras in Hyperbolic Geometry. *Let* (A, B, C) *be a triangle in the hyperbolic plane* $\mathbb{H}$ *with right angle at C. The hyperbolic Pythagoras type statement is:*

$$cosh(c) = cosh(a)cosh(b).$$

Proof: The half-lines $L^+ = \{q_t \mid q_t = ((1-t)(X^2+1)+t(X-1)^2),\ t \in [0,1[\}$ and $Y^+ = \{r_s \mid r_s = (X^2+s^2),\ s \in [1,+\infty[\}$ in $\mathbb{H}_I$ meet at (X^2+1) with right angles. Indeed the isometry $(P(X)) \mapsto X^2 P(\frac{1}{X}))$ fixes point wise the halfline Y^+ and fixes globally the line L supporting L^+. Every triangle (A,B,C) with right angle at C can be moved by an isometry such that $C = (X^2+1)$, $B = q_t \in L$ and $A = r_s \in Y$ hold. Previous computations of $d_{\mathbb{H}}$ yield

$$\cosh(a) = \frac{1}{2\sqrt{t(1-t)}}, \cosh(b) = \frac{s^2+1}{2s}$$

and

$$\cosh(c) = 1 + \frac{(2t-1)^2 + \left(s - \sqrt{1-(1-2t)^2}\right)^2}{2s\sqrt{1-(1-2t)^2}} =$$

$$\frac{s^2+1}{2s\sqrt{1-(1-2t)^2}} = \frac{1}{2\sqrt{t(1-t)}} \frac{s^2+1}{2s}$$

The result follows.

The Euclidean Pythagoras Theorem reads $c^2 = a^2 + b^2$, which can be interpreted as an equality of areas. On spheres, Euclidean lengths of intervals on great circles can be measured by numbers in $[0, 2\pi]$. The Spherical Pythagorean Theorem reads $\cos(c) = \cos(a)\cos(b)$. It is natural to ask for an interpretation of the Pythagorean Theorems in hyperbolic and spherical geometry. See[1] for a more geometric proof and also for how the Euclidean Pythagoras Theorem is hidden in the hyperbolic and spherical Theorems.

In planar Euclidean geometry twice the area $2V$ of a triangle (A,B,C) with right angle at C can be computed in two different ways: $2V = ab$ and $2V = hc$ where h is the length of the height to the hypotenuse to c. So $ab = hc$ holds. The following result provides an analogue in hyperbolic geometry.

Theorem 4.18 Hyperbolic Sinh Product Theorem. *Let* (A,B,C) *be a triangle in the hyperbolic plane* $\mathbb{H}$ *with right angle at C. Let h be the length of the height* *perpendicular to the hypotenuse. Then*

$$sinh(a)\,sinh(b) = sinh(h)\,sinh(c).$$

Proof: The foot point P of the height to the hypotenuse divides the hypotenuse in two pieces of length c', c''. We choose the piece of length c' to be incident with the summet B.

The logic of our proof is to use the result in order to have a candidate value for the quantity $h>0$. Now we build the candidate quadrilateral (A, P, B, C) by computing first candidate values for c', c'' and by gluing the triangles (A, P, C) and (B, P, C) along the common edge PC. The points A, P, B should by aligned since the angle at P is right by construction in both triangles. The punch line of the proof is to check $c' + c'' = c$, which proves that the points A, P, B are indeed aligned, see figure 20. This will be done by checking $\cosh(c' + c'') = \cosh(a)\cosh(b)$.

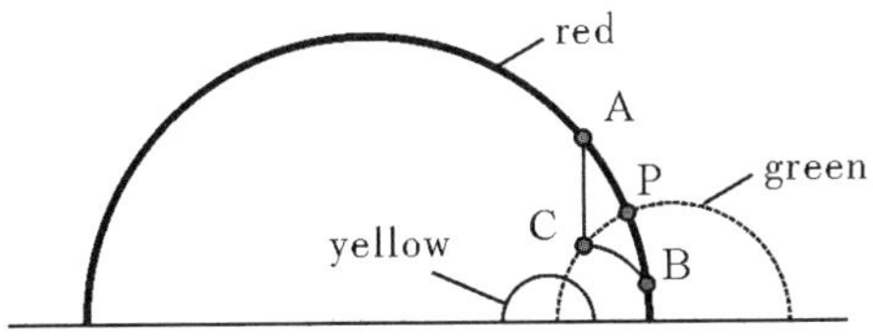

Figure 20 Triangle ABC with height CP and right angle C.

(Red and yellow lines are symmetric by point involution C.

The green line is the common perpendicular of the red and the yellow line).

The candidate value for h is implicitly given by

$$\sinh(h) = \frac{\sinh(a)\sinh(b)}{\sinh(c)}.$$

It follows

$$\cosh(h) = \sqrt{1 + \sin^2(h)} = \sqrt{1 + \frac{\sinh^2(a)\sinh^2(b)}{\sinh^2(c)}}.$$

From the hyperbolic Pythagoras Theorem in the triangles APC and BPC with right angles at P one deduces candidate values for c', c''

$$\cosh(c') = \frac{\cosh(a)}{\sqrt{1 + \frac{\sinh^2(a)\sinh^2(b)}{\sinh^2(c)}}} = \frac{\sinh(c)\cosh(a)}{\sqrt{\sinh^2(a)\sinh^2(b) + \sinh^2(c)}}$$

and

$$\cosh(c'') = \frac{\cosh(b)}{\sqrt{1 + \frac{\sinh^2(a)\sinh^2(b)}{\sinh^2(c)}}} = \frac{\sinh(c)\cosh(b)}{\sqrt{\sinh^2(a)\sinh^2(b) + \sinh^2(c)}}$$

and hence, using $\cosh^2 = 1+\sinh^2$, $\cosh(c) = \cosh(a)\cosh(b)$, also

$$\sinh(c') = \sqrt{-1 + \frac{\sinh^2(c)\cosh^2(b)}{\sinh^2(c) + \sinh^2(a)\sinh^2(b)}} =$$

$$\sinh(b)\sqrt{\frac{\sinh^2(c) - \sinh^2(a)}{\sinh^2(c) + \sinh^2(a)\sinh^2(b)}} =$$

$$\sinh(b)\sqrt{\frac{\cosh^2(c) - \cosh^2(a)}{\sinh^2(c) + \sinh^2(a)\sinh^2(b)}} =$$

$$\frac{\sinh^2(b)\cosh(a)}{\sqrt{\sinh^2(c) + \sinh^2(a)\sinh^2(b)}}$$

and also

$$\sinh(c'') = \frac{\sinh^2(a)\cosh(b)}{\sqrt{\sinh^2(c) + \sinh^2(a)\sinh^2(b)}}.$$

We prepare the check of $c = c' + c''$ by starting from the cosh addition formula:

$$\cosh(c' + c'') = \cosh(c')\cosh(c'') + \sinh(c')\sinh(c'').$$

First

$$\cosh(c')\cosh(c'') = \frac{\sinh^2(c)\cosh(a)\cosh(b)}{\sinh^2(c) + \sinh^2(a)\sinh^2(b)}.$$

Next

$$\sinh(c')\sinh(c'') = \frac{\sinh^2(a)\sinh^2(b)\cosh(a)\cosh(b)}{\sinh^2(c) + \sinh^2(a)\sinh^2(b)}.$$

Now, clearly, ouf!, $\cosh(c' + c'') = \cosh(a)\cosh(b) = \cosh(c)$.

In planar Euclidean geometry the trigonometric functions are defined as ratios of lengths. The following result provides an analogue in hyperbolic geometry.

Theorem 4.19 *Let (A, B, C) be a triangle in the hyperbolic plane $\mathbb{H}$. The measurement of angles is given by the Riemannian metric of $\mathbb{H}$. Assume that the angle at C is right, i.e. $\gamma = \frac{\pi}{2}$. Then $\sin(\alpha) = \frac{\sinh(a)}{\sinh(c)}$ holds.*

Proof: Construct a sequence $(C_n)_{n\in\mathbb{N}}$ as follows: put $C_0 = C$. Let C_1 be the foot point of the orthogonal projection of C_0 to the hypotenuse of (A, B, C). Let C_2 be the foot point of the orthogonal projection of C_1 to the hypotenuse of (A, C_0, C_1), see figure 21. Inductively, let C_{n+1} be the foot point of the orthogonal projection of C_n to the hypotenuse of (A, C_{n-1}, C_n). Claim:

$$\lim_{n\to\infty} C_n = A.$$

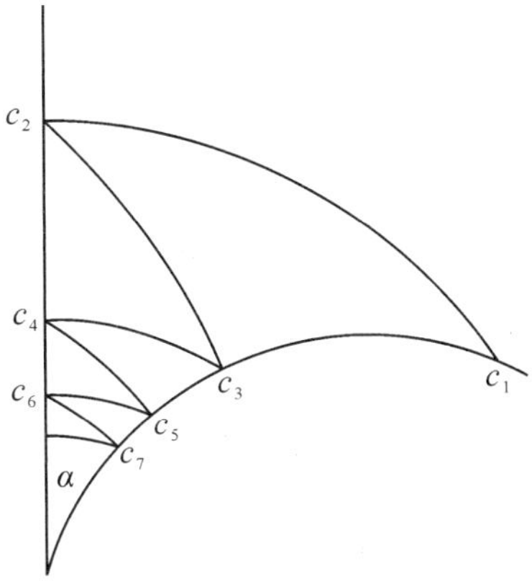

Figure 21 Zigzag of perpendicular segments

Observe, that the point C_{2n+2} is in between the points A and C_{2n}. The sequence of distances $n \mapsto d_{\mathrm{H}}(A, C_{2n})$ is monotonously decreasing, hence convergent. It follows the sequence of the points C_{2n} has a limit, say C'. Analogously, the sequence of points C_{2n+1} has a limit, say B'. Assuming, $C' \neq A$ leads to a contradiction, namely the triangle $AB'C'$ would have right angles at B' and C', contradicting the fact that the sum of the angles of a triangle is strictly less than the sum of two right angles. Hence the claim.

So all lengths of the triangles (A, C_n, C_{n+1}) tend to 0 if $n \to \infty$. The coordinate z : $\mathbb{H} = \mathbb{H}_l \to \mathbb{C}_+$ is an isometry into $(\mathbb{C}_+, \rho_{\mathbb{C}_+})$. The Riemannian metric $\rho_{\mathbb{C}_+}$ and the Euclidean metric $\rho_{\mathbb{C}}$ are conformal. Hence,

$$\lim_{n\to\infty} \frac{d_{\mathbb{H}}(C_n, C_{n+1})}{d_{\mathbb{H}}(A, C_n)} = \lim_{n\to\infty} \frac{d_{\mathbb{C}_+}(z(C_n), z(C_{n+1}))}{d_{\mathbb{C}_+}(z(A), z(C_n))} =$$

$$\lim_{n\to\infty} \frac{d_{\mathbb{C}}(z(C_n), z(C_{n+1}))}{d_{\mathbb{C}}(z(A)\ z(C_n))} = \sin(\alpha)$$

where $\alpha \in]0, \frac{\pi}{2}[$ is the angle at A of the triangle (A, B, C) or at $z(A)$ of the triangle $(z(A), z(B), z(C))$ with segments of half circles as sides. Using the Taylor expansion of the sinh function, one shows

$$\lim_{n\to\infty} \frac{\sinh(d_{\mathbb{H}}(C_n, C_{n+1}))}{\sinh(d_{\mathbb{H}}(A, C_n))} = \lim_{n\to\infty} \frac{d_{\mathbb{H}}(C_n, C_{n+1})}{d_{\mathbb{H}}(A, C_n)} = \sin(\alpha).$$

By the previous Hyperbolic Sinh Product Theorem the most left above limit is stationary from its first term on. The result follows.

As a consequence, by using identities between elementary functions, follows:

Theorem 4.20 *Let* (A, B, C) *be a triangle in the hyperbolic plane* $\mathbb{H}$. *Assume that the angle at C is right, i.e.* $\gamma = \frac{\pi}{2}$ *Then*

$$\sin(\alpha) = \frac{\sinh(a)}{\sinh(c)}$$

$$\cos(\alpha) = \frac{\tanh(b)}{\tanh(c)} = \frac{\sinh(b)\cosh(a)}{\sinh(c)}$$

$$\tan(\alpha) = \frac{\tanh(a)}{\sinh(b)} = \frac{\sinh(a)}{\cosh(a)\sinh(b)}.$$

The following theorems describe the three basic couplings of lengths of sides and angles for hyperbolic triangles.

Theorem 4.21 Hyperbolic Cosine Law. *Let* (A, B, C) *be a triangle in* $\mathbb{H}$. *The* Hyperbolic Cosine Law *states*:

$$\cosh(a) = \cosh(b)\cosh(c) - \sinh(b)\sinh(c)\cos(\alpha)$$

$$\cosh(b) = \cosh(a)\cosh(c) - \sinh(a)\sinh(c)\cos(\beta)$$

$$\cosh(c) = \cosh(a)\cosh(b) - \sinh(a)\sinh(b)\cos(\gamma).$$

Proof: Let P be the foot point of the height from A. Let a' be the length of BP, and a'' the length PC. Let h be the length of the height AP. Let α' be the angle BAP and α'' the angle PAC.

With the addition formulae

$$\cosh(a) = \cosh(a')\cosh(a'') + \sinh(a')\sinh(a'')$$

$$\cos(\alpha) = \cos(\alpha')\cos(\alpha'') - \sin(\alpha')\sin(\alpha'')$$

and the hyperbolic Pythagoras Theorem and Th. 4.20 one gets

$$\cosh(b)\cosh(c) - \sinh(b)\sinh(c)\cos(\alpha' + \alpha'') =$$

$$\cosh(\alpha')\cosh(\alpha'')\cosh^2(h) -$$

$$\sinh(b)\sinh(c)\left(\frac{\sinh(h)\cosh(a')}{\sinh(c)}\frac{\sinh(h)\cosh(a'')}{\sinh(b)} - \frac{\sinh(\alpha')}{\sinh(c)}\frac{\sinh(a'')}{\sinh(b)}\right) =$$

$$(\cosh^2(h) - \sinh^2(h))(\cosh(a')\cosh(a'') + \sinh(a')\sinh(a'')) = \cosh(a)$$

Theorem 4.22 Hyperbolic Sine-Sinh Law. *Let* (A,B,C) *be a triangle in* $\mathbb{H}$. *The* Hyperbolic Sine-Sinh Law *states*:

$$\frac{\sin(\alpha)}{\sinh(a)} = \frac{\sin(\beta)}{\sinh(b)} = \frac{\sin(\gamma)}{\sinh(c)}.$$

Proof: The symmetric expression

$$\frac{1 - \cosh^2(a) - \cosh^2(b) - \cosh^2(c) + 2\cosh(a)\cosh(b)\cosh(c)}{\sinh^2(a)\sinh^2(b)\sinh^2(c)}$$

reduces by simplification to $\dfrac{\sin^2(\alpha)}{\sinh^2(a)}$.

Theorem 4.23 Angular Hyperbolic Cosine Law. *Let* (A,B,C) *be a triangle in* $\mathbb{H}$. *The Angular Hyperbolic Cosine Law states*:

$$-\cos(\alpha) = \cos(\beta)\cos(\gamma) - \sin(\beta)\sin(\gamma)\cosh(a)$$

$$-\cos(\beta) = \cos(\alpha)\cos(\gamma) - \sin(\alpha)\sin(\gamma)\cosh(b)$$

$$-\cos(\gamma) = \cos(\alpha)\cos(\beta) - \sin(\alpha)\sin(\beta)\cosh(c).$$

Proof: Compute $\cos(\beta)$, $\cos(\gamma)$ using the Hyperbolic Cosine Law, next compute $\sin(\beta)$ and $\sin(\gamma)$. The expression $\cos(\beta)\cos(\gamma) - \sin(\beta)\sin(\gamma)\cosh(a)$ will simplify to $-\cos(\alpha)$.

We remember that the function $\cos: [0,\pi] \to [-1,1]$ is a strictly monotonously decreasing bijection. The reciprocal bijection is the function $\arccos: [-1,1] \to [0,\pi]$. Remember: $\arccos(h) = \frac{1}{i}\log(h + i\sqrt{1 - h^2})$. From the Angular Hyperbolic Cosine Law we deduce:

Theorem 4.24 *Let* (A,B,C) *be a triangle in* $\mathbb{H}$. *We have*

$$\alpha = \arccos\left(\frac{\cosh(a) - \cosh(b)\cosh(c)}{\sinh(b)\sinh(c)}\right).$$

The angles β, γ *are determined by the same expression after a cyclic permutation.*

The function $\cosh: [0, +\infty[\to [1, +\infty[$ is strictly monotonously increasing. The reciprocal function is arcCosh : $[1,+\infty[\rightarrow: [0,+\infty[$. Remember: $\text{arcCosh}(h) = \log(h + \sqrt{h^2 - 1})$. From the Angular Hyperbolic Cosine Law we deduce:

Theorem 4.25 *Let (A,B,C) be a triangle in $\mathbb{H}$. We have*

$$a = arcCosh\left(\frac{\cos(\alpha) + \cos(\beta)\cos(\gamma)}{\sin(\beta)\sin(\gamma)}\right).$$

The side lengths b, c are determined by an analogous expression after a cyclic permutation.

For right hyperbolic triangles simplifications occur:

Theorem 4.26 *Let (A,B,C) be a triangle in $\mathbb{H}$ with right angle at C. The coupling lengths-angle becomes:*

$$\cosh(a) = \cos(\alpha) / \sin(\beta)$$

$$\cosh(b) = \cos(\beta) / \sin(\alpha)$$

$$\cosh(c) = \coth(\alpha)\coth(\beta).$$

Natural questions concern the trigonometry of more general triangles in the hyperbolic plane $\mathbb{H}$. Instead of encoding a triangle by its summets, it is more convenient to define a triangle by the triple of lines $(\boldsymbol{a}, \boldsymbol{b}, \boldsymbol{c})$ that carry the sides of the triangle. The line $\mathbf{a}$ carries the side BC etc. If the three lines intersect pairwise in three points, one recovers the notion of a usual triangle. If one or more pairs of lines do not intersect, the triple $(\boldsymbol{a}, \boldsymbol{b}, \boldsymbol{c})$ defines a general hyperbolic triangle.

Pairs of lines $(\boldsymbol{a}, \boldsymbol{b})$ in the hyperbolic plane $\mathbb{H}$ that do not intersect are of two kinds. Let $\gamma' \in \mathbb{R}$ be the infimum of the distance $d_{\mathbb{H}}(P,Q)$ with $P \in \mathbf{a}$ and $Q \in \mathbf{b}$. If $\gamma' > 0$ the lines are called *strictly disjoint*, if $\gamma' = 0$ the lines are called *asymptotic*.

Most general triangles are triples $(\mathbf{a}, \mathbf{b}, \mathbf{c})$ of pairwise strictly disjoint lines. Let A be the shortest geodesic segment that joins $\mathbf{b}, \mathbf{c}$, etc. The three geodesic segments A, B, C together with three geodesic segments on the lines $(\boldsymbol{a}, \boldsymbol{b}, \boldsymbol{c})$ build a hexagon $H(\boldsymbol{a}, \boldsymbol{b}, \boldsymbol{c})$ with right angles. Let a, b, c be the lengths of the segments carried by $(\boldsymbol{a}, \boldsymbol{b}, \boldsymbol{c})$ and let α', β', γ' be the lengths of the segments A, B, C. Observe that all quantities are hyperbolic lengths, and a combinatorial central symmetry exchanges the roles of a, b, c and α', β', γ', see figure 22.

The basic trigonometric relation for most general triangles $(\boldsymbol{a}, \boldsymbol{b}, \boldsymbol{c})$ and the

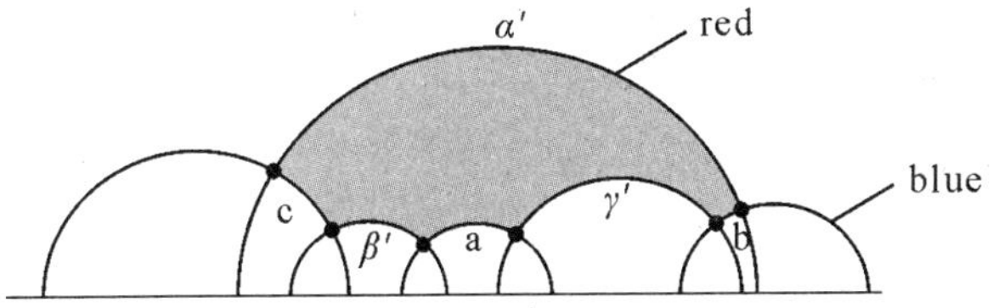

Figure 22 **Right-angled hexagon. The red lines are common perpendiculars to the blue lines**

corresponding right angled hexagons $H(a, b, c)$ is given by

Theorem 4.27 Hyperbolic Cosine Law for ⊥-hexagons. *With the notation from above the following identities hold.*

$$\cosh(a) = -\cosh(b)\cosh(c) + \sinh(b)\sinh(c)\cosh(\alpha')$$

$$\cosh(\alpha') = -\cosh(\beta')\cosh(\gamma') + \sinh(\beta')\sinh(\gamma')\cosh(a).$$

Before giving a proof we need to study pairs of lines in $\mathbb{H}$. In particular we need expressions for the angle if they intersect and for the shortest distance if they do not intersect.

Let K, L be two distinct oriented lines in $\mathbb{H} = \mathbb{H}_I$ that intersect in $\mathbb{H}$. By an isometry we transform for some $s \in]-1,+1[$ the pair (K, L) into the pair (C, L_s) where C is the oriented line $\{t((X-1)^2) + (1-t)((X+1)^2) \mid t \in [0,1[\}$ and L_s is the oriented line $\{(X-s)^2 + r^2 \mid r > 0\}$. The lines C and L_s are oriented by the parameters $t \in]0,1[$ and $r \in]0,+\infty[$. At the intersection point of C and L_s appear four sectors oriented by the restriction of the z- coordinate orientation of $\mathbb{H}$: at precisely one of those four oriented sectors the union of boundary legs with the induced orientation form the oriented boundary of this oriented sector. The oriented angle $\alpha(K, L)$ between C and L_s is the angle of this sector. Switching from z -coordinate to $\bar{z}$ -coordinate orientation changes this sector to the opposite sector and does not change the angle α. Changing the orientation on one line only changes the angle from α to $\pi - \alpha$.

We define the oriented cross ratio $\mathrm{CR}(K, L)$ of a pair of intersecting oriented lines K, L as

$$\mathrm{CR}(K,L) = \mathrm{CR}(C, Ls) = \mathrm{cr}(-1, 1, s, \infty) = \frac{1+s}{2}.$$

For two lines K, L that are strictly disjoint we orient the lines such that their union becomes the oriented boundary of the z-coordinate oriented region in between K and L. By an isometry we transform the pair (K,L) for some $r \in]1,+\infty[$ to the pair (C,C_r), C as before and $C_r = \{t(X+r)^2+(1-t)(X-r)^2 \mid t \in [0,1[\}$. The shortest distance from C to C_r is realized by the geodesic segment that connects (X^2+1) and (X^2+r^2). Its length is $\log(r)$.

We define the oriented cross ratio $\mathrm{CR}(K,L)$ of a pair of intersecting oriented lines K,L as

$$\mathrm{CR}(K,L) = \mathrm{CR}(C,Cr) = cr(-1,1,r,-r) = \frac{(r+1)^2}{4r}.$$

The pair (K,L) of oriented lines can also be transformed to the pair (C,L_s) with $s = \dfrac{r^2+1}{2r}$.

From previous computations we deduce.

Theorem 4.28 *Let K,L be two oriented intersecting lines with oriented angle α. If (K,L) is congruent to (C,L_s) as above for some $-1<s<1$, then the angle α and its cosine are given by*

$$\cos(\alpha) = 2\mathrm{CR}(K,L)-1=2\mathrm{CR}(C,L_s)-1= s$$
$$\alpha = \arccos(2\mathrm{CR}(K,L)-1).$$

Theorem 4.29 *Let K,L be two strictly disjoint lines. If (K,L) is congruent to (C,C_r) as above for some $r>1$, and also to (C,L_s) for $s=\frac{1}{2}(r+\frac{1}{r})$, then the distance from K to L is given by*

$$d_{\mathbb{H}}(K,L)= d_{\mathbb{H}}(C,C_r)=\log(r)=\mathrm{arcCosh}(2\mathrm{CR}(K,L)-1)$$

and

$$cosh(d_{\mathbb{H}}(K,L)) = s = 2CR(K,L) - 1$$

holds.

Proof: Hyperbolic Cosine Law for $\perp$-hexagons. Due to the central combinatorial symmetry of order 6 it suffices to proof only one identity. First we orient the hexagon according to the z-coordinate orientation and name the sides a, C, b, A, c, B. The letters a, b, c stand also for the lengths of the corresponding sides. The lengths of A,B,C are denoted by α', β', γ'. The side a is carried by the oriented line $a = (t(X+a_2)^2+(1-t)(X+a_1)^2), t \in [0,1]$. We introduce similar notation for the other sides. We get 12 distinct points on $\mathbb{R}\cup\{\infty\}$ which appear in the following cyclic order:

$$a_1,\ B_2,\ C_1,\ a_2,\ b_1,\ C_2,\ A_1,\ b_2, c_1,\ A_2,\ B_1,\ c_2.$$

For convenience of calculation, assume that all differ from ∞ and that they appear in increasing order according to the order of $\mathbb{R}$. The six right angles

$$\sphericalangle aC,\ \sphericalangle Cb,\ \sphericalangle bA,\ \sphericalangle Ac,\ \sphericalangle cB,\ \sphericalangle Ba$$

between oriented lines lead to the cross-ratio equations

$$\frac{1}{2}=\mathrm{CR}(aC)=\mathrm{CR}(Cb)=\mathrm{CR}(bA)=\mathrm{CR}(Ac)=\mathrm{CR}(cB)=\mathrm{CR}(Ba).$$

Hence to

$$\frac{1}{2}=\frac{(C_1-a_1)(C_2-a_2)}{(a_2-a_1)(C_2-C_1)}=\frac{(b_1-C_1)(b_2-C_2)}{(C_2-C_1)(b_2-b_1)}=\frac{(A_1-b_1)(A_2-b_2)}{(b_2-b_1)(A_2-A_1)}=$$

$$\frac{(c_1-A_1)(c_2-A_2)}{(A_2-A_1)(c_2-c_1)}=\frac{(B_1-c_1)(B_2-c_2)}{(c_2-c_1)(B_2-B_1)}=\frac{(a_1-B_1)(a_2-c_2)}{(B_2-B_1)(a_2-a_1)}.$$

Using the trigonometric identity $\cosh^2-1=\sinh^2$, rearranging and squaring, the identity that has to been proved becomes equivalent to the following identity that only uses cosh functions

$$(\cosh(a)-\cosh(b)\cosh(c))^2-(\cosh^2(b)-1)(\cosh^2(c)-1)\cosh^2(\alpha')=0.$$

One has

$$\cosh(a)=2CR(BC)-1=2\frac{(C_1-B_1)(C_2-B_2)}{(B_2-B_1)(C_2-C_1)}-1$$

$$\cosh(b)=2CR(CA)-1=2\frac{(A_1-C_1)(A_2-C_2)}{(C_2-C_1)(A_2-A_1)}-1$$

$$\cosh(c)=2CR(AB)-1=2\frac{(B_1-A_1)(B_2-A_2)}{(A_2-A_1)(B_2-B_1)}-1$$

$$\cosh(\alpha')=2CR(bc)-1=2\frac{(c_1-b_1)(c_2-b_2)}{(b_2-b_1)(c_2-c_1)}-1.$$

Now it is straightforward to check the identity by a tedious calculation.

Remark. In spherical geometry no embedded right-angled hexagons exist. However, every spherical triangle Δ can be completed to an immersed spherical right-angled hexagon $H_\Delta=(A, B, C)$. To do this, extend each pair of sides of Δ beyond their intersection point until reaching a pair of points realizing the maximal distance along their supporting lines. Connecting at three places those pairs of points by shortests segments constructs an immersed right-angled spherical hexagon. Here, the lengths of these segments correspond to the angles of the triangle Δ. At the vertex A of Δ one adds a double right-angled spherical triangle. To both sides b, c one adds at A segments of equal length α''. By the spherical Pythagoras Theorem the length α'' is given by $\cos(\alpha'') = \cos^2(\alpha)$.

Using notation as above, the spherical length α' of the added segment between the lines supporting the sides b, c is equal to the angle α of the triangle Δ. Using consistent notation, the lengths of the sides of the hexagon H_Δ are in cyclic order $\alpha', \alpha'' + b + \gamma'', \gamma', \gamma'' + a + \beta'', \beta', \beta'' + c + \alpha''$.

A Spherical Cosine Law holds for the $\perp$-hexagon H_Δ which in fact reduces to the Spherical Cosine Law for the triangle Δ.

The triangle Δ can be retrieved from the immersed hexagon H_Δ as the triangle spanned by its double points.

Exercise 11: *Let $p = (p_i)_I$ be a countable system of points in $\mathbb{H}$, weighted by a weight function $w : I \to \mathbb{R}_{\geqslant 0}$ with $\sum_I w_i = 1$. Assume that the set $\{p_i\} \subset \mathbb{H}$ is of finite diameter. Define the energy $E(q;\ p,\ w)$ of (p, w) with respect to a point $q \in \mathbb{H}$ by $E(q;p,w) \overset{def}{=} -1 + \sum_I w_i \cosh(d_{\mathbb{H}}(q, p_i))$. Show that the map $q \in \mathbb{H} \mapsto E(q;p,w) \in \mathbb{R}$ achieves its minimum at a unique point $b(p,\ w)$.*

Hint: Show that the restriction of this map to a geodesic in $\mathbb{H}$ is strictly convex.

Exercise 12: *Show, in case that the cardinality of I is finite, that $b(p,w)$ depends differentiably upon the multi-point p and the weights w. We call the point $b(p,w)$ the energy-barycenter of the weighted multi-point (p,w).*

Exercise 13: *Construct hexagons with 6 equal angles in $\mathbb{H}$. Let a, b, c the lengths of 3 sides that pairwise do not have a vertex in common and let $\alpha \in [0, \frac{2\pi}{3}]$ be the common angle. Compute the three other lengths.*

Exercise 14: *Let $h = (A_1, A_2, \cdots, A_6)$ and $h' = (A_1', A_2', \cdots, A_6')$ be hyperbolic hexagons with oriented numberings of the vertices. Assume h to be right angled, h' to have angles $> \frac{\pi}{2}$ and that the sides of h' have smaller length then the correspond-*

ing side in h. Let $B=b(A_1,A_2,\cdots,A_6)$, $B'=b(A_1',A_2',\cdots,A_6')$ *be the energy-barycenters. Show that there exists a unique isometric inclusion of* h' *in* h, *such that* $B=B'$ *and the points* $B=B'$, A'_1, A_1 *are aligned. We call such an inclusion a rigid inclusion. If requiring alignment of the other pairs of vertices,* h' *admits six rigid inclusions in h.*

Exercise 15: Busemann's axiom for negative curvature. *In a hyperbolic triangle ABC the length of the segment joining the mid-points of the sides AB and AC is strictly less than half the length of the side BC.*[16].

Together with right angled triangles, the Chayyam-Saccheri and Lambert quadrilaterals are basic building blocks in hyperbolic and spherical trigonometry.

A Lambert quadrilateral is a quadrilateral $AOBC$ with three right angles, say at A, O and B. A Chayyam-Saccheri quadrilateral is a quadrilateral $ABCD$ with right angles at B, C and sides AB and CD of equal length.

A generalized Lambert quadrilateral is a quadrilateral with three right angles, say at A, O and B such that the sides opposite to the sides OA and OB do not necessarly meet. A generalized Lambert quadrilateral is up to isometry characterized by the lengths $|AO|$, $|BO|$. We distinguish three cases:

—The (ordinary) ones: the opposite sides meet in a point C,

—The ideal ones: the opposite sides do not meet, but have asymptotic ends,

—The trans-ideal ones: the opposite sides do not meet, and the ends are not asymptotic.

One can think of the rays $[O,A[$ and $[O,B[$ as orthogonal coordinate axes X_+, Y_+ and the points $A\in X_+$, $B\in Y_+$ as the orthogonal projections of the existing, or non-existing point C of the quadrilateral. Think of the numbers $x=\tanh(|OA|)$, $y=\tanh(|OB|)$ as "" coordinates of the "point" C. If $A\notin X_+$ but $A\in X$ where X is the line carrying X_+, then define the coordinate number by $x=-\tanh(|OA|)$. Extend the definition of the coordinate y accordingly.

Now, the hyperbolic plan $\mathbb{H}$ has coordinates $p\in\mathbb{H}\mapsto(x(p),y(p))\in\mathbb{R}^2$. Not every pair (a,b) of numbers is realized as coordinates of a point $p\in\mathbb{H}$. Let $\mathbb{K}$ be the open unit disc in $\mathbb{R}^2$.

Theorem 4.30 Kleinian Model $\mathbb{K}$. *The map* $p\in\mathbb{H}\mapsto(x(p),y(p))\in$

$\mathbb{K}$ is a bijection. Images of hyperbolic lines are chords in $\mathbb{K}$. The hyperbolic metric $d_{\mathbb{H}}$ is transformed to the Hilbert metric $d_{\mathbb{K}}$. The space $(\mathbb{K}, d_{\mathbb{K}})$ is the so called Kleinian model for the hyperbolic plane.

Proof: Let X, Y be lines in $\mathbb{H}$ that intersect each other with a right angle at the point O. Think of X, Y as coordinate axes. For $p \in \mathbb{H}$ let p_X, O, p_Y, p be the Lambert quadrilateral where p_X, p_Y are the projections of p on the axes. Denote by α, β the angles pOp_X, pOp_Y. Observe $\cos(\alpha)^2 + \cos(\beta)^2 = 1$ since $\alpha + \beta = \frac{\pi}{2}$.

From $\cos(\alpha) = \frac{x(p)}{\tanh(|Op|)}$ and $\cos(\beta) = \frac{y(p)}{\tanh(|Op|)}$ follows $\tanh(|Op|)^2 = x(p)^2 + y(p)^2$. By varying p over $\mathbb{H}$ the quantity $\tanh(|Op|)$ varies over $[0,1[$. Now it follows that the map $p \in \mathbb{H} \mapsto (x(p), y(p)) \in \mathrm{K}$ is a bijection. We leave finishing the proof as an exercise. Hint: the coordinate map is equivariant with respect to rotation of $\mathbb{H}$ with center O and rotations of $\mathbb{R}^2$ with center $(0,0)$.

From this proof also follows

Theorem 4.31 *A generalized Lambert quadrilateral AOB with $a = \tanh(|AO|)$, $b = \tanh(|BO|)$ is ordinary if $a^2 + b^2 < 1$, ideal if $a^2 + b^2 = 1$, and trans-ideal if $a^2 + b^2 > 1$.*

In the forthcoming proof of the Uniformisation Theorem we will use that the lengths u, v of two adjacent edges of a right-angled hyperbolic hexagon satisfy $\tanh(u)^2 + \tanh(v)^2 > 1$. Indeed, four consecutive edges define a trans-ideal Lambert quadrilateral. Consequently

Theorem 4.32 Degeneration of hyperbolic $\perp$-hexagons. *Let $(H_n)_{n \in \mathbb{N}}$ be a sequence of labelled hyperbolic $\perp$-hexagons. Let d_n be the distance between the lines that support the edge U_n and the opposite edge U'_n. If the edge length u_n of the edge U_n tends to 0 for $n \to \infty$, then the edge length v_n of an adjacent edge V_n tends to ∞ with*

$$v_n \geqslant \operatorname{arctanh}\sqrt{(1 - \tanh(u_n)^2)}.$$

The distance d_n tends to ∞ with

$$d_n \geqslant \operatorname{arctanh}\left(\sqrt{1 - \tanh(u_n)^2 - \tanh\left(\frac{u_n}{2}\right)^2}\right).$$

Proof: The first inequality follows from $\tanh(u_n)^2+\tanh(v_n)^2>1$. For the second inequality observe that a Saccheri quadrilateral S with bottom edge U_n and two perpendicular sides of length $A=arctanh\sqrt{1-tanh(u_n)^2}$ can be placed inside H_n. Let h be the height of S, i.e. the distance between U_n and the opposite edge U_n'' in S. Observe $d_n \geqslant h$. The Saccheri quadrilateral S is the union of two Lambert quadrilaterals L, L' Let δ be the length of the diagonal in L' that connects the midpoint of U_n with the acute angle of L'. Now observe, by using "Cartesian coordinates" in L' and the hyperbolic Pythagoras Theorem,

$$\tan(h)^2+\tanh\left(\frac{u_n}{2}\right)^2=\tanh(\delta)^2 \geqslant \tanh(A)^2.$$

Hence,

$$d_n \geqslant h \geqslant \operatorname{arctanh}\sqrt{1-\tanh(u_n)^2-\tanh\left(\frac{u_n}{2}\right)^2}.$$

Ευκλείδης από την Αλεξάνδρεια (300 π.Χ.–270 π.Χ.), Euclid of Alexandria, cited as ὁ στοιχειώτης, author of the Elements, was a Greek mathematician. His axiomatic approach to reality after 2300 years still remains a main method of study. Moreover today, his approach creates realities even before that they become visible by our eyes or are detected by our experiments.

Omar Khayyám (1048–1131) was a Persian mathematician, astronomer, philosopher, and poet.

Giovanni Girolamo Saccheri (1667–1733) was an Italian philosopher and mathematician.

Johann Heinrich Lambert (1728–1777) was a Swiss mathematician, physician.

4.4 Hyperbolic Area

The angular excess $\epsilon(ABC)=\pi-\alpha-\beta-\gamma$ of a spherical triangle $\delta(ABC)$ was discovered as a measure of area by Albert Girard (1595–1632), a French-Dutch mathematician. A direct inspection shows that the angular excess behaves in an additive way under geodesic subdivision.

A similar behavior is known in hyperbolic geometry for the angular defect $\delta(ABC) = \pi - \alpha - \beta - \gamma$ that was introduced by Lambert.

Let $\mu_{\mathbb{H}}$ be the Lebesgue measure on $\mathbb{H}$ induced by the Riemannian metric $g_{\mathbb{H}}$ of Gaussian curvature −1. Similarly on the Euclidean unit sphere $\mathbb{S}$ let $\mu_{\mathbb{S}}$ be the Lebesque measure induced by the Riemannian metric $g_{\mathbb{S}}$ of Gaussian curvature +1.

In both geometries by integration we get an area function defined on triangles that behaves in an additive way under geodesic subdivision:

$$A_{\mathbb{H}}(ABC) = \int_{\Delta(ABC)} d\mu_{\mathbb{H}}, A_{\mathbb{S}}(ABC) = \int_{\Delta(ABC)} d\mu_{\mathbb{S}}.$$

The defect/excess functions and the area functions are moreover invariant by isometries.

It follows that the angular defect/excess functions and the area functions are proportional. So there exist gauge constants $\lambda_{\mathbb{H}}, \lambda_{\mathbb{S}}$ such that for triangles ABC in $\mathbb{H}$or $\mathbb{S}$ the following formulas hold.

$$A_{\mathbb{H}}(ABC) = \lambda_{\mathbb{H}}\delta(ABC), A_{\mathbb{S}}(ABC) = \lambda_{\mathbb{S}} \in (ABC).$$

In order to calibrate those gauge constants an example will suffice.

For the spherical geometry the half sphere considered as a triangle ABC with vertices on the equator gives

$$A_{\mathbb{S}}(ABC) = 2\pi = \pi + \pi + \pi - \pi = \epsilon(ABC).$$

This shows $\lambda_{\mathbb{S}} = 1$.

We have used that the total area of the unit two sphere $\mathbb{S}$ is 4π as computed by Archimedes of Syracuse (BC 287−212), a Greek mathematician, physicist, engineer, and astronomer[7].

Let ABC in $\mathbb{H}$ be the triangle with image $z(\Delta(ABC))$ by the coordinate z in $\mathbb{C}_+$ that is limited by the lines $L_{-1,\infty}, L_{-1,1}, L_{1,\infty}$. The angles are $\alpha = \beta = \gamma = 0$. One computes

$$\delta(ABC) = \pi - 0 - 0 - 0 = \pi,$$

$$A_{\mathbb{H}}(ABC) = \int_{z(\Delta(ABC))} \frac{dx \Lambda dy}{y^2} = \int_{-1}^{+1} dx \int_{\sqrt{1-x^2}}^{+\infty} \frac{dy}{y^2} = \int_{-1}^{+1} \frac{dx}{\sqrt{1-x^2}} = \pi$$

and concludes $\lambda_{\mathbb{H}} = 1$.

As application, a regular N-gon P_N with right angles in $\mathbb{H}$, $N \geqslant 5$, has area

$(N-4)\frac{\pi}{2}$. Indeed, P_N is the union of $2N$ triangles with angles $\frac{\pi}{N}, \frac{\pi}{2}, \frac{\pi}{4}$.

This union is not disjoint, but the union of their interiors is. Even more generally, the area of an N-gon P_N with angles $\alpha_1, \alpha_2, \cdots, \alpha_N$ is $(N-2)\pi - \sum_i \alpha_i$.

4.5 A compact hyperbolic surface of genus $g \geqslant 2$

With the help of hyperbolic trigonometry for every genus $g \geqslant 2$ we can construct a compact hyperbolic surface.

Theorem 4.33 *For any $g \geqslant 2$, there exists a compact hyperbolic surface S_g of genus g. The hyperbolic area of S_g is $-2\pi\chi(S_g)$. The surface is a 4g fold branched cover of the sphere $\Sigma_{1,1/4g,1/4g}$ with 3 orbifold angles $\frac{\pi}{1}, \frac{\pi}{4g}, \frac{\pi}{4g}$. The covering map is a Belyi map.*

A hyperbolic surface S is a manifold given by families $(U_\alpha \subset \mathbb{H})_{\alpha \in A}$, $(U_{\beta\alpha} \subset U_\alpha)$ and $(\phi_{\alpha\beta} : U_{\alpha\beta} \to U_{\beta\alpha})_{(\alpha,\beta) \in A \times A}$. Note that the subsets U_α are open subsets in $\mathbb{H}$. Moreover, the maps $\phi_{\alpha\beta} : U_{\alpha\beta} \to U_{\beta\alpha}$ preserve all the structure that we have in the hyperbolic plane $\mathbb{H}$. This means that the map $\phi_{\alpha\beta} : U_{\alpha\beta} \to U_{\beta\alpha}$ is the restriction of an automorphism $\Phi_{\alpha\beta} : \mathbb{H} \to \mathbb{H}$. In particular $\phi_{\alpha\beta}$ is differentiable, so S is a differentiable manifold. But also $\Phi_{\alpha\beta}$ preserves the fields $p \in \mathbb{H} \mapsto \text{Hess}_p$ and $p \in \mathbb{H} \mapsto J_p$, so S is equipped with a Riemannian metric and also with a complex structure. Since the local geometry is the local geometry inherited from the hyperbolic plane, we say that S is a hyperbolic surface.

Proof: Let $g \in \mathbb{N}$, $g > 1$. First we construct a hyperbolic triangle T, see figure 23, with angles $\frac{\pi}{2}, \frac{\pi}{4g}, \frac{\pi}{4g}$. This is possible, since $\frac{\pi}{2} + \frac{\pi}{4g} + \frac{\pi}{4g} < \pi$. It is a triangle with a right angle. The hypotenuse has length $\text{arcCosh}\left(\frac{\cos(\pi/4g)^2}{\sin(\pi/4g)^2}\right)$ and both catheti are of equal length $\text{arcCosh}\left(\frac{\cos(\pi/4g)}{\sin(\pi/4g)}\right)$. We put $8g$ such triangles together and construct a regular $4g$ -gon P in the hyperbolic plane $\mathbb{H}$ with angles $\frac{2\pi}{4g}$ and side length 2arcCosh $\left(\frac{\cos(\pi/4g)}{\sin(\pi/4g)}\right)$ .The $4g$ -gon P is the pave of a tessellation of the hyperbolic plane $\mathbb{H}$. We will describe the manifold S with $8g+1$ charts $U_0, U_1, U_2, \cdots, U_{8g}$. The open set U_0 is the interior of the $4g$ -gon P. We number its vertices following the boundary of P and the midpoints of the edges by $A_1, A_2, \cdots, A_{8g}$. Numberings are cyclic, i.e. $A_{8g+j} = A_j$. Let $E_1, E_2, \cdots, E_{8g}$ be the (half) edges: $E_i = A_iA_{i+1}, 1 \leqslant i \leqslant 8g$. Let U_i be an open $\in$ - tubular neighborhood of the edge E_i. Here $0 < \epsilon \ll arcoos\left(\frac{\cos(\pi/4g)}{\sin(\pi/4g)}\right)$. In order to describe the manifold S we have to define subsets $U_{ji} \subset U_i$ and a family $\phi_{ji}: U_{ji} \to U_{ij}$ of gluing maps.

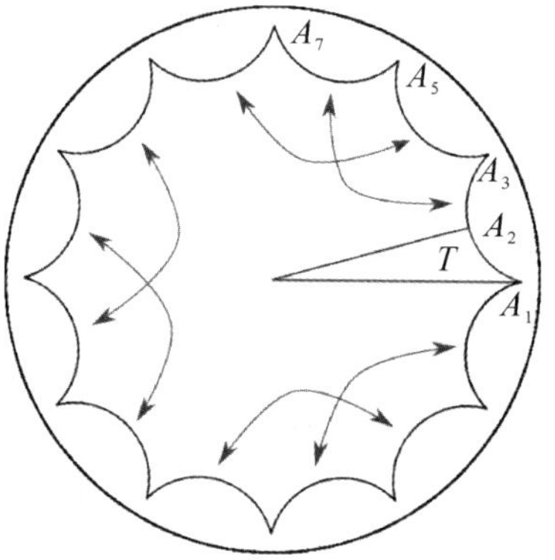

Figure 23 Hyperbolic 12-gon in Poincaré disc with identifications

If $U_i \cap U_j \neq \phi$ we put $U_{ij} = U_i \cap U_j = U_{ji}$ and $\phi_{ij} = Id_{U_j \cap U_i}: U_{ij} \to U_{ji}$. For $k = 0, 1, 2, \cdots, g-1$ define

$$U_{4k+6,4k+1} \stackrel{def}{=} U_{4k+1}, U_{4k+5,4k+2} \stackrel{def}{=} U_{4k+2}$$

$$U_{4k+8,4k+3} \stackrel{def}{=} U_{4k+3}, U_{4k+7,4k+4} \stackrel{def}{=} U_{4k+4}.$$

We orient the edges E_i from A_i to A_{i+1} if i odd, otherwise from A_{i+1} to A_i. For $k = 0, 1, 2, \cdots, g-1$, let

$$\Phi_{4k+6,4k+1}: \mathbb{H} \to \mathbb{H}$$

be the isometry with $\Phi_{4k+6,4k+1}(U_0) \cap U_0 = \phi$ that maps the oriented edge E_{4k+1} to the oriented edge E_{4k+6}. Let

$$\Phi_{4k+5,4k+2}: \mathbb{H} \to \mathbb{H}$$

be the isometry with $\Phi_{4k+5,4k+2}(U_0) \cap U_0 = \phi$ that maps the oriented edge E_{4k+2} to the oriented edge E_{4k+5}. The isometries $\Phi^{\pm 1}_{4k+6,4k+1}$, $\Phi^{\pm 1}_{4k+5,4k+2}$ correspond to the green arrows in the figure. Let $\phi_{4k+6,4k+1}$, $\phi_{4k+5,4k+2}$ be the restrictions to $U_{4k+6,4k+1}$, $U_{4k+5,4k+2}$. Let $\sim$ be the equivalence relation on $\dot{\bigcup}_{0\leqslant i\leqslant 8g} U_i$ generated by the gluings

$$p \sim \phi_{i,j}(p),\ p \in U_{ij},\ U_i \cap U_j \neq \phi,$$

$$p \sim \phi_{4k+6,4k+1(p)},\ p \in U_{4k+6,4k+1},$$

$$p \sim \phi_{4k+5,4k+2(p)},\ p \in U_{4k+5,4k+2}.$$

The manifold $S_g = S \overset{def}{=} \dot{\bigcup}_{0\leqslant i\leqslant 8g} U_i/\sim$ is now defined.

The $4g$ -gon P is the union of $8g$ triangles with angles $\frac{\pi}{2}, \frac{\pi}{4g}, \frac{\pi}{4g}$. Each triangle maps by $q: \dot{\bigcup}_{0\leqslant i\leqslant 8g} U_i \to S \overset{def}{=} \dot{\bigcup}_{0\leqslant i\leqslant 8g} U_i/\sim$ injectively to S. In S we will have $(2+2g)$ vertices, $12g$ edges and $8g$ triangles. Hence $\chi(S) = (2+2g) - 12g + 8g = 2 - 2g$ is the Euler characteristic and the genus of S equals g. For Belyi maps, and Belyi's Theorem, see the book by Ernesto Girondo and Gabino Gonzales-Diάz[39].

The same construction works for $g = 1$. Let P be a square in the Euclidean plane. We introduce vertices $A_1, A_2, \cdots, A_8$ in the plane as before, also open sets set $U_0, U_1, \cdots, U_8$ and corresponding glueings ϕ_{ij}. The resulting surface will be a surface of genus 1, i.e. a torus, but with an Euclidean structure.

A genus 0 surface can be obtained by starting out with two discs. No Euclidean motion will allow us to glue them in order to make a manifold. But don't worry, a surface with spherical geometry is already present, the unit two sphere S^2 in Euclidean three space.

Exercise 16: *Study the topology of the surface* $\{p \in \mathbb{C}^2 \mid w(p)^2 = z(p)^5 - 1\}$.

Exercise 17: *Compute the genus of the Fermat surface* $\{p \in P^2(\mathbb{C}) \mid x(p)^d + y(p)^d + z(p)^d = 0\}$ *of degree d.*

In spherical, Euclidean and hyperbolic geometry a triangle is determined up to isometry by its side lengths. Hence the area is a function of the side lengths. It is interesting to know explicit expression for the area.

Theorem 4.34 Heron, Huilier. *For a triangle ABC with sides of length a, b, and c, and semi-perimeter s. In spherical geometry, the angular excess $\epsilon(ABC)$ is* *given by Huilier's formula*

$$\tan(\frac{\epsilon(ABC)}{4}) = \sqrt{\tan(\frac{s}{2})\tan(\frac{s-a}{2})\tan(\frac{s-b}{2})\tan(\frac{s-c}{2})}.$$

In hyperbolic geometry, the angular defect δ(ABC) is given by

$$\tan(\frac{\delta(ABC)}{4}) = \sqrt{\tanh(\frac{s}{2})\tanh(\frac{s-a}{2})\tanh(\frac{s-b}{2})\tanh(\frac{s-c}{2})}.$$

In Euclidean geometry, the area A is given by Heron's formula

$$A = \sqrt{s(s-a)(s-b)(s-c)}.$$

4.6 The Riemann Sphere $\mathbb{C} \cup \{\infty\}$

The hyperbolic plane $\mathbb{H} = \mathbb{H}_I$ in above construction was a subset in the quotient space $S/\sim$ where we started with the set

$S = \{\phi: \mathbb{R}[X] \to F \mid \phi$ *surjective ring homomorphism to a field*$\}$

In order to have a better understanding of the set S we use a coordinate Ev_X on this set. Consider $\mathbb{R}$ as a subfield in $\mathbb{C}$ and denote the underlying set of the less common field F_1 by $\{\infty\}$. Here"∞" is a symbol with as only property: $\infty \notin \mathbb{C}$. Remembering that the only fields that can be the target of such a ring homomorphism are the fields $\mathbb{R} \subset \mathbb{C}$ and F_1, we define the bijective coordinate $\mathrm{Ev}_X: S \to \mathbb{C} \cup \{\infty\}$ by the evaluation $\mathrm{Ev}_X(\phi) = \phi(X) \in \mathbb{C} \cup \{\infty\}$. Now identify S and $\mathbb{C} \cup \{\infty\}$ via Ev_X. As natural topology T on $\mathbb{C} \cup \{\infty\}$, hence on S, choose the only compact topology that on $\mathbb{C}$ induces the usual norm topology. This topological space (S, T) is homeomorphic to the 2 sphere S^2.

Bernhard Riemann, by using the coordinates $z, \frac{1}{z}$ on $\mathbb{C}$ and on $(\mathbb{C} \setminus \{0\}) \cup \{\infty\}$ respectively has made $\mathbb{C} \cup \{\infty\}$ to a Riemann surface of genus 0. See section 7.

Coordinates $z, \frac{1}{z}: \mathbb{P}^1(\mathbb{C}) \to \mathbb{C} \cup \{\infty\}$ allow to identify the space $\mathbb{P}^1(\mathbb{C})$ of vector subspaces of dimension 1 in $\mathbb{C}^2$ and $\mathbb{C} \cup \{\infty\}$. Namely define $z(L)$, $L \in \mathbb{P}^1(\mathbb{C})$, by $z(L) = \frac{a}{b}$ with $(a, b) \in L \setminus \{0\}$.

More general, a similar coordinates allow for any field K to identify the projective space $\mathbb{P}^1(K)$ of 1-dimensional subspaces in K^2 and $K \cup \{\infty\}$.

5 Examples of Geometry

5.1 The Space of Norms

In the above presentation of the hyperbolic plane $\mathbb{H}_l$ we first introduced a set E of points, each point was representing a mathematical object of some kind. In a next step one studies how those points interact. In this way the set obtains a rich structure and becomes a space E. The next example is based on private communication with Bernard Mischler [Mis], who has taught me the following.

Let V be a vector space. Let $\mathbb{B}=\mathbb{B}(V)$ be the set of norms on V. The structure will be an internal composition law

$$\mu : \mathbb{B}\times\mathbb{B}\to\mathbb{B}.$$

In his first step Mischler introduces a map Diagr: $\mathbb{B}\times\mathbb{B}\times V\to\mathbb{D}(\mathbb{P}_+)$ to the space of Newton diagrams $\mathbb{D}(\mathbb{P}_+)$ in $\mathbb{P}_+ \overset{def}{=} \mathbb{R}_+\times\mathbb{R}_+$. A Newton diagram in $\mathbb{P}_+$ is a closed convex subset D in $\mathbb{P}_+$ such that the intersections of D with each axis $\{(a,b)\in\mathbb{P}_+ \mid a=0\}$ or $\{(a,b)\in\mathbb{P}_+ \mid b=0\}$ is non bounded. The set of Newton diagrams itself has an interesting geometry, which we will not explain further here, except that in particular, for each Newton diagram D one has a number $\alpha(D)\in\mathbb{R}$ namely the area of $\mathbb{P}_+\setminus D$.

Given two norms N,M on V and a vector $u\in V$, the Newton diagram Diagr$(N,M)(u)$ attached to N, M, u is the set

$$Diagr(N,M)(u) \overset{def}{=} \{(r,s)\in\mathbb{P}_+ \mid B^N(0,r)\cap B^M(u,s)\neq\phi\}.$$

In other words, Diagr$(N,M)(u)$ is the set of pairs of radii $(r,s)\in\mathbb{P}_+$ such that the closed N-ball with center $0\in V$ and radius r intersects the closed

M-ball with center $u \in V$ and radius s. The binary composition μ of norms $(N, M) \mapsto \mu(N,M)$ is defined as follows: the $\mu(N,M)$-norm of $u \in V$ is given by

$$\mu(N,M)(u)^2 = 2\alpha(\mathrm{Diagr}(N,M)(u))$$

Theorem 5.1 Bernard Mischler. *Let V be a real vector space with basis $(e_1, e_2, \cdots, e_n)$. Let N be the l^1-norm*

$$N(u) = \| u \|_{l^1} = \sum_{1 \leqslant i \leqslant n} |x_i(u)|$$

and M the l^∞-norm

$$M(u) = \| u \|_{l^\infty} = Max_{1 \leqslant i \leqslant n} |x_i(u)|.$$

Then $\mu(N,M)$ is the l^2-norm

$$\mu(N,M)(u) = \| u \|_{l^2} = \Big(\sum_{1 \leqslant i \leqslant n} |x_i(u)|^2 \Big)^{1/2}.$$

An immediate consequence is

Theorem 5.2 *Il a linear map $A: V \to V$ on a based vector space is contracting the l^1-and the l^∞-norms, then A contracts the l^2-norm.*

We have learned once more that set of mathematical objects of some given type has a rich structure and geometry. Figure 24 shows interpolation of l^1-and l^∞-norms.

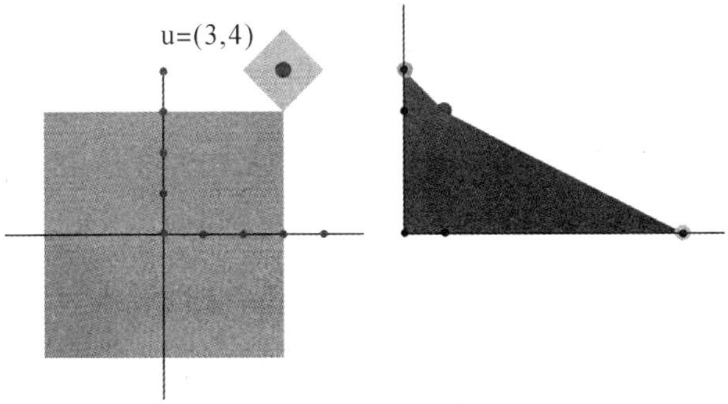

Figure 24 Interpolation of l^1-and l^∞-norms. Twice the red area is the l^2-norm of $u = (3,4) = (3,3) + (0,1)$.

Exercise 1: *Work out the inequalities that are hidden in above theorem, say for cases $Dim(V) = 2, 3, 10$.*

Exercise 2: *Let $\| ? \|$ be a norm on $\mathbb{R}^n$ that takes integral values at vectors* *with integral coordinates. Show that the unit ball of* $\| ? \|$ *is the convex hull of a finite set.*

The following example was explained at the Topology Seminar 1977 in Orsay by Adrien Douady (1935–2006), a french mathematician, and shows that the conclusion of the above exercise does not hold, if one assumes that the norm takes rational values at vectors with integral coordinates. The norm on $\mathbb{R}^2$ of Adrien has as unit ball the convex hull of the union of the two discs of Euclidean radius 1 and centers at $(-1,0)$ and $(1,0)$.

The above exercise is the key step in the study of the Thurston norm on the cohomology group $H^1(M,\mathbb{Z}) \otimes_{\mathbb{Z}} \mathbb{R}$ of 3-manifolds M.

5.2 Combinatorial Geometry

As example, let $E = \mathrm{Grass}_{4,2}(F_2)$ be the set of 2-dimensional linear subspaces in the 4-dimensional vector space F_2^4 over the field F_2 with two elements. We want to study structures on the set E.

The 2-point function $(a,b) \in E \times E \mapsto \delta(a,b) = 2 - \mathrm{Dim}_{F2}(a \cap b)$ is a metric on E. The group $\mathrm{GL}_4(F_2)$ acts transitively on E, but does not act transitively on the set $E \times E \setminus E$ of distinct pairs. Indeed, the metric δ takes only the values $0,1,2$. The group $\mathrm{GL}_4(F_2)$ acts by isometries on (E,δ).

Exercise 3: *Is* $GL_4(F_2)$ *the full group of isometries of* (E,δ)?

A ball $B^\delta(a,1)$ has 19 elements. If $\delta(a,b) = 2$, then $\# B^\delta(a,1) \cap B^\delta(b,1) = 9$ and if $\delta(a,b) = 1$ then $\# B^\delta(a,1) \cap B^\delta(b,1) = 14$. In particular, (E,δ) is a homogeneous metric space with integral metric, of diameter 2, with balls of radius 1 having 19 elements and mutual intersections having 9 or 14 elements. In short, we say it is a $(19,14,9)$-triple space.

Many questions arise: For which triples (a,b,c) does there exist a (a,b,c) triple space? Are $\mathrm{Grass}_{4,2}(F_q)$ with the metric $\delta(a,b) = 2 - \mathrm{Dim}_{Fq}(a \cap b)$ the only such spaces?

5.3 Spaces of Involutions

Remember that the spaces of involutions acting fixed point free on $P^1(\mathbb{R})$ or $P^1(\mathbb{C})$ that preserve the 4-point function given by cross ratio are models for the hyperbolic spaces $\mathbb{H}^2$ and $\mathbb{H}^3$. The Busemann boundary of $\mathbb{H}^2$ can be identified with the real projective line $P^1(\mathbb{R})$. Switching the endpoints of the geodesics that pass through a point $p \in \mathbb{H}^2$ is a fixed point free involution I_p of $P^1(\mathbb{R})$ that preserves the cross ratio. A similar construction identifies points $p \in \mathbb{H}^3$ with cross ratio preserving fixed point free involutions I_p of $P^1(\mathbb{C})$. The involutions I_p extend to isometric involutions of $\mathbb{H}^2$ and $\mathbb{H}^3$. In short, points p are identified with isometric involutions that have p as only fixed point. At the fixed point p the differential of the involution I_p is the $-\mathrm{Id}$ involution of the tangent space at p.

This last formulation was used by Élie Cartan as axiom in the definition of an important class of geometric spaces[20,21,22]. A *Riemannian symmetric space* is a connected Riemannian manifold X such that each point $p \in X$ is fixed point of an isometric involution I_p with $D_p I_p = -\mathrm{Id}_{T_pX}$.

First examples are the Euclidean spaces, spheres, projective spaces and hyperbolic spaces. There are many more. A basic example is the space of Euclidean norms on $\mathbb{R}^n$ with unit balls of volume normalized by 1. This space can be parametrized by the homogeneous space $SL(n, \mathbb{R})/SO(n)$.

Symmetric spaces and Involutions are central in Geometry, Mathematics and Physics,…, see the books by Helgason [H] and by Knus, Merkurjev, Rost and Tignol[56].

6 Differential Topology of Surfaces

6.1 0- and 1-deRham cohomology of surfaces

Cohomology appears as soon as one wishes to understand globally problems that one can solve locally. The cohomology will be a book keeping device for the obstructions preventing the existence of global solutions provided the existence of local solutions. This is very philosophical and not a definition of cohomology! There exist many different types of cohomology theories and it is far from being true that all the global problems with local solutions can be understood through an appropriate cohomology theory.

Let us move to an example to explain this idea. Le S be a compact, connected, oriented surface of genus g. Let ω be a 1-differential form on S. We want to understand the possibility of finding a function f on S with $df = \omega$. We already know the answer locally: the answer is locally yes if and only if the form ω is closed, i.e. if $d\omega = 0$ holds. So, the answer to the question whether exists a function on S with $df = \omega$ has a chance to be yes only if $d\omega = 0$ holds. Given two 1-forms ω_1, ω_2 on S, the problem of solving $df_1 = \omega_1$ is equivalent to the problem of solving $df_2 = \omega_2$ as soon the difference 1-form $\omega_1 - \omega_2$ is *exact*, i.e. if $dg = \omega_1 - \omega_2$ for a function g holds. So the following quotient vector space measures how impossible it is to solve the equation $df = \omega$ with unknown function f:

$$\{\omega \in \Omega^1(S) \mid d\omega = 0\} / \{df \mid f \in \Omega^0(S)\}$$

where we have used the notation $\Omega^1(S)$ for the vector space of all 1-differential forms on S and the notation $\Omega^0(S)$ for the vector space of all functions on S.

This quotient vector space, denoted by $H^1_{dR}(S)$, of the space of closed 1-forms modulo the space of exact 1-forms on S is called the *first deRham cohomology group* of S in honour of the Swiss mathematician George deRham (1903–1990).

More generally, let M be a differentiable manifold. The quotient vector spaces

$$\{\omega \in \Omega^k(M) \mid d\omega = 0\} / \{d\eta \mid \eta \in \Omega^{k-1}(M)\}, \quad k = 0, 1, 2, \cdots$$

measure how possible (better impossible) it is to solve the equation $d\eta = \omega$ with $\eta \in \Omega^{k-1}(M)$ for given $\omega \in \Omega^k(M)$ satisfying the necessary condition $d\omega = 0$. This quotient vector space is denoted by $H^k_{dR}(M)$ and is called the kth deRham cohomology group of M. Its dimension is called the kth Betti number of M in honour of the Italian mathematician Enrico Betti "1823–1892". If $H^k_{dR}(M) = 0$ the equation $d\eta = \omega$ will have global solutions for those $\omega \in \Omega^k(M)$ with $d\omega = 0$. If Dim $(H^k_{dR}(M)) = $ n there will be n linearly independent "reasons", called *obstructions* , for the impossibility of solving the equation $d\eta = \omega$.

Theorem 6.1 *Let S be a compact, oriented, connected surface of genus g. Then* $Dim(H^1_{dR}(S)) = 2g$.

Proof: We only consider the case $g \geqslant 2$. Remember, that the surface S can be obtained as $S \stackrel{\text{def}}{=} \dot{\bigcup}_{0 \leqslant i \leqslant 8g} U_i / \sim$. We map the open sets $U_i \subset \mathbb{H}$ by the coordinate $w : \mathbb{H}^2 \to \mathbb{D}$ to the Poincaré disc. The open set $w(U_i)$ in $\mathbb{D}$ is still denoted by U_i. Let $U \stackrel{\text{def}}{=} \bigcup_{0 \leqslant i \leqslant 8g} U_i \subset \mathbb{D}$. It is an open star-shaped subset in $\mathbb{D} \subset \mathbb{C} = V$. Let ω be a closed 1-differential form on S given by a family of forms $\omega_i : U_i \to V^*$. This family defines a closed form ω_U on U. Since U is star-shaped there exists a function $f_U : U \to \mathbb{R}$ with $df_U = \omega_U$. Each time we use a gluing transformation $\phi_{ij} : U_{ij} \to U_{ji}$, we have to check that the solution f_U is invariant under this gluing. This means for the function f_U that for all $p \in U_{ij}$ the values $f_U(p)$ and $f_U(\phi ij(p))$ coincide. This leads to necessary conditions for being able to define the function f_U on S , namely the equations,

$$f_U(\phi ij(p)) - f_U(p) = \int_{[p, \phi ij(p)]} \omega_U = 0, p \in U_{ij}.$$

Here $[p, \phi ij(p)]$ is the segment in $\mathbb{D}$ on the hyperbolic line through the points $p, \phi ij(p)$. The open sets $U_{i,j}$ are path connected, so if the above condition is fulfilled for one $p \in U_{i,j}$ then the conditions are full filled for all $p \in U_{i,j}$. The above necessary conditions reduce to a finite list of conditions.

We take for points p the midpoints A_{2h}, $h = 1, 2, \cdots, 4g$, of the edges of P. The obstructions t_k, s_k are the numbers

$$t_K = \int_{[A_{8k-6}, A_{8k-2}]} \omega_U \ , \ S_K = \int_{[A_{8k-4}, A_{8k}]} \omega_U$$

and the above necessary conditions ask for the vanishing of the numbers t_k, s_k.

The oriented segment $[A_{8k-6}, A_{8k-2}]$ closes in the surface S up to a cycle a_k. Also the oriented segment $[A_{8k-4}, A_{8k}]$ closes in S to a cycle b_k. We can also express the obstructions as

$$t_K = \int_{ak} \omega \ , \ S_K = \int_{bk} \omega$$

which are in fact linear maps t_k, s_k : $\Omega^1(S) \to \mathbb{R}$. If all obstructions vanish, the function f_U becomes a function f on S solving $df = \omega$. We have proved Dim $(H^1_{dR}(S)) \leqslant 2g$.

The cycles a_k, b_h are pairwise disjoint, except for the pairs (a_k, b_k) that intersect on S in one point like coordinate axes intersect in the plane.

We proceed to describe a construction of a list α_k, β_k, $1 \leqslant k \leqslant g$, of closed 1-forms with$t_k(\beta_h) = - s_k(\alpha_h) = \delta^k_h$, $1 \leqslant k, h \leqslant g$. We have used here the Kronecker symbol δ^k_h with values $\delta^k_h = 0$ if $k \neq h$ and $\delta^k_h = 1$ if $k = h$.

The circle a_k has a cylindrical tubular neighborhood C_k on S since S is orientable. Let $g_k : C_k \to \mathbb{R}$ be a function that is identical 1 near one boundary component of C_k and identically 0 near the other boundary component. Let dg_k be its differential. It is crucial is that g_k does not extend to a function on S with vanishing differential on $S \setminus C_k$ but dg_k extends (by 0 outside from C_k) to a smooth 1-differential form on S. Let α_k be the extension of dg or of $-dg$ by 0 on S such that all obstructions evaluate to 0 except $\int_{bk} \alpha_k = -1$. The construction of β_k in a tubular neighborhood of b_k is similar with $\int_{ak} \beta_k = 1$.

This proves that the obstructions are linearly independent. Now the equality Dim $(H^1_{dR}(S)) = 2g$ follows.

A system of oriented cycles a_i, b_i as above is called a *symplectic marking*. The corresponding system of 1-differential forms α_i, β_i, $1 \leqslant i \leqslant g$, as in above proof provide a basis $([\alpha_i],[\beta_i])$, $1 \leqslant i \leqslant g$, for real vector space $H^1_{dR}(S,\mathbb{R})$ as for the complex vector space $H^1_{dR}(S,\mathbb{C})$. For each closed 1-differential form ω its cohomology class $[\omega]$ expands as

$$[\omega] = \sum_{i=1}^{g} \int_{a_i} \omega[\beta_i] - \int_{b_i} \omega[\alpha_i].$$

Observe $\int_S \partial_i \wedge \beta_j = \delta_i^j$ and $\int_S \alpha_i \wedge \alpha_j = \int_S \beta_i \wedge \beta_j = 0$.

Theorem 6.2 Green-Riemann relation. *For closed 1-differential forms ω_1, ω_2 on a closed oriented surface S of genus $g \geqslant 1$ with a symplectic marking of cycles a, b the following identity holds:*

$$\int_S \omega_1 \Lambda \omega_2 = \sum_{i=1}^{g} \int_{a_i} \omega_1 \int_{b_i} \omega_2 - \int_{b_i} \omega_1 \int_{a_i} \omega_2.$$

Proof: Both sides are alternating bilinear in the arguments ω_1, ω_2. Replacing an argument ω by $\omega + df$ does not change the values of both sides. Replacing the arguments by expansions

$$\omega = \sum_{i=1}^{g} \int_{a_i} \omega\beta_i - \int_{b_i} \omega\alpha_i$$

does not change the values. Clearly the identity holds for pairs with entries from α_i, β_j.

The differential df of a function f measures the local behaviour of a function. The Theorem of Michel Rolle (1652–1719), a French mathematician, implies that a function f with $df=0$ is constant along every differentiable path. A connected differentiable manifold is also connected by differentiable paths. It follows that the restrictions of a function f with $df=0$ to the connected components of a differentiable manifold are constant functions. In particular:

Theorem 6.3 *For a connected non empty manifold M the space $H^0_{dR}(M)$ is the space of constant functions and $Dim(H^0_{dR}(M))=1$.*

Let a be a simple closed regularly parametrized curve on a compact orientable surface S of genus $g > 0$. We can extend the parametrization to an embedding of a cylinder $\Gamma : S^1 \times [-1,+1] \to S$ such that $t \in S^1 \mapsto \Gamma(t,0) \in S$ parametrizes the curve a. The image of Γ is called a collar neighborhood of the curve a. Let $\chi : [-1,+1] \to \mathbb{R}$ be a function with such that $\chi'(s) \geqslant 0$, $\chi(+1)-\chi(-1)=1$ and $\chi'(s)=0$ near ± 1. The push-forward 1-differential form

$\Gamma_*(d\chi)$ on the image of Γ extends by 0 to a 1-differential form $\alpha(a)$ on S. Let b be a closed parametrized curve in S that intersects a in one point such that speeds of a and b at this point are linearly independent. One has $\int_b \alpha(a) = \pm 1$. More general, $\int_b \alpha(a) \in \mathbb{Z}$ counts with sign how many times a curve b goes through the collar neighborhood of the curve a.

Exercise 1: *Do the computation of $H^1_{dR}(S_g)$ for remaining the cases of genus $g = 0, 1$.*

Exercise 2: *Compute $H^1_{dR}(K)$ for the Klein bottle K.*

Exercise 3: *Compute $H^1_{dR}(P^2(\mathbb{R}))$.*

Exercise 4: *Let $A: \mathbb{R}^2 \to S^1 \times S^1$ be the map $p \in \mathbb{R}^2 \mapsto (e^{2\pi i x(p)}, e^{2\pi i y(p)}) \in S^1 \times S^1$. Let $\phi: S^1 \times S^1 \to S^1 \times S^1$ be a diffeomorphism of the torus. Construct a diffeomorphism $\Phi: \mathbb{R}^2 \to \mathbb{R}^2$ satisfying $\Phi(0) = 0$ and $A \circ \Phi = \phi \circ A$. Construct a linear map $\Psi: \mathbb{R}^2 \to \mathbb{R}^2$ such that $\Psi - \Phi$ is bounded. Show that Ψ maps $A^{-1}(1,1)$ into $A^{-1}(1,1)$. Identify $H^1_{dR}(S^1 \times S^1)$ and $\mathbb{R}^2$ such that Ψ becomes the induced map by Φ on $H^1_{dR}(S^1 \times S^1)$. Show that Ψ induces a diffeomorphism ψ of $S^1 \times S^1$, satisfying $A \circ \Psi = \psi \circ A$, that is homotopic, even isotopic, to ϕ.*

Exercise 5: *The augmented mapping class group of the torus $T^2 = S^1 \times S^1$ is the quotient group $AMod(T^2) = Diff(T^2)/Diff_0(T^2)$, where $Diff_0(T^2)$ is the group of diffeomorphisms that are homotopic or isotopic to the identity.*

Show that the groups $AMod(T^2)$ and $GL(2, \mathbb{Z})$ are isomorphic.

6.2 Hyperbolic plane again, now $\mathbb{H} = \mathbb{H}_J$

We work with different personalities. We define the hyperbolic plane as a set by

$$\mathbb{H} = \{J \in Hom(\mathbb{R}^2, \mathbb{R}^2) J \circ J = J^2 = -Id_{\mathbb{R}^2},\ J \text{ left oriented}\}$$

Remember $\mathbb{H}$ for hyperbolic and J since the personalities are linear complex structures on $\mathbb{R}^2$. Let $J \in \mathbb{H}$. From $J \circ J = J^2 = -Id_{\mathbb{R}^2}$ it follows that for all $u \in \mathbb{R}^2, u \neq 0$, the vectors u, $J(u)$ are linearly independent. The imposed condition namely : J *left oriented* means that the pair of vectors $(u, J(u))$ and the pair (e_1, e_2) of standard basis vectors give equal orientations to $\mathbb{R}^2$. We can represent J by a real two-by-two matrix $\begin{pmatrix} h & x \\ k & y \end{pmatrix}$. The condition of left orientation implies $k > 0$. The condition $J \circ J = J^2 = -Id_{\mathbb{R}^2}$ implies that the eigenvalues are $i, -i$, so Trace$(J) = 0$, meaning $y = -h$. The condition also implies Det$(J) = 1$, so $x = \frac{-h^2 - 1}{k}$. Representing elements of $\mathbb{H}$ by matrices we conclude

$$\mathbb{H} = \{ \begin{pmatrix} h & * \\ k & -h \end{pmatrix} \mid h, k \in \mathbb{R}, k > 0, * = \frac{-h^2 - 1}{k} \}.$$

What are the symmetries, the interactions in $\mathbb{H}$? Is there a geometry defined by lines or by a two point function?

A base change $f_1 = P(e_1)$, $f_2 = P(e_2)$, $P \in GL^+(2, \mathbb{R})$ acts on $\mathbb{H}_J$ by $(P, J) \mapsto P \circ J \circ P^{-1}$. Here $GL^+(2, \mathbb{R})$ is the group of linear automorphisms of $\mathbb{R}^2$ that preserve orientation.

We define as a line in $\mathbb{H}_J$ a subset L that is maximal for the following property: given $p, q, p', q' \in L \subset \mathbb{H}_J$ the compositions $p \circ q$ and $p' \circ q'$ commute in $GL^+(2, \mathbb{R})$. This definition is based on the composition of elements in $\mathbb{H}_J$ with values in $GL^+(2, \mathbb{R})$. Think of this composition as an interaction. The effective group of symmetries is the group $PSL(2, \mathbb{R})$. We get a symmetric two point function $T: \mathbb{H}_J \times \mathbb{H}_J \to \mathbb{R}$ with positive values by putting $T(p, q) \overset{\text{def}}{=} -\frac{1}{2} Trace(p \circ q)$. The two point function $d_{\mathbb{H}_J}: \mathbb{H}_J \times \mathbb{H}_J \to \mathbb{R}$ with

$$d_{H_J}(p, q) \overset{def}{=} \log(T(p, q) + \sqrt{T(p, q)^2 - 1})$$

is a symmetry invariant distance function.

Remember that the group $PSL(2, \mathbb{R})$ acts by homographic transformations on $\mathbb{C}_+$. The coordinate

$$Fix: \mathbb{H}_J \to \mathbb{C}_+, \begin{pmatrix} h & * \\ k & -h \end{pmatrix} \mapsto a + b_i \in \mathbb{C}_+$$

where $a + bi \in \mathbb{C}_+$ is the fixed point of the homographic transformation

$$u \in \mathbb{C}_+ \mapsto \frac{hu + *}{ku - h} \in \mathbb{C}_+, * = \frac{-h^2 - 1}{k}.$$

We have $a+b_i=\frac{h}{k}+\frac{i}{k}$. The coordinate Fix is an equivariant bijection with respect to the symmetries by PSL(2, $\mathbb{R}$). One should not be surprised that Fix maps lines in $\mathbb{H}_J$ to half circles perpendicular to the real axes in $\mathbb{C}_+$, and that the composition $\Pi \circ$ Fix maps lines in $\mathbb{H}=\mathbb{H}_J$ to lines in $\mathbb{H}_I$. The inverse map

$$\mathrm{Xif}: \mathbb{C}_+ \to \mathbb{H}_J$$

is given by

$$a+b_i \in \mathbb{C}_+ \mapsto Xif(a+bi)=\begin{pmatrix} a/b & * \\ 1/b & -a/b \end{pmatrix} \in \mathbb{H}_J.$$

Theorem 6.4 *The tangent space $T_J(\mathbb{H}_J)$ at $J\in\mathbb{H}_J$ is the vector space of all endomorphisms h of $\mathbb{R}^2$ that anti-commute with J.*

Proof: Up to first order an endomorphism h deforms J to an almost complex structure $J+h$ on $\mathbb{R}^2$ if $J\circ h+h\circ J=0$ since

$$(J+h)^2=J^2+J\circ h+h\circ J+h\circ h$$

and $J^2=-\mathrm{Id}$.

The following theorem constructs a natural J-field on the manifold $\mathbb{H}_J$. The hyperbolic plane has a natural complex structure.

Theorem 6.5 *The map $J_J: h\in T_J\mathbb{H}_J \mapsto h\circ J\in T_J\mathbb{H}_J$ defines a J-field on $\mathbb{H}_J$*

.

Proof: For $h\in T_J\mathbb{H}_J$ the endomorphism $k=h\circ J$ anti-commutes with J. Indeed,

$$k\circ J+J\circ k=h\circ J\circ J+J\circ h\circ J=h\circ J\circ J-h\circ J\circ J=0.$$

Clearly $J_J\circ J_J=-Id_{T_J\mathbb{H}_J}$

Theorem 6.6 *The coordinate $Fix:\mathbb{H}_J\to\mathbb{C}_+\subset\mathbb{C}$ is (J_J, m_i)-holomorphic.*

Proof: The map Fix is equivariant for the transitive holomorphic actions of $\mathrm{PGL}^+(2,\mathbb{R})$ on $(\mathbb{H}_J, J_J)$ and on $(\mathbb{C}_+, m_i)$. The map Fix is (J_J, m_i) holomorphic at the point $\begin{pmatrix} 0 & -1 \\ 1 & 0 \end{pmatrix}\in\mathbb{H}_J$.

Exercise 6: *Let $J_1, J_2, \cdots, J_n$ be n different points in $\mathbb{H}_J$. Put $J_{n+1}=J_1$. We assume that $J_{k+1}=J_{k-1}\circ J_k\circ J_{k-1}$ for $k=1,2,\cdots,n$ hold. Show that the images Fix (J_k) are the vertices of a regular right-angled n-gon, $n\geqslant 5$, in $\mathbb{C}_+$.*

Exercise 7: *Given $J\in\mathbb{H}_J$ and $\theta\in\mathbb{R}/2\pi\mathbb{Z}$ define $J(\theta): \mathbb{R}^2\to\mathbb{R}^2$ by J*

$(\theta)(u) \stackrel{def}{=} \sin(\theta) J(u) + \cos(\theta) u$. *Show that* $(\theta, u) \mapsto J(\theta)(u)$ *defines a faithful linear action of the the circle group* $\mathbb{R}/2\pi\mathbb{Z}$ *on* $\mathbb{R}^2$. *Define a hyperbolic plane* $\mathbb{H} = \mathbb{H}_p$ *as the set of faithful linear actions of the group* $\mathbb{R}/2\pi\mathbb{Z}$ *on* $\mathbb{R}^2$.

Exercise 8: *In* $\mathbb{H}_I$ *we have a notion of energy-barycenter. How about* $\mathbb{H}_J$? *Let* (p, w) *be a weighted multi-point in* $\mathbb{H}_J$. *For* $q \in \mathbb{H}_J$ *let* R_q *be the rotation of* $\mathbb{H}_J$ *with center* q *and constant angular speed* 1. *Compute according to Newton's law the kinetic energy* $K(q; p, w)$ *of the motion of the multi-point* (p, w). *Think of the points* p_i, w_i *as point mass. Does the function* $q \mapsto K(q; p, w)$ *achieve a unique minimum at a point* $k(p, w)$? *Do we have* $k(p, w) = b(p, w)$?

6.3 Reminder: Multi-Linear Algebra

Let V be a real vector space of finite dimension and let $J: V \to V$ be a linear map with $J \circ J = -\mathrm{Id}_V$. Using J we can multiply vectors u in V by complex numbers $\lambda = a + bi$ in such a way that V together with this multiplication is a complex vector space. The multiplication λu is defined for $T\lambda = a + bi \in \mathbb{C}$ by

$$\lambda u \stackrel{\text{def}}{=} au + bJ(u).$$

We denote by $\Lambda^k(V, \mathbb{C})$ the complex vector space of all maps:

$$\omega : V^k \to \mathbb{C}$$

that are $\mathbb{R}$-multi-linear and alternating. Remember, $\mathbb{R}$-multi-linear means that the map

$$(u_1, u_2, \cdots, u_k) \in V^k \mapsto \omega(u_1, u_2, \cdots, u_k) \in \mathbb{C}$$

is $\mathbb{R}$-linear in each of its arguments. *Alternating* means that if in ω one exchanges two arguments u_i, u_j, $1 \leqslant i < j \leqslant k$, the value of

$$\omega(u_1, u_2, \cdots, u_k) \in \mathbb{C}$$

gets multiplied by -1. Since the target space of $\omega : V^k \to \mathbb{C}$ is the $\mathbb{C}$-vector space $\mathbb{C}$ the space $\Lambda^k(V, \mathbb{C})$ becomes a $\mathbb{C}$-vector space: the addition $\omega_1 + \omega_2$ is defined as

$$(\omega_1 + \omega_2)(u_1, u_2, \cdots, u_k) \stackrel{def}{=} \omega_1(u_1, u_2, \cdots, u_k) + \omega_2(u_1, u_2, \cdots, u_k)$$

and the multiplication $\lambda\omega$ is defined as

$$(\lambda\omega)(u_1, u_2, \cdots, u_k) \overset{def}{=} \lambda\omega(u_1, u_2, \cdots, u_k).$$

It is important to observe that the map

$$(u_1, u_2, \cdots, u_k) \in V^k \mapsto \omega(u_1, u_2, \cdots, u_k) \in \mathbb{C}$$

is only $\mathbb{R}$-linear and not $\mathbb{C}$-linear in each of its arguments.

Exercise 9: *Let $\sigma : E \to E$ be a permutation of a finite set E. Minimal non empty subsets $A \subset E$ that are stable by σ are called σ-orbits. Define $orb(\sigma)$ as the partition of E in σ-orbits. Let $\#orb(\sigma)$ be the length of the partition, i.e. the number of σ-orbits. Define the signature of the permutation σ by:*

$$sign(\sigma) = (-1)^{\#E - \#orb(\sigma)}.$$

Prove that the signature of a transposition equals -1. Prove that the signature is multiplicative: $sign(\sigma_1 \circ \sigma_2) = sign(\sigma_1) sign(\sigma_2)$. Show that the above definition of alternating is consistent.

Let $\Lambda_J^{k-l,l}(V,\mathbb{C})$, $l = 0, 1, \cdots, k$, be the subspace of $\Lambda^k(V, \mathbb{C})$ of all maps $\omega : V^k \to \mathbb{C}$ that satisfy

$$\omega(\lambda u_1, \lambda u_2, \cdots, \lambda u_k) = \lambda^{k-l} \bar{\lambda}^{-l} \omega_1(u_1, u_2, \cdots, u_k), \lambda \in \mathbb{C}.$$

The spaces $\Lambda_J^{k-l,l}(V,\mathbb{C})$, $l = 0, 1, \cdots, k$, are $\mathbb{C}$-sub-vector spaces.

Theorem 6.7 *The space $\Lambda^k(V, \mathbb{C})$ is the direct sum of its sub-vector spaces $\Lambda_J^{k-l,l}(V,\mathbb{C})$, $l=0,1,\cdots,k$. In formula:*

$$\Lambda^k(V,\mathbb{C}) = \bigoplus_{l=0}^{l=k} \Lambda_J^{k-l,l}(V,\mathbb{C}).$$

Proof: For $v = (u_1, u_1, \cdots, u_k) \in V^K$, $\omega \in \Lambda_J^{k-l,l}(V,\mathbb{C})$, $\lambda = e^{it}$ we have $\omega(e^{it} v) = e^{(k-2l)it} \omega(v)$. We define a projector $\P_J^{k-l,l} : \Lambda^k(V,\mathbb{C}) \to \Lambda^K(V,\mathbb{C})$ with image $\Lambda_J^{k-l,l}(V,\mathbb{C})$ by

$$(\P_J^{k-l,l}\omega)(v) = \frac{1}{2\pi} \int_0^{2\pi} e^{(2l-k)it} \omega(e^{it} v)\, dt.$$

It suffices to observe

$$\P_J^{k-l,l} = 0, l \notin \{0, 1, 2, \cdots, k\}, \sum_{l \in \mathbb{Z}} \P_J^{k-l,l} = Id_{\Lambda^k(V,\mathbb{C})}.$$

Exercise 10: *Compute the dimension of $\Lambda^k(V, \mathbb{C})$ as a function of $n = Dim(V)$ and k.*

6.4 Reminder: Holomorphic functions in one complex variable

Let U be an open subset in $\mathbb{C}$. A local piece-wise closed smooth path in U is a closed smooth path $\gamma: [0,1] \to U$ that takes its values in a disc $B(p,r) = \{q \in \mathbb{C} \mid |p-q| < r\}$ which is contained in U.

Holomorphic functions on U, open in $\mathbb{C}$, are complex valued continuous functions for which all path integrals $\int_\gamma f dz$ over local piece-wise smooth closed paths in U vanish.

Holomorphic functions have many properties. The following theorem provides three more ways of characterising holomorphic functions. The first two (i) and (ii) apply to a continuous function.

Theorem 6.8 *Let U be an open subset in $\mathbb{C}$ and let f be a complex valued continuous function on U. The following statements are equivalent:*

(i) *f is holomorphic.*

(ii) *the 1-differential form fdz is closed.*

(iii) *the function f is continuously differentiable and its differential df is $\mathbb{C}$-linear.*

(iv) *the function f in each subdisc $B(p, r) \subset U$ is given by a convergent power series.*

Proof: (i) implies (ii): remember, the value of $d(fdz)$ at $q \in U$ on vectors $u, v \in \mathbb{C}$ is given by

$$(d(fdz))_q(u,v) = \lim_{s \to 0, s>0} \frac{1}{s^2} \int_{\partial P_q(u,v,s)} fdz$$

a scaled limit of path integrals over boundaries of parallelograms. By (i)

$$\int_{\partial P_q(u,v,s)} = 0$$

holds for $q \in U$, $u, v \in \mathbb{C}$ and $s > 0$ with $P_q(u,v,s) \subset U$.

Hence $d(fdz) = 0$.

(ii) implies (iii): let $D = B(p,r) \subset U$ be a subdisc in U. On D the closed form fdz is exact. Let $F: D \to \mathbb{C}$ be a function with $dF = fdz$.

Remember that dg for a complex valued function g on U splits as $dg = d'g + d''g$ in $\mathbb{C}$-linear and anti-$\mathbb{C}$-linear parts.

Observe $dF = d'F$ and $d''F = 0$. The function F being continuously differentiable, from $d(dF) = 0$ follows $d''d'F = 0$. Hence F is harmonic, and in particular smooth.

From $dF = fdz$ it follows that f is smooth, in particular continuously differentiable, on D and also on U. Since f is smooth, the formula $d(fdz) = d''f \wedge dz = 0$ applies, and $d''f = 0$ follows. From $d''f = 0$ follows $df = d'f$ showing that the differential of f is $\mathbb{C}$-linear.

(iii) implies (iv): let $B(p,r) \subset U$ be a subdisc in U such that its closure is also a subset of U. For $q \in B(p,r)$ and $0 < \rho < r - |q - p|$ let $R(p,q,r,\rho)$ be the closure of $B(p,r) \setminus B(q,\rho)$ in U. The function $g = \frac{f}{z(q) - z}$ is smooth and $d(gdz) = 0$. It follows by Stokes's theorem that the path integral of gdz along the oriented boundary of $R(p,q,r,\rho)$ vanishes.

Evaluating separately on each boundary component yields

$$\int_{\partial+B(q,\rho)} \frac{fdz}{z(q) - z} = \int_{\partial+B(p,r)} \frac{fdz}{z(q) - z}.$$

The left hand side is independent of ρ since no ρ appears in the right hand side. Its value is $2\pi i f(q)$, which can be seen by taking the limit for $\rho \to 0$. In conclusion

$$f(q) = \frac{1}{2\pi i} \int_{\partial+B(p,r)} \frac{fdz}{z(q) - z}$$

which shows the interesting and fundamental fact that the value of the function f at $q \in B(p,r) \subset U$ is determined by the restriction of f to the boundary of the disc $B(p,r)$.

The integral expression for $f(q)$ expands into a power series.

$$f(q) = \frac{1}{2\pi i}\int_{\partial + B(p,r)} \frac{fdz}{z(q) - z} =$$

$$\frac{1}{2\pi i}\int_{\partial + B(p,r)} \frac{fdz}{(z(q) - z(p)) - (z - z(p))} =$$

$$\frac{1}{2\pi i}\int_{\partial + B(p,r)} \frac{fdz}{\frac{z(q) - z(p)}{z - z(p)} - 1}.$$

Along the path of integration $\left| \frac{z(q) - z(p)}{z - z(p)} \right| = \frac{|q - p|}{r}$ 1 holds, which permits an expansion using the geometric series

$$\frac{1}{2\pi i}\int_{\partial + B(p,r)} \sum_{n=0}^{\infty} (z(q) - z(p))^n \frac{fdz}{(z - z(q))^{n+1}} =$$

with
$$\sum_{n=0}^{\infty} a_n (z(q) - z(p))^n$$

$$a_n = \frac{1}{2\pi i}\int_{\partial + B(p,r)} \frac{fdz}{(z - z(q))^{n+1}}.$$

If using the coordinate function $u = z - z(p)$ at p centred one has $du = dz$ and more simply the power series expression in u for f

$$f = \sum_{n=0}^{\infty} a_n u^n$$

with
$$a_n = \frac{1}{2\pi i}\int_{\partial + B(p,r)} \frac{fdu}{u^{n+1}}$$

(*iv*) implies (*i*): path integration and summation commute for convergent power series. For a closed local path $\gamma : [0,1] \to U$ with values in a disc

$B(p, r) \subset U$ and coordinate $u = z - z(p)$ at p centred one gets

$$\int_\gamma fdz = \int_\gamma fdu = \int_\gamma \sum_{n=0}^{\infty} a_n u^n du =$$

$$\sum_{n=0}^{\infty} \int_\gamma a_n u^n du = \sum_{n=1}^{\infty} a_n (u(\gamma(0)))^{n+1} - a_n (u(\gamma(1)))^{n+1} = 0.$$

(iv) implies (*ii*): differentiation and summation commute for convergent power series. The property $d(fdz) = 0$ is local, hence it suffices to work in discs $B(p,r) \subset U$. So working with the at p coordinate $u = z - z(p)$, one gets $d(fdz) = d(fdu) = (\sum_{n=1}^{\infty} na_n u^{n-1}) du \wedge du = 0$

Let $f: U \to \mathbb{C}$ be a holomorphic function on U open in $\mathbb{C}$. From (ii) follows that the differential df is can be written in a unique way as $df = gdz$ for a function g on U. The function g is called the complex derivative of f and is sometimes denoted by f' or by $\frac{\partial f}{\partial z}$. From (iv) follows that the complex derivative f' of a holomorphic function f is holomorphic too.

Let $(f_n)_{n \in \mathbb{N}}$ be a sequence of holomorphic functions on U open in $\mathbb{C}$. Suppose that the sequence converges uniformly on each compact subset in U. It is well known that the limit $f = \lim_{n \to \infty} f_n$ is a continuous function on U. From (i) follows that the function f is holomorphic. Indeed, for a local closed path $\gamma: [0, 1] \to U$ the image of γ is compact and path integration commutes with taking uniform limits, hence

$$0 = \lim_{n \to \infty} \int_\gamma f_n dz = \int_\gamma \lim_{n \to \infty} f_n dz = \int_\gamma f dz$$

which proves.

Theorem 6.9 *The limit function for uniform convergence on compact subsets of a sequence of holomorphic functions on an open subset in $\mathbb{C}$ is holomorphic.*

Proof: See above.

The characterisation (i), due to the Italian mathematician Giacinto Morera (1856–1909), is very useful, since heriditary with respect to taking limits for the uniform convergence on compacta in the domain of functions.

The characterisation (iv) allows to define interesting functions, for example the exponential function $e^z = \sum_{n=0}^{\infty} \frac{z^n}{n!}$, trigonometric functions $cos(z) = \sum_{k=0}^{\infty} (-1)^k \frac{z^{2k}}{(2k)!}$ and many more.

Exercise 11: *The function $\omega = \sum_{n=0}^{\infty} z^{n!}$ is holomorphic in the open unit disc D. Let U be open and connected in $\mathbb{C}$. Assume $D \subset U$ and $D \neq U$.*

Prove that ω does not extend to a holomorphic function on U. Hint: try to define $\omega(\mu)$ for a root of unity μ.

Exercise 12: *The function $\Theta = \sum_{n=0}^{\infty} z^{n^2}$ is holomorphic in the open unit disc D. Does Θ extend to an open neigborhood of -1?*

A zoom in an open subset U of $\mathbb{C}$ is a pair of nested discs $(B(p,r) \subset B(p,2r))$, $p \in U, r > 0$, such that the closure in $\mathbb{C}$ of $B(p,2r)$ is a subset of U. A zoom-covering of U is a family $(B(p_j,r_j) \subset B(p_j,2r_j))_{j \in J}$ of zooms in U such that the inner discs $B(p_j,r_j)$ cover U. Every open subset U in $\mathbb{C}$ admits a countable zoom-covering. For a continuous function f on U and subset A in U denote by $\|f\|_A$ the least upper bound of $|f|$ on A. So,

$$\|f\|_A = \mathrm{Sup}_{a \in A} |f(a)|$$

Exercise 13: *For every zoom-cover $(B(p_j,r_j) \subset B(p_j,2r_j))_{j \in J}$ of an open subset U in $\mathbb{C}$ there exists a countable subset J_0 in J such that $(B(p_j,r_j) \subset B(p_j,2r_j))_{j \in J0}$ is still a zoom-cover of U.*

Exercise 14: *Let $C^0(U, \mathbb{C})$ be the space of complex continuous functions on an open subset U of $\mathbb{C}$ equipped with the topology of uniform convergence on compacta in U. Let $Z = (B(p_j,r_j) \subset B(p_j,2r_j))_{j \in \mathbb{N}}$ be a countable zoom-cover of U indexed by the natural numbers. For $f, g \in C^0(U,\mathbb{C})$ define*

$$d_Z(f,g) = \sum_{j=0}^{\infty} \frac{1}{2^j} \frac{\|f-g\|_{B(p_j,2r_j)}}{1 + \|f-g\|_{B(p_j,2r_j)}}$$

and show that d_Z is a metric on $C^0(U, \mathbb{C})$ with the topology of uniform convergence on compacta in U.

Exercise 15: *Balls for d_Z in $C^0(U,\mathbb{C})$ are convex. The function $n(f) = d_Z(f, 0)$ is not a norm, but satisfies $n(f+g) \leqslant n(f) + n(g)$.*

The following theorems and their consequences were discovered by the French mathematician Paul Antoine Aristide Montel (1876–1975).

Theorem 6.10 *Let $(B(p,r) \subset B(p,2r))$ be a zoom in an open subset U of $\mathbb{C}$. For a holomorphic function f on U the inequality*

$$\|f'\|_{B(p,r)} \leqslant \frac{1}{r} \|f\|_{B(p,2r)}$$

holds. The restriction of f to $B(p,r)$ is Lipschitz continuous with Lipschitz constant $\frac{1}{r}\|f\|_{B(p,2r)}$.

Proof: For $q \in B(p,r)$ the disc $B(q,r)$ is contained in $B(p,2r)$. Hence

$$f'(q) = \frac{1}{2\pi i}\int_{\partial + B(q,r)} \frac{fdu}{u^2} fdu$$

where u is the at q coordinate $u = z - z(q)$. For $q \in B(p, r)$ follows

$$|f'(q)| \leqslant \frac{1}{2\pi} \frac{\|f\|_{B(q,r)}}{r^2} 2\pi r = \frac{1}{r} \|f\|_{B(p,2r)}$$

and hence $\|f'\|_{B(p,r)} \leqslant \frac{1}{r} \|f\|_{B(p,2r)}$.

For $q_0, q_1 \in B(p,r)$ one has $f(q_1) - f(q_0) = \int_{[q_0,q_1]} f' dz$. Hence, the Lipschitz continuity on $B(p,r)$ with the claimed constant follows

$$|f(q_1) - f(q_0)| \leqslant \frac{1}{r} \|f\|_{B(p,2r)} |q_1 - q_0|, q_0, q_1 \in B(p,r).$$

Theorem 6.11 *Let* $(f_n)_{n \in \mathbb{N}}$ *be a sequence of holomorphic functions on* B(p,2r) *such that for* $M \in \mathbb{R}$ *the estimates* $\|f_n\|_{B(p,2r)} \leqslant M$, $n \in \mathbb{N}$ *hold. Then there exists a subsequence* $(f_{nk})_{k \in \mathbb{N}}$ *and a holomorphic function* g *on* B(p,r) *such that*

$$\lim_{k \to \infty} \|f_{nk} - g\| B(p,r) = 0$$

Proof: Let $p_i, i \in \mathbb{N}$, be an enumeration of the points in $B(p,2r)$ with rational real and imaginairy parts. For each i the values $f_n(p_i), n \in \mathbb{N}$, belong to the closed disc centred at $0 \in \mathbb{C}$ of radius M. Hence for each i there exists a subsequence $(f_{n_k^i})_{k \in \mathbb{N}}$ such that the sequence of values $(f_{n_k^i}(p_i))_{k \in \mathbb{N}}$ converges. For each i the subsequences $(f_{n_k^{i+1}})_{k \in \mathbb{N}}$ can be chosen as subsequence of $(f_{n_k^i})_{k \in \mathbb{N}}$. The diagonal subsequence $(f_{n_k^k})_{k \in \mathbb{N}}$ is then such that at each point p_i the sequence of its values converges to a value $g(p_i)$.

The Lipschitz inequalities

$$|g(p_i) - g(p_j)| \leqslant \frac{M}{r} |p_i - p_j|, i,j \in \mathbb{N},$$

are preserved by taking limits.

The partially defined Lipschitz continuous functiong can be extended in a unique way to a Lipschitz continuous function $g: B(p,r) \to \mathbb{C}$ with Lipschitz constant $\frac{M}{r}$.

One has

$$\lim_{k \to \infty} \|f_{n_k^k} - g\|_{B(p,r)} = 0.$$

Indeed, assume the contrary, i.e. the existence of e>0, of a subsequence

$(f_{m_h})_{h\in\mathbb{N}}$ of $(f_{n_k})_{k\in\mathbb{N}}$ and of a sequence of points $(q_h)_{h\in\mathbb{N}}$ in $B(p,r)$ such that $\|f_{m_h}(q_h)-g(q_h)\|_{B(p,r)}\geqslant\epsilon$. By taking a subsequence we may achieve that the points q_h converge to a point q in the closure of $B(p,r)$. Noe choose $p_i\in B(p,r)$ with $|q-p_i|<\frac{r}{8M}\epsilon$. There exists H such that $|q_h-q|<\frac{r}{8M}\epsilon$, $h\geqslant H$. Observe $|q_h-p_i|<\frac{r}{4M}\epsilon$, hence $\|f_{m_h}(q_h)-f_{m_h}(p_i)\|_{B(p,r)}\geqslant\frac{1}{4}\epsilon$ and $\|g(q_h)-g(p_i)\|_{B(p,r)}\geqslant\frac{1}{4}\epsilon$. It follows $\|f_{m_h}(p_i)-g(p_i)\|\geqslant\frac{1}{2}\epsilon$, $h\geqslant H$, contradicting $\lim_{h\to\infty}f_{mh}(p_i)=g(p_i)$.

The function g is holomorphic, since it is a uniform limit of holomorphic functions.

In a finite dimensional normed real or complex vector space $(V,\|\ \|_V)$ compacta are precisely the closed and bounded subsets. For instance closed balls $\{v\in V\mid \|v\|_V\leqslant R\}$ are compact. This property is characteristic for finite dimensional spaces by a theorem of the Hungarian mathematician Frigyes Riesz (1880–1956),

Theorem 6.12 *Let $(V,\|\ \|_V)$ be a real or complex normed vector space. Equivalent are:*

(i) V is finite dimensional.

(ii) the closed unit ball in V is compact.

Proof: Clearly $(i)\Rightarrow(ii)$. The following proves the implication $(ii)\Rightarrow(i)$.

The closed unit ball $B_1\subset V$ being compact is covered by finitely many balls

$$B(v_1,\frac{1}{2}),B(v_2,\frac{1}{2}),\cdots,B(v_k,\frac{1}{2})$$

For $v\in V$, $v\neq 0$, put $\omega=\frac{1}{\|v\|V}v\in B_1$. The vector w belongs to $B(v_{i_1},\frac{1}{2})$ for some $1\leqslant i_1\leqslant k$. Hence $w=v_{i1}+w_1$ with $2w_1\in B_1$. Again vector $2w_1$ belongs to $B(v_{i_2},\frac{1}{2})$ for some $1\leqslant i_2\leqslant k$. Hence $\omega=v_{i_1}+\frac{1}{2}v_{i_2}+\omega_2$ with $4w_2\in B_1$. Repeating one gets for $n\in\mathbb{N}$ an expansion

$$w=v_{i_1}+\frac{1}{2}v_{i_2}+\cdots+\frac{1}{2^{n-1}}v_{i_2}+w_n$$

with $2^n w_n \in B_1$. This expansion can be rewritten as a linear combination with positive coefficients of the vectors $v_1, v_2, \cdots, v_k$ yielding

$$\omega = a_1(n) v_1 + \cdots + a_k(n) v_k + w_n$$

with $a_i(n) \in [0,2]$ and $2^n w_n \in B_1$. Observe $\lim_{n\to\infty} w_n = 0$. Moreover the coefficients $a_i(n)$ satisfy $a_i(n) \leqslant a_i(n+1) \leqslant 2$. Putting $a_i = \lim_{n\to\infty} a_i(n)$ one gets

$$w = a_1 v_1 + \cdots + a_k v_k, \ a_i \geqslant 0$$

showing that $v = \| v \|_V w$ is in the positive cone generated by the vectors v_i. One concludes that the vector space V is of finite dimension $< k$.

We turn back to the space $C^0(U, \mathbb{C})$ with metric d_Z given by a countable zoom-cover $Z = (B(p_j, r_j) \subset B(p_j, 2r_j))_{j\in J}$. The space $\hbar(U, \mathbb{C})$ of holomorphic functions is a closed subspace in $C^0(U, \mathbb{C})$ by a previous theorem. The following theorem, due to Montel, describes the compacta in $\hbar(U, \mathbb{C})$.

Theorem 6.13 *Let $M = (M_j)_{j\in J}$ be a system of real numbers > 0. The set*

$$K_M = \{f \in \hbar(U, \mathbb{C}) \mid \|f\|_{B(p_j, 2r_j)} \leqslant M_j, j \in J\}$$

is compact. Moreover, for every compact set K in $\hbar(U, \mathbb{C})$ there exists a system $M = (M_j)_{j\in J}$ of numbers with $K \subset K_M$.

Proof: The topology on K_M is given by the metric d_Z. In order to prove that K_M is compact, it suffices to show that every sequence $(f_n)_{n\in\mathbb{N}}$ in K_M has a subsequence that converges to an element g in K_M. First identify J, the index set of the zoom Z, with $\mathbb{N}$. So $j \in J = \mathbb{N}$. By the previous theorem there exist subsequences $(f_{n_k^j})_{k\in\mathbb{N}}$ that converge for the norm $\| \ \|_{B(p_j, r_j)}$ to a holomorphic function g_j on $B(p_j, r_j)$. The subsequences can be chosen such that for each $j \in \mathbb{N}$ the subsequence $(f_{n_k^{j+1}})_{k\in\mathbb{N}}$ is a subsequence of $(f_{n_k^j})_{k\in\mathbb{N}}$.

The diagonal subsequence $(f_{n_k^k})_{k\in\mathbb{N}}$ converges for the distance d_Z to a function g that agrees for every $j \in J$ with the holomorphic function g_j on $B(p_j, r_j)$. The function g is holomorphic on U since the balls $B(p_j, r_j)$ cover U. Finally $g \in K_M$ since inequalities like $\|f_n\|_{B(p_j, 2r_j)} \leqslant M_j$ are preserved after taking limits.

6.5 J-Laplace operator and metric

Let (S, J) be a connected compact surface with J-field J. We assume that the surface S is defined by charts $U_\alpha \subset V$. The first Laplace operator $\Delta_J : \Omega^0(S, \mathbb{R}) \to \Omega^2(S, \mathbb{R})$ is the map $f \in \Omega^0(S, \mathbb{R}) \mapsto d(df \circ J) \in \Omega^2(S, \mathbb{R})$ that transforms a function to a differential 2-form.

Let $\omega \in \Omega^2(S, \mathbb{R})$ be a volume form on S such that for all $p \in S$ and all $u \in T_pS, u \neq 0$, we have $\omega_p(u, Ju) > 0$. The given J-field orients the surface S. A volume form ω also orients the surface S. The inequalities $\omega_p(u, Ju) > 0$ just mean that both orientations agree.

From the pair of fields (J, ω) we deduce a new field of bilinear maps $g(J, \omega)$ that in a chart $U_\alpha \subset V$ is given by $p \in U_\alpha \mapsto g_{\alpha,p}$ where $g_{\alpha,p} : V \times V \to \mathbb{R}$ is the bilinear map

$$(u, v) \in V \times V \mapsto \omega_{\alpha,p}(u, J_{\alpha,p}(v)) \in \mathbb{R}.$$

The field $g(J, \omega)$ on S defines a Riemannian metric $g = g(J, \omega)$ on S which depends on the data of the J-field J and the volume form ω, both with the same orientation. The endomorphism J_p fixes the form ω_p since $\mathrm{Det}(J_p) = 1$.

It follows that

$$g_p(u, v) = \omega_p(u, Jv) = \omega_p(Ju, J^2v) = \omega_p(Ju, -v) = \omega_p(v, Ju) = g_p(v, u).$$

Hence g_p is symmetric, also clearly bilinear, and positive by construction, so a scalar product. The point-wise action of J is isometric and the volume form of the Riemannian metric $g(J, \omega)$ coincides with the form ω.

From a volume form ω on S we get an operator

$$\%_\omega : \Omega^2(S, \mathbb{R}) \to \Omega^0(S, \mathbb{R})$$

as follows. For $\eta \in \Omega^2(S, \mathbb{R})$ the function $\%_\omega(\eta)$ is the unique function f - satisfying $\eta = f\omega$. We define the second Laplace operator

$$\Delta_{J,\omega} : \Omega^0(S, \mathbb{R}) \to \Omega^0(S, \mathbb{R})$$

by $\Delta_{J,\omega} \overset{\text{def}}{=} \%_\omega \circ \Delta_J$. The operator $\Delta_{J,\omega}$ transforms a function to a function.

The choice of a J-field J a a volume form ω on a differential surface S, opens the possibility to apply a wide range of mathematical and physical methods to study the triple (S, J, ω). Given a triple (S, J, ω), we can measure the length of curves, compute curvature, and make many more measurements since on S we have the Riemannian metric $g_{J,\omega}$. We can study the eigenfunctions and eigenvalues of the operator $\Delta_{J,\omega}$ on functions, also on the space $\mathrm{Bal}(S, \omega)$ of balanced functions f with $\int_S f\omega = 0$. The restriction of $\Delta_{J,\omega}$ to $\mathrm{Bal}(S,\omega)$ has a regularized determinant $Z(S,J,\omega) \in \mathbb{R}$. So one can optimize the quantity $\omega \mapsto Z(S,J,\omega)$ keeping (S,J) fixed. This was done and initiated by Alexander Markovich Polyakov, a Russian-American physicist, yielding spectacular results. We will not explain these results[5].

6.6 J-surfaces

A J-surface is a pair (S,J) of a manifold S with charts in $\mathbb{R}^2$ and a J-field on it. Examples are $(\mathbb{R}^2, J)$ where the J field is constant with value $\begin{pmatrix} 0 & -1 \\ 1 & 0 \end{pmatrix}$. This example is very important, it corresponds to $\mathbb{C}$ with the multiplication m_i by i. The torus is the surface $T^2 \overset{\text{def}}{=} \mathbb{R}^2/2\pi\mathbb{Z}^2$. The previous J field m_i is constant, hence $2\pi\mathbb{Z}^2$-periodic and descends to the torus T^2, which then as J-surface is denoted by $\mathbb{C}/\Gamma$, Γ being the standard lattice $\Gamma \overset{\text{def}}{=} 2\pi\mathbb{Z} + 2\pi i\mathbb{Z}$. Stretching by the factor 2π, transforms lattice $\Gamma \overset{\text{def}}{=} \mathbb{Z} + i\mathbb{Z}$ into $\Gamma \overset{\text{def}}{=} 2\pi\mathbb{Z} + 2\pi i\mathbb{Z}$. The J-tori $\mathbb{R}^2/2\pi\mathbb{Z}^2$ and $\mathbb{R}^2/\mathbb{Z}^2$ are diffeomorphic as J-surfance. We can vary the lattice by putting $\Gamma_\tau \overset{\text{def}}{=} \mathbb{Z} + \tau\mathbb{Z}$, $\tau \in \mathbb{C}_+$, and this way obtain many J-tori $\mathbb{C}/\Gamma_\tau$.

A more general construction of a J-field on an oriented surface uses the notion of energy-barycenter in $\mathbb{H} = \mathbb{H}_J$. Let S be an oriented differential surface given by a finite family of charts $U_\alpha \subset \mathbb{R}^2$. Let $J_\alpha : U_\alpha \to \mathbb{H}_J = \mathbb{H}_J(\mathbb{R}^2)$ be a family of oriented differentiable J-fields. We want to construct a J-field on the surface S. The construction uses a differentiable partition of unity χ_α subordinated to the given system of charts. For a point $p \in S$ with representatives $p_1, p_2, \cdots, p_k$ in charts $U_{\alpha_1}, U_{\alpha_2}, \cdots, U_{\alpha_K}$ we define $J(p)$ as the barycenter of $J_{\alpha_1}(p_1)$, $J_{\alpha_2}(p_2)$, $\cdots, J_{\alpha_K}(p_k)$ with weights $\chi(p_1), \chi(p_2), \cdots, \chi(p_k)$. This construction provides many J-surfaces.

For an oriented real vector space V of dimension two, let $H_J(V)$ be the space of $J \in \mathrm{End}(V)$ with $J^2 = -\mathrm{Id}_V$ and matching orientation. We have seen that $H_J(V)$ carries the geometry of a hyperbolic plane.

Let S be an oriented, compact and connected differentiable surface. Let $\mathbb{J}(TS)$ be the space of J-fields on S that matching the orientation of S. The space $\mathbb{J}(TS)$ is equipped with a natural metric, namely the following. Let J_0, J_1 be two J-fields on S. For $p \in S$ the values $J_{0,p}, J_{1,p}$ take place in $\mathbb{H}_J(T_p(S))$ which is naturally a model for the hyperbolic plane. The natural distance on $\mathbb{J}(TS)$ is

$$dist_J(J_0, J_1) = Supremum_{p \in S} dist_{\mathbb{H}_J(Tp(S))}(J_{0,p}, J_{1,p}).$$

The topological space $\mathbb{J}(TS)$ with its distance dist_J is naturally path connected by geodesic paths, namely for $p \in S$ let $t \in [0,1] \mapsto J_{p,t} \in \mathbb{H}_J(T_p(S))$ be the geodesic in $\mathbb{H}_J(V)$ with constant speed from $J_{0,p}$ to $J_{1,p}$, V being the oriented 2-dimensional vector space $T_p(S)$.

We have repeatedly used the word natural. Here it just means that the distance dist_J and the above geodesic segments $[J_0, J_1]$ are preserved by the action of the group of orientation preserving diffeomorphisms of the surface S.

In real dimension two a J-field $J: S \to \text{End}(TS)$ on a differentiable surfaces defines a canonical structure of a holomorphic manifold on S. In order to obtain this structure it suffices to locally construct J-holomorphic functions. This is the issue of next theorem, which is in fact a local rigidity theorem for J-fields in dimension 2.

Theorem 6.14 Local rigidity of J-fields in real dimension two. *Let V be a real two dimensional vector space. Let $J: V \to End(V)$ be a J-field. For all $p \in V$ there exists an open neighborhood U of p and a smooth injective map $z: U \to \mathbb{C}$ such that at all $q \in U$ its differential $(Dz)_q$ is of real rank 2 and satisfies $(Dz)_q(J_q(h)) = i(Dz)_q(h), h \in V$.*

In other words, for $p \in V$ there exists a complex coordinate function $z: U \to \mathbb{C}$ on an open neighborhood of p that is (J, m_i)-holomorphic. The local coordinate functions of the theorem show that locally near each point $p \in V$ the J-field J is isomorphic to the standard J-field m_i on $\mathbb{C}$ near $z(p)$.

The proof uses the Toric Laplace Inversion Theorem:

Theorem 6.15 Toric Laplace Inversion. *The Laplace operator*

$$f \mapsto \left(-\frac{\partial^2 f}{\partial^2 x} - \frac{\partial^2 f}{\partial^2 y}\right) dx \wedge dy$$

is an isomorphism between the Fréchet spaces of smooth functions f and smooth

2-differential forms ω on the 2-torus $T^2 = \mathbb{R}^2/\mathbb{Z}^2$ with $\int_{T^2} f dx \wedge dy = 0$ and $\int_{T^2} \omega = 0$ respectively.

Proof: A continuous function f on the torus T^2 is represented by a Fourier series

$$\sum_{(n,m) \in \mathbb{Z}^2} a_{n,m} e^{2\pi i(nx+my)}$$

with

$$a_{n,m} = \int_0^1 \int_0^1 f(x,y)\, e^{-2\pi i(nx+my)}\, dxdy.$$

The coefficients $a_{n,m}$ are bounded by the supremum norm $\| f \|_{\sup}$ of f. More is true, the coefficients tend to 0 if (n, m) tends to infinity. For $2k$ -times continuously differential functions f the coefficients tend faster to 0, more precisely $(n^2 + m^2)^k a_{n,m}$ tend to 0 if (n, m) tends to infinity. A converse holds: a function f on T^2 is smooth if and only if for all $k \in \mathbb{N}$ the Fourier coefficients $a_{n,m}$ tend to 0 such that $(n^2 + m^2)^k a_{n,m}$ tend also to 0. Since $a_{n,m}(-\frac{\partial^2 f}{\partial^2 x} - \frac{\partial^2 f}{\partial^2 y}) = 4\pi^2(n^2 + m^2) a_{n,m}(f)$ the operator $f \mapsto (-\frac{\partial^2 f}{\partial^2 x} - \frac{\partial^2 f}{\partial^2 y}) dx \wedge dy$ is an isomorphism of Fréchet spaces between the spaces of functions with $a_{0,0}(f) = 0$ and of forms ω with integral 0.

Proof: Local Rigidity of J -fields in real dimension 2. Assume p to be the origin of V and let e_1, e_2 be a basis for V with $J_p(e_1) = e_2$. Let x, y be the corresponding linear coordinates on V. Let $\chi : V \to [0,1]$ be a smooth function with $\chi(q) = 1$ if $|x(q)|, |y(q)| \leqslant \frac{1}{4}$ and $\chi(q) = 0$ if $|x(q)| \geqslant \frac{1}{2}$ or $|y(q)| \geqslant \frac{1}{2}$. For $s \in]0,1]$ put $\chi_s(q) = \chi(\frac{1}{s} q)$. Let J_0 on $P = \{q \in V \mid |x(q)|, |y(q)| \leqslant 1\}$ be the constant J -field $J_q = J_p$. For $q \in P$, let $t \in [0,1] \mapsto J(t,q) \in H_J(V)$ be the geodesic from $J_{0,q}$ to J_q. For $s \in]0,1]$, let J_s be the J -field on P defined by $J_{s,q} = J(\chi_s(q), q)$. Observe $\lim_{s \to 0} J_s = J_0$.

For $s \in]0,1]$, define $U_s = \{q \in P \mid |x(q)|, |y(q)| < \frac{s}{4}\}$ and observe that on the open neighborhood U_s of p the fields J_s and J agree.

The J-fields J_s correspond to J-fields, again denoted by J_s, on the torus $T = \mathbb{R}^2/\mathbb{Z}^2$. The 1-differential form dx corresponds to a 1-form, again and with a slight abuse denoted by dx on T. For smooth functions f with $\int_T f dx \wedge dy = 0$ on T we consider the equation

$$d((dx + df) \circ J_s) = 0$$

which can be rewritten as

$$\Delta_{J_s}(f) = - d(dx \circ J_s).$$

By the Toric Laplace Inversion, the equation for $s = 0$ has the only solution $f = 0$. The operator Δ_{J_s} for s close to 0 is close to the operator $\Delta_{J_0} = \Delta$ of the Toric Laplace Inversion theorem, so also invertible. Hence for $s > 0$ but small enough, the above equation has a solution f_s that in the C^∞-Fréchet topology is close to the function 0. Observe $dx + df_s \neq 0$ at p. Fix such an s.

Put $\omega_s = (dx + df_s) - i(dx + df_s) \circ J_s \in \Omega^1(U_s, \mathbb{C})$. Observe $d\omega_s = 0$. Note $\omega_s \circ J_s = i\omega_s$. Let $z: U_s \to \mathbb{C}$ be the function

$$z(q) = \int_{[p,q]} \omega.$$

Observe that the function z is (J, m_i)-holomorphic since it is (J_s, m_i)-holomorphic and $J_s = J$ on U_s. The function z is a (J, m_i)-holomorphic coordinate at p on an open neighborhood $U' \subset U_s$ of p since $(Dz)_p \neq 0$.

We introduce the term z-structure. We call a system of (U_a, z_a), $a \in A$, of charts on a differential manifold M with values in $\mathbb{C}^d$ a *z-structure* on M if the transition maps are holomorphic. Such a system of charts is termed in short as holomorphic atlas. Two z-structures (U_a, z_a), $a \in A$, and (U_b, z_b), $b \in B$, are equivalent if all transition maps between charts U_a and U_b are holomorphic. A holomorphic structure is a z-structure up to equivalence of holomorphic atlases.

The main result of this section affirms that in real dimension 2 every J-structure determines a z-structure and a unique compatible holomorphic structure. In fact, the proof of the local rigidity theorem yields more: In real dimension 2 every smooth family J_t of J-structures determines a smooth family z_t of z-structures.

7 Riemann Surfaces

7.1 Riemann surfaces as z- and as J- surface

A *Riemann surface* is a differentiable manifold with charts in $\mathbb{C}$ and holomorphic transition maps. In short we can say that a Riemann surface is a surface with a z-structure. It follows from the Local Rigidity of J-Fields Theorem, that a Riemann surface can also be defined as a differentiable manifold S of dimension two, together with a J-field on it. Having those two equivalent definitions implies:

Theorem 7.1 *Let S be a differentiable surface. The set $Z(S)$ of holomorphic structures on S has a natural topology, namely the compact-open topology on the space of J-fields. On a compact surface, the topology is induced by the metric $d_{Z(S)}$ of maximal point-wise distance in the hyperbolic plane and the action of diffeomorphisms on $Z(S)$ is by isometries.*

Since the point-wise values of J-fields in real dimension two take place in the hyperbolic plane we conclude:

Theorem 7.2 *Let S be an oriented differentiable surface. The space $Z(S)$ of holomorphic structures on S is path connected. Moreover between two points there exists the path that traces point-wise geodesics in the hyperbolic plane.*

As we will see later, a little more effort not using the two definitions of Riemann surface, but merely the proof of the local rigidity of J-fields will give:

Theorem 7.3 *Let Σ be a Riemann surface of genus 1. Then Σ is biholomorphic to $\mathbb{C}/\Gamma_\tau$, $\tau \in \mathbb{C}_+$, for a suitable lattice Γ_τ in $\mathbb{C}$.*

7.2 Natural structures on the space $\mathbb{J}(TS)$

Let S be a connected compact oriented surface. Let $\mathbb{J}(TS)$ be the space of all smooth J-fields on S, that agree with the orientation of S. The space $\mathbb{J}(TS)$ is a manifold of infinite dimension, it has charts in a complex Fréchet space.

The group of orientation preserving diffeomorphisms $\mathrm{Diff}^+(S)$ of the oriented surface S acts on $\mathbb{J}(TS)$. Define a *natural structure* on the space $\mathbb{J}(TS)$ to be a $\mathrm{Diff}^+(S)$-invariant structure.

An important example of a natural structure are the point-wise geodesic paths $t \in \mathbb{R} \mapsto J_t \in \mathbb{J}(TS)$ that we have already encountered. This structure assigns to a pair of points $J_0, J_1 \in \mathbb{J}(TS)$ a parametrized segment $[J_0, J_1] \subset \mathbb{J}(TS)$ consisting of a map $t \in [0,1] \mapsto J_t \in \mathbb{J}(TS)$ that traces at every point $p \in S$ a geodesic of constant speed in the hyperbolic plane $J_{t,p} \in \mathbb{H}_J(T_pS)$.

Let us denote a point in $\mathbb{J}(TS)$ by (S, J) or simply by J. The tangent space $T_J\mathbb{J}(TS)$ at $J \in \mathbb{J}(TS)$ is the space of smooth fields $H: S \to \mathrm{End}(TS)$ of endomorphisms of the tangent space TS, that point-wise anti-commute with the J-field J. Indeed, from

$$(J+H)^2 = -\mathrm{Id} + H \circ J + J \circ H + H \circ H$$

it follows that $J + H$ satisfies $(J+H)^2 = -\mathrm{Id}$ up to order 1 if and only if H anti-commutes with J point-wise. At a point $p \in S$, the value H_p is a linear map $H_p: T_pS \to T_pS$ with $H_p \circ J_p + J_p \circ H_p = 0$. Hence, almost clearly:

Theorem 7.4 *The map J°: $H \in T_J(\mathbb{J}(TS)) \mapsto J \circ H \in T_J(\mathbb{J}(TS))$ is a natural complex structure J° on the manifold $\mathbb{J}(TS)$. In other words, the group of orientation preserving diffeomorphisms of S acts by J°-holomorphic automorphisms of $\mathbb{J}(TS)$.*

Proof: If H anti-commutes with J, then $J^\circ(H) = J \circ H$ anti-commutes also with J, so, J° is an endomorphism of the tangent bundle $T(\mathbb{J}(TS))$. Clearly, $J^\circ \circ J^\circ = -\mathrm{Id}_{T\mathbb{T}(TS)}$. So, J° is an almost complex structure on $\mathbb{J}(TS)$.

The structure J° is integrable. Indeed, we will construct a J°-holomorphic atlas on the Fréchet-manifold $\mathbb{J}(TS)$.

Let the oriented surface S be presented by an atlas (U_α, ϕ_α) such that the charts U_α have compact closure in S and such that the images $\phi_\alpha(U_\alpha) \subset \mathbb{R}^2$ are a fixed open disc $U \subset \mathbb{R}^2$.

Let F be the Fréchet manifold of smooth bounded fields $J: U \to \mathbb{H}_J(\mathbb{R}^2) = \mathbb{H}_J$. Bounded here means that $J(U) \subset \mathbb{H}_J$ is bounded in the hyperbolic plane and that all partial derivatives are 2×2-matrices with bounded coefficients. The Fréchet topology is given by the family of C^k-norms. Postcomposing $J \in F$ with the complex coordinate Fix : $\mathbb{H}_J \to \mathbb{C}_+$ shows that the Fréchet manifold F is identified with an open subset Fix $F = \{\text{Fix} \circ J \mid J \in F\}$ in the complex linear Fréchet space $C_b^\infty(U, \mathbb{C})$ of all bounded smooth maps from U to $\mathbb{C}$, that admit moreover a smooth extension to the closure $\overline{U}$.

The (integrable almost) complex structure on Fix$F$ is the linear structure m_i. The post composition with Fix is (J°, m_i)-holomorphic, so the almost complex structure J° on F is integrable too.

The coordinate map $\phi_\alpha: U_\alpha \to U$ induces $\phi_\alpha^*: J(U_\alpha) \to F$, which is J°-biholomorphic. So, J° on $J(U_\alpha)$ is integrable too.

The restriction maps $R_\alpha: \mathbb{J}(TS) \to J(U_\alpha)$ are J°-holomorphic and define the complex Fréchet manifold structure. It follows that J° on $\mathbb{J}(TS)$ is integrable too.

Our next aim is the construction of a natural (pre-)symplectic structure ω° on $\mathbb{J}(TS)$. We need some preparations.

Given $J \in \mathbb{J}(TS)$ on a surface S, let (U_α) be an open cover of S, such that each U_α admits a (bijective) holomorphic coordinate $z_\alpha: U_\alpha \to U \subset \mathbb{C}$. A tangent vector $H \in T_J\mathbb{J}(TS)$ is given by a compatible system $H_\alpha \in T_{m_i}J(U)$. Each H_α is a field on U of 2×2-matices that anti-commute with m_i, or equivalently the field $p \in U \mapsto H_{\alpha,p}$ is a field of traceless symmetric matrices.So

$$H_{\alpha,p} = \begin{pmatrix} a(p) & b(p) \\ b(p) & -a(p) \end{pmatrix}$$

Observe

$$m_i \circ H_{\alpha,p} = \begin{pmatrix} b(p) & -a(p) \\ -a(p) & -b(p) \end{pmatrix}, \quad H_{\alpha,p} \circ m_i = \begin{pmatrix} -b(p) & a(p) \\ a(p) & b(p) \end{pmatrix}.$$

Define the norm of a matrix $\begin{pmatrix} a & b \\ b & -a \end{pmatrix}$ as $\sqrt{a^2+b^2}$. Let $D \subset T_{m_i}\mathbb{J}(TU)$ be the space of smooth traceless symmetric fields of 2×2−matrices

$$p \in U \mapsto d(p) = \begin{pmatrix} a(p) & b(p) \\ b(p) & -a(p) \end{pmatrix}$$

of norm< 1. The map

$$E : D \rightarrow \mathbb{J}(TU)$$

$$d \in D \mapsto (p \mapsto (E(d))_p) = \frac{1}{\sqrt{1-a(p)^2-b(p)^2}}\begin{pmatrix} a(p) & -1+b(p) \\ 1+b(p) & -a(p) \end{pmatrix}$$

smoothly parametrizes an open neighborhood N_{mi} of m_i in $\mathbb{J}(TU)$.

Note that the anti-commutator $[A,B]_+ = AB + BA$ of traceless symmetric 2×2-matrices evaluates to a multiple of the identity matrix.

Keeping the notation U, $\mathbb{J}(TU)$, $m_i \in \mathbb{J}(TU)$, N_{m_i}, E, D as before, we obtain:

Theorem 7.5 *For $H \in T_{m_i}\mathbb{J}(TU)$ the field*

$$E(d) \in N_{m_i} \mapsto \widetilde{H} \overset{def}{=} H + \frac{1}{4} Trance([H, E(d) - m_i]_+) E(d)$$

is a smooth tangent vector field $\widetilde{H}$ on N_{m_i} that extends H.

Proof: Putting $X_{E(d)} = \frac{1}{4}\operatorname{Trace}([H, E(d) - m_i]_+) E(d)$, observe $X_{E(0)} = 0$ since $E(0) = m_i$. So the field of 2×2-matrices $p \in U \mapsto H_p + (X_{E(d)})_p$ extends the field $p \in U \mapsto H_p$. Observe

$$[H + X_{E(d)}, E(d)]_+ = [H, E(d)]_+ + [X_{E(d)}, E(d)]_+ = \\ [H, E(d) - m_i]_+ + [X_{E(d)}, E(d)]_+$$

and

$$[H, E(d) - m_i]_+ = \begin{pmatrix} \lambda & 0 \\ 0 & \lambda \end{pmatrix}$$

$$[E(d), E(d)]_+ = \begin{pmatrix} -2 & 0 \\ 0 & -2 \end{pmatrix}.$$

So, by putting $X = \frac{1}{4}\operatorname{Trace}([H, E(d) - m_i]_+) E(d)$ makes that $H+X$ and $E(d)$ anti commute, hence $H + X \in T_{E(d)}\mathbb{J}(TU)$.

The above proof even shows little more, namely that the tangent vectors $H \in T_J \mathbb{J}(TS)$ extend explicitly smoothly to a tangent vector field over an open neighborhood N_J of J in $\mathbb{J}(TS)$. Put $D_J = \{ d \in T_J \mathbb{J}(TS) \mid \mathrm{Det}(d_p + J_p) > 0, p \in S \}$. The map

$$E: d \in D_J \to \mathbb{J}(TS),\ d \mapsto \frac{1}{\sqrt{Det(d+J)}}(d+J)$$

is a parametrization of an open neighborhood N_J of J in $\mathbb{J}(TS)$. The expression

$$\widetilde{H}_{E(d)} = H + \frac{1}{4}\mathrm{Trace}([H, E(d) - J]_+) E(d)$$

extends $H \in T_J \mathbb{J}(TS)$ to a vector field over N_J.

Theorem 7.6 *The expression*

$$\omega^\circ_J(H,K) = -TraceHJK,\ J \in \mathbb{J}(TS),\ H,K \in T_J(\mathbb{J}(TS))$$

defines a natural non-degenerate closed 2-differential form ω° on the Fréchet manifold $\mathbb{J}(TS)$ with values in the space $C^\infty(S, \mathbb{R})$ of real functions on S. For $H \in T_J(\mathbb{J}(TS))$, the function $\omega^\circ_J(H, J^\circ H)$ is non-negative, and moreover positive at $p \in S$ if $H_p \neq 0$.

Proof: Clearly $\omega^\circ_J(H,K)$ is linear in its arguments H and K. From $KJ = -JK$ and the property TraceAB = TraceBA its anti-symmetry follows:

$$\omega^\circ_J(H,K) = -\mathrm{Trace}\, HJK = \mathrm{Trace}\, HKJ = \mathrm{Trace}\, KJH = -\omega^\circ_J(K,H)$$

so the expression defines a 2-differential form ω° on $\mathbb{J}(TS)$.

The 2-form ω° is closed. Indeed, for $J \in \mathbb{J}(TS)$, $H,K,L \in T_J(\mathbb{J}(TS))$ let $\widetilde{H}$, $\widetilde{K}$, $\widetilde{L}$ be extensions over N_J. In order to prove $d\omega^\circ = 0$ we evaluate at $J \in N_J$

$$d\omega^\circ(\widetilde{H},\widetilde{K},\widetilde{L}) = \widetilde{H}\omega^\circ(\widetilde{K},\widetilde{L}) - \widetilde{K}\omega^\circ(\widetilde{H},\widetilde{L}) + \widetilde{L}\omega^\circ(\widetilde{H},\widetilde{K}) -$$
$$\omega^\circ([\widetilde{H},\widetilde{K}]_{Lie},\widetilde{L}) + \omega^\circ([\widetilde{H},\widetilde{L}]_{Lie},\widetilde{K}) - \omega^\circ([\widetilde{K},\widetilde{L}]_{Lie},\widetilde{H})$$

The first term at J is the directional derivative in the direction $H \in T_J \mathbb{J}(TS)$ of the function $J' \in N_J \mapsto \mathring{\omega}_{J'}(\widetilde{K}_J', \widetilde{L}_J') = -Trace\, \widetilde{K}_{J'} J' \widetilde{L}_{J'}$. One contribution, the partial derivative with respect to J', is $-$Trace KHL. So for all three first terms we collect the contributions

$$-\mathrm{Trace}(KHL - HKL + HLK).$$

The remaining six contributions of the two partial derivatives from the first three terms cancel against the last three terms. So finally

$$(d\omega^{\circ}(\widetilde{H},\widetilde{K},\widetilde{L}))_J = - Trance(KHL - HKL + HLK)$$

Products with three factors like KHL anti-commute with J, so Trace $KHL = 0$. We conclude that ω° is a closed 2-form on $\mathbb{J}(TS)$.

Locally, expressed in suitable coordinates, a field J is the constant field $\begin{pmatrix} 0 & -1 \\ 1 & 0 \end{pmatrix}$ and a field H that anti-commutes with J is of the form $\begin{pmatrix} a(p) & b(p) \\ b(p) & -a(p) \end{pmatrix}$.

The function $p \mapsto (\omega^{\circ}(H, J^{\circ} H))_p$ on S is the non-negative function $p \mapsto 2(a(p)^2 + b(p)^2)$, which is positive at p if $H_p \neq 0$.

Much later we will study the *moduli spaces* M_g and the *Teichmüller spaces* $\mathbb{T}_g$. At this point we can already give definitions, but many justifications have to be postponed at this stage of the study.

Let S_g be a compact, oriented, connected surface of genus $g \geqslant 0$. The space M_g is the quotient as metric space of $J(TS_g)$ by the group $\mathrm{Diff}^{+}(S_g)$ of oriented diffeomorphisms of S_g. The Teichmüller space $\mathbb{T}g$ is the quotient of $J(TS_g)$ by the group $\mathrm{Diff}_0(S_g)$ of diffeomorphisms of S_g that are homotopic to the identity. More precisely, the group Φ being $\mathrm{Diff}^{+}(S_g)$ or $\mathrm{Diff}_0(S_g)$, the distance between orbits $\Phi^* a, \Phi^* b \in J(S_g)/\Phi$, $a, b \in J(TS_g)$ is the infimum of the distances in $J(TS_g)$ between $(S_g, \phi^* a), (S_g, \psi^* b)$, $\phi, \psi \in \Phi$.

It turns out that $\mathbb{T}_g$ is a smooth manifold of real dimension $6g - 6$ if $g \geqslant 2$, of real dimension 2 if $g = 1$ and of dimension 0 if $g = 0$. The complex structure J° on $J(TS_g)$ is invariant by the action of diffeomorphisms, hence will induce a complex structure on $\mathbb{T}_g$, provided that $\mathbb{T}_g$ is naturally a smooth manifold and that the orbits of the group of diffeomorphisms have J°-invariant tangent spaces. In a later section will be proved that indeed $\mathbb{T}_g$ is a smooth complex manifold.

Also the Uniformization Theorem will be proved. It provides a Riemann surface S of genus $g \geqslant 1$ with a natural Riemannian metric of constant curvature. Let μ be the corresponding natural measure. The form ω° on $\mathbb{J}(TS)$ together with the measure μ define a natural symplectic form $\omega^{\circ,\mu}$ on $\mathbb{J}(TS)$ by

$$\omega^{\circ,\mu}(H,K) = \int_S \omega^{\circ}(H,K)\, d\mu$$

Theorem 7.7 *The pair* $(J^{\circ}, \omega^{\circ,\mu})$ *defines a natural Kähler structure on* $\mathbb{J}$

(TS). *If S is compact, of genus $g \geqslant 1$ the structure $(J^{\circ}, \omega^{\circ,\mu})$ induces a natural Kähler structure on the Teichmüller space $\mathbb{T}_g$ and on the moduli space M_g.*

7.3 J-fields and Integrability in higher dimension

The above decomposition as a direct sum can be done point-wise in case of a J-manifold. Let M be a manifold with charts U_α in a vector space V and let J be a J-field on M given locally by fields $J_\alpha : U_\alpha \to J(V)$. At each point $p \in M$, the tangent space at p is identified with V. Fields on M that are locally maps $U_\alpha \to \Lambda(V, \mathbb{C})$ are k-differential forms with values in $\mathbb{C}$. The infinite dimensional $\mathbb{C}$-vector space of these forms is denoted by $\Omega(M, \mathbb{C})$. The previous theorem applies point wise and gives a direct sum decomposition

$$\Omega^k(M,\mathbb{C}) = \bigoplus_{l=0}^{l=k} \Omega_J^{k-l,l}(M,\mathbb{C}).$$

The previously point-wise defined projectors $\P_J^{k-l,l}$ give projectors

$$\P_J^{k-l,l} : \Omega^k(V,\mathbb{C}) \to \Omega^k(V,\mathbb{C})$$

with images $\Omega_J^{k-l,l}(V,\mathbb{C})$. It is interesting how the exterior differentials $d^k : \Omega^k(V,\mathbb{C}) \to \Omega^{k+1}(V,\mathbb{C})$ intertwine with the projectors $\P_J^{k-l,l}$ and $\P_J^{k+1-h,h}$.

In the case of a complex manifold, i.e. a manifold M with charts U_α in $\mathbb{C}^n$ and holomorphic transition maps $\phi_{\beta\alpha}$ the underlying J-field intertwines in a special way with the projectors $\P^{*,*}$. In a chart U_α the forms $\omega \in \Omega^{k-l,l}(M, \mathbb{C})$ can be written in a special way in terms of the coordinate differentials $dz_i, d\bar{z}_j$ namely, as a linear combination of forms

$$f dz_{a_1} \wedge \cdots \wedge dz_{a_{k-1}} \wedge d\bar{z}_{b_1} \wedge \cdots \wedge d\bar{z}_{b_l}$$

with $1 \leqslant a_1 < a_2 < \cdots < a_{k-l} \leqslant n$ and $1 \leqslant b_1 < b_2 < \cdots < b_l \leqslant n$. It follows that $d^k : \Omega^k(M, \mathbb{C}) \to \Omega^{k+1}(M, \mathbb{C})$ maps the space $\Omega^{k-l,l}(M,\mathbb{C})$ into the sum of two summands of the decomposition:

$$d^k(\Omega^{k-l,l}(M,\mathbb{C})) \subset \Omega^{k+1-l,l}(M,\mathbb{C}) \oplus \Omega^{k-l,l+1}(M,\mathbb{C}).$$

With the notation $\Omega^{p,q}(M, \mathbb{C}) = \Omega^{k-l,l}(M, \mathbb{C})$ we have $d^{p+q}(\Omega^{p,q}(M, \mathbb{C})) \subset \Omega^{p+1,q}(M, \mathbb{C}) \oplus \Omega^{p,q+1}(M, \mathbb{C})$. Remember that for spaces $\Omega_J^{k-l,l}(V, \mathbb{C})$ or projectors $\P_J^{k-l,l}$ on a complex manifold associated to the underlying J-field we have omitted the index J in the notations. In particular, for a J -field that underlies a complex manifold structure it follows that the composition

$$\P^{0,2}\circ d^1 : \Omega^{1,0}(M,\mathbb{C})\to\Omega^{0,2}(M,\mathbb{C})$$

evaluates to 0.

What happens for J -fields that do not necessary underly a holomorphic structure on the manifold M ? It was observed by Albert Nijenhuis (1926–2015), a Dutch-American mathematician, that the map $\P_J^{0,2}\circ d^1$ is tensorial, which means that for each point $p\in M$ and for each $\omega\in\Omega_J^{1,0}(M,\mathbb{C})$ the value $(\P_J^{0,2}\circ d^1(\omega))_p$ of $\P_J^{0,2}\circ d^1(\omega)$ at the point p only depends on the value ω_p of ω at the point p. The map $\P_J^{0,2}\circ d^1$ is called the Nijenhuis tensor N_J.

A J -field on a manifold M is called integrable if the field underlies a holomorphic structure on M. We have already proved the following result of Nijenhuis:

Theorem 7.8 $N_J = 0$ *for an integrable J-field J.*

The reciprocal statement is true according to a deep result of August Newlander, a USA mathematician, and Louis Nirenberg (1925–2020), a Canadian USA mathematician[74].

Theorem 7.9 *A J-field J on a manifold is integrable if* $N_J = 0$ *holds.*

We already gave a proof for J -fields on 2-dimensional manifolds. For the higher dimensional cases we give references to the literature. See the more elementary proof by Bernard Malgrange for C^∞ fields and the even more elementary proof by André Weil for real analytic fields[65].

In real even dimension $4,6,\cdots$ a J -structure can not be upgraded in general to a z -structure.

Exercise 1: *First, show that the map* $\P^{0,2}\circ d^1 : \Omega^{1,0}(M,\mathbb{C})\to\Omega^{0,2}(M,\mathbb{C})$ *is smoothly linear and deduce that the* $\P^{0,2}\circ d^1$ *map is tensorial.*

7.4 Integrability of fibred J -fields

Let $E = B\times S$ be the product of a holomorphic manifold B and a smooth surface S. Let $\sigma : B\to\mathbb{J}(TS)$ be a smooth map from B to the complex Banach manifold $\mathbb{J}(TS)$ of J-fields on the surface S. The map σ defines a J-field J_σ on E as follows. The tangent space T_pE at $p=(b,s)$ decomposes as direct sum of the tangent spaces $T_pE = T_bB \oplus T_sS$ and $J_{\sigma,p} = J_b \oplus \sigma(b)_s$.

The J-field J_σ is partially integrable. On B its J-field $b \mapsto J_{B,b}$ is integrable by assumption and on the fibers $\{b\} \times S$ the fields $\sigma(b)$ are integrable by a previous Theorem. The following theorem simplifies the integrability condition of Nijenhuis for the field J_σ.

Theorem 7.10 Fibered Integrability Criterion. *Let $E=B\times S$ be the product of a holomorphic manifold B and a smooth surface S. Let $\sigma: B \to \mathbb{J}(TS)$ be a smooth map from B to the complex Banach manifold $\mathbb{J}(TS)$ of J-fields on the surface S. The field J_σ on E is integrable if and only if the map σ is holomorphic.*

Proof: Let $\frac{\partial}{\partial t_1}, \frac{\partial}{\partial t_2}, \cdots, \frac{\partial}{\partial t_{2n}}$ be local coordinate vector fields on B such that $J(\frac{\partial}{\partial t_k}) = \frac{\partial}{\partial t_{k+n}}, k = 1\cdots n$, holds. This is possible to achieve since B *is a* holomorphic manifold. Let $\frac{\partial}{\partial s_1}, \frac{\partial}{\partial s_2}$ be local smooth coordinate vector fields on S. It suffices to compute the Nijenhuis tensor $N_{J_\sigma}(X,Y)$ for X being a coordinate vector field on B and Y being a coordinate vector field on S.

Using the expression of Nijenhuis and Woolf[75] for the Nijenhuis tensor

$$N_J(X,Y)=[JX,JY]_{\text{Lie}}-[X,Y]_{\text{Lie}}-J[JX,Y]_{\text{Lie}}-J[X,JY]_{\text{Lie}}$$

it simplifies here for the field J_σ on $B \times S$ to

$$N_{J_\sigma}(X,Y)=[J_\sigma X, J_\sigma Y]\text{Lie}-J_\sigma[X, J_\sigma Y]\text{Lie}.$$

since X, $J_\sigma X$, Y are coordinate vector fields on $B \times S$. Notice

$[X, J_\sigma Y]_{\text{Lie}}=((D\sigma)(X))(Y), [J_\sigma X, J_\sigma Y]_{\text{Lie}}=((D\sigma)(J_\sigma X))(Y)$

and at $(b, s) \in B \times S$

$$(J_\sigma)_{b,s}Ys = \sigma(b)Ys,\ (J_\sigma)_{b,s}X_b = J_{B,b}X_b.$$

So, $N_{J_\sigma} = 0$ if and only if for all coordinate vector fields X, Y as above

$$((D\sigma)(J_\sigma X))(Y)= J_\sigma((D\sigma)(X))(Y)$$

or more expanded at $(b,s) \in B \times S$

$$((D\sigma)_b(J_{B,b}X_b))(Y_s) = (((D\sigma)(J_\sigma X))(Y))_{b,s} =$$

$$(J_\sigma((D\sigma)(X))(Y))_{b,s} = (\sigma(b))_s(((D\sigma)_b(X_b))(Y_s))$$

hold. This formula (which is written with many brackets) means precisely that the map $\sigma : B \to \mathbb{J}(TS)$ is $(J_B, J_{J(S)})$-holomorphic. With the Newlander Nirenberg Theorem it follows that the field J_σ on $B \times S$ is integrable if and only if the map $\sigma : B \to \mathbb{J}(TS)$ is holomorphic.

7.5 Analysis of Laplace operators on J-surfaces

In the proofs of the two main theorems, namely Uniformisation Theorem and Analytic characterisation of genus, the following property of the Laplace operator $\Delta_J : \Omega^0(S, \mathbb{R}) \to \Omega^2(S, \mathbb{R})$ on a J-surface (S, J) will be of crucial importance. Remember that the spaces $\Omega^0(S, \mathbb{R})$ and $\Omega^2(S, \mathbb{R})$ are spaces of smooth, i.e. C^∞, sections.

Theorem 7.11 Laplace Inversion Theorem, version 1. *Let* (S, J) *be a compact connected J-surface. Let* ω *be a smooth volume form on S. The kernel and co-kernel of the continuous operators on Fréchet spaces* $\Delta_J : \Omega^0(S, \mathbb{R}) \to \Omega^2(S, \mathbb{R})$ *and* $\Delta_{J,\omega} : \Omega^0(S, \mathbb{R}) \to \Omega^0(S, \mathbb{R})$ *are of dimension one. The kernel of* Δ_J *is the space of constant functions. The image of* Δ_J *is the space of* 2*-forms* ω *with* $\int_S \omega = 0$.

Theorem 7.12 Laplace Inversion Theorem, version 2. *Let* (S, J) *be a compact connected J-surface. Let* ω_0 *be a smooth volume form on S of total volume* 1. *The operator*

$$\Delta_J^+ : \Omega^0(S, \mathbb{R}) \to \Omega^2(S, \mathbb{R})$$

defined by

$$f \in \Omega^0(S, \mathbb{R}) \mapsto \Delta_J(f) + \left(\int_S f\omega_0\right) \omega_0 \in \Omega^2(S, \mathbb{R})$$

is an isomorphism of Fréchet spaces.

These theorems imply each other. There are several methods of proof. Since the operator Δ_J is an elliptic partial differential operator, the theory of Fredholm operators applies.

For version 2 we supply a proof that uses Potential Theory. Its origins are in the work of Peter Gustav Lejeune Dirichlet, Axel Harnack[47], Robert Brown (1773–1858), a Scottish botanist, who observed the so called Brownian motion,

Tibor Radó[85] and Oskar Perron[78]. The mathematical treatment of Brownian motion is initiated in the work of Albert Einstein (1879–1955), a Swiss-American physicist[34], Norbert Wiener (1894–1964), an American mathematician[104], and Paul Pierre Lévy (1886–1971), a French mathematician[61]. The proof of the Laplace Inversion Theorem needs a preparation that uses Brownian motion and constructs meromorphic differentials with only two first order poles.

Theorem 7.13 Two point Green function. *Let (S, J) be a compact connected J-surface. Given two distinct points $p, q \in S$ there exist a Δ_J harmonic real function $h_{p,q}$ on $S \setminus \{p, q\}$ such that the J-holomorphic $(1,0)$ form $\omega_{p,q} = dh_{p,q} - idh_{p,q} \circ J$ has poles at p and q with residues $+1$ and -1 respectively.*

Proof: Let ω_0 be a J-oriented volume form on S. The proof uses the Brownian motion on the Riemannian surface $(S, g(J, \omega_0))$[98]. Choose local z coordinates z_p, z_q centred at p, q respectively. Put $b_p(r) = \{a \in S \mid |z_p(a)| < r\}$ and $b_q(r) = \{a \in S \mid |z_q(a)| < r\}$. For $r > 0$ and small enough, use Brownian motion on $S_{p,q,r} = S \setminus b_p(r) \cup b_q(r)$ in order to construct a real function $h_{p,q,r}$ on $S_{p,q,r}$ that is harmonic in the interior of $S_{p,q,r}$ and with boundary values $\frac{\pm 1}{2\pi}\log(r)$. The function $h_{p,q}$ is the limit function for $r \to +0$ of the functions $h_{p,q,r}$. The function $h_{p,q}$ is a Green function with poles p, q and moreover in the sense of distribution or Cauchy principal values solves the equation $\Delta_J(h_{p,q}) = \delta_p - \delta_q$. The J-holomorphic $(1,0)$-form $\omega_{p,q} = dh_{p,q} - idh_{p,q} \circ J$ has poles at p and q with residues $+1$ and -1 respectively.

For further study of Brownian Motion see the book[4] of Marc Yor (1949–2014), a French mathematician and for Distributions the book[93] of Laurent Schwartz (1915–2002), a French mathematician. Cauchy principal values give first examples of distributions.

Proof: of Laplace Inversion Theorem, version 2. Let $M_0^2(S)$ be the set of Radon measures of total mass 2 and integral 0. It is a compact convex set in the dual space with its weak topology of the Banach space $C^0(S, \mathbb{R})$ of real continuous functions on S. Its extremal points are the measures $m_{p,q} = \delta_p - \delta_q$, $p, q \in S$, $p \neq q$, where δ_r is the Dirac measure concentrated at $r \in S$. The integrable function $h_{p,q}$ of the previous theorem satisfies $\Delta_J(h_{p,q}) = m_{p,q}$ in the sense of distributions of Laurent Schwartz or principal values of AugustinLouis Cauchy. The Banach space is separable and therefore the space $M_0^2(S)$ is metrizable. The Krein-Milman Theorem of Mark Grigorjewitsch Krein and David Milman, represents a point $\omega \in M_0^2(S)$ as a limit of convex combinations of points in the closure of the set of extremal points $EM_0^2(S)$. Since the space $M_0^2(S)$ is metrizable, even a strengthening, due to Gustave Choquet of the Krein-Milman theorem applies and a probability measure μ_ω on $M_0^2(S)$ may be chosen with support in the set of extremal points such that the representation

$$\omega = \int_{EM_0^2(S)} m_{p,q} d\mu(p,q)$$

holds. It follows that for every $\omega = M_0^2(S)$ the integrable function

$$h_\omega = \int_{EM_0^2(S)} h_{p,q} d\mu(p,q)$$

satisfies $\Delta_J(h_\omega) = \omega$. The function h_ω is unique up to a constant function by the maximum principle. If ω is smooth, the function h_ω is smooth too by standard regularity theory.

If $\omega \in \Omega^2(S)$ is not in $M_0^2(S)$ we first replace ω by $\omega - (\int_S \omega)\omega_0$. After scaling eventually ω will be in $M_0^2(S)$ and we apply the above.

The operator Δ_J^+ being continuous, injective and surjective is an isomorphism of Fréchet spaces by the Banach-Schauder isomorphism Theorem treated in a later section.

Spectral Theory provides an other proof for version 1. The operator $\Delta_{J,\omega}$ maps functions to functions, so the notion of eigenvalue and eigenvector make sense. A function $f \neq 0$ on S is an eigenvector if the functions f and $\Delta_{J,\omega}(f)$ are proportional, i.e.

$$\Delta_{J,\omega}(f) = \lambda f.$$

The factors λ that appear are the eigenvalues of the operator $\Delta_{J,\omega}$.

The following "work horse" theorem states essential results from spectral theory.

Theorem 7.14 Spectral work horse. *The operator $\Delta_{J,\omega}$ has countably many eigenvalues $(\lambda_n)_{n \in \mathbb{N}}$. The eigenvalues λ_n are real non negative numbers, which can be labelled in increasing order such that*

$$0 = \lambda_0 < \lambda_1 \leqslant \lambda_2 \leqslant \cdots$$

holds. Moreover, for every $T \in \mathbb{R}$ *the number* $\Lambda(T)$ *of eigenvalues in* $[0,T]$ *is finite. The asymptotics of the growth of* $\Lambda(T)$ *for* $T \to +\infty$ *is deduced from the law of Weyl and Karamata:*

$$\lim_{n\to\infty} \frac{\lambda_n}{n} = \frac{1}{4\pi}\int_S \omega.$$

There exists a system of eigenvectors $(e_n)_{n\in\mathbb{N}}$ *which are smooth functions on* S *with*

$$\int_S e_n^2\omega = 1, \int_S e_n e_m \omega = 0, 0 \leqslant n < m.$$

Every smooth function f *on* S *admits a unique expansion in eigenfunctions*

$$f = \sum_0^\infty a_n e_n$$

which is uniformly convergent in the Fréchet space of smooth functions. One has for every $k \in \mathbb{N}$

$$\lim_{n\to\infty} n^k a_n = 0.$$

Conversely, a series $\sum_0^\infty a_n e_n$ *with* $\lim_{n\to\infty} n^k a_n = 0$, $k \in \mathbb{N}$, *defines a smooth function by summation.*

Jovan Karamata, (1902–1967) was a Serbian mathematician and Professor at the University of Geneva.

In short, one can say that the properties given by Fourier's theory for smooth functions and the operator $-\frac{d^2}{d\theta^2}$ on the circle $S^1 = \mathbb{R}/2\pi\mathbb{Z}$ hold for smooth functions and the operator $\Delta_{J,\omega}$ on a J-surface S. Even more generally, these properties hold for the Laplace operator

$$\Delta_M = *d*d : \Omega^0(M) \to \Omega^0(M)$$

on a compact Riemannian manifold (M, g) of dimension $d \geqslant 1$. The law concerning the growth of the eigenvalues depends on the dimension. For $T > 0$ let $\Lambda_M(T)$ be the dimension of the space spanned by eigenfunctions for eigenvalues $\lambda \in [0,T]$. Then the law of Weyl and Karamata becomes

$$\lim_{T\to\infty} \frac{\Lambda_M(T)}{T^{d/2}} = \frac{\beta(d)}{(2\pi)^d} Vol_g(M)$$

where $\beta(d)$ is the volume of the unit ball in Euclidean space of dimension d. As illustration, the cases of the circle S^1 of length 2π and the round unit two sphere S^2 in $\mathbb{R}^3$ of area 4π match the law.

The eigenfunctions on the circle S^1 are

$$\frac{1}{2\pi},\frac{1}{\sqrt{\pi}}\sin(\theta),\frac{1}{\sqrt{\pi}}\cos(\theta),\frac{1}{\sqrt{\pi}}\sin(2\theta),\frac{1}{\sqrt{\pi}}\cos(2\theta),\frac{1}{\sqrt{\pi}}\sin(3\theta),\frac{1}{\sqrt{\pi}}\cos(3\theta),\cdots$$

and the corresponding eigenvalues $0,1,1,4,4,9,9,\cdots$. Weyl's Law in dimension 1 is

$$\lim_{T\to\infty}\frac{\Lambda_{s^1}(T)}{\sqrt{T}}=\lim_{T\to\infty}\frac{2([\sqrt{T}]+1)}{\sqrt{T}}=2=\frac{\beta(1)}{2\pi}\text{Length}(S^1)$$

The eigenvalues and eigenspaces of the Laplace operator ΔS^2 on the round sphere S^2 of radius 1 in Euclidean 3-space $\mathbb{R}^3$ are explicitly known. The space of restrictions of homogeneous harmonic polynomials $F(x,y,z)$ on Euclidean 3-space of degree d to the sphere S^2 is the kernel of the operator $\Delta_{S^2}-d(d+1)$ Id. The eigenvalues are $0,2,6,12,20,\cdots,d(d+1),\cdots$ with multiplicity $2d+1$ for the eigenvalue $d(d+1)$, $d\geqslant 0$. Observe

$$\lim_{T\to\infty}\frac{\Lambda_{s^2}(T)}{T}=\lim_{d\to\infty}\frac{\Lambda_{s^2}(d(d+1))}{d(d+1)}=$$

$$\lim_{d\to\infty}\frac{(d+1)^2}{d(d+1)}=1=\frac{\beta(2)}{(2\pi)^2}Area(S^2).$$

For more about Riemannian Geometry and in particular about Weyl-and Karamata's Law, study the impressive book[9] of Marcel Berger, (1927–2016) a French mathematician.

Proof of Laplace Inversion Theorem, version 1. Let $f=\sum_0^\infty a_n e_n$ be in the kernel of $\Delta_{J,\omega}$. We have

$$0=\Delta_{J,\omega}(f)=\sum_1^\infty \lambda_n a_n e_n$$

From the uniqueness of the expansion in eigenfunctions of the function 0 it follows that $\lambda_n a_n=0$, $n=1,2,\cdots$. Hence $a_n=0$, $n>0$, since $\lambda_n>0$, $n>0$. We conclude $f=a_0 e_0$ and $\text{Dim}(\text{Kernel}(\Delta_{J,\omega}))=1$. The space of constant functions is of dimension one and subspace of the kernel, hence equal to the kernel of $\Delta_{J,\omega}$.

All smooth functions $g = \sum_0^\infty b_n e_n$ with $b_0 = 0$ are contained in the image of $\Delta_{J,\omega}$. Indeed, put $f = \sum_1^\infty \frac{b_n}{\lambda_n} e_n$ and we have $\Delta_{J,\omega}(f) = g$. It follows that the dimension of the co-kernel equals one.

The operator $\% \omega : \Omega^2(S, \mathbb{R}) \to \Omega^0(S, \mathbb{R})$ is a linear isomorphism, hence the dimensions of kernel and co-kernel of Δ_J are one. Moreover, $\mathrm{Kern}(\Delta_J) = \mathrm{Kern}(\Delta_{J,\omega})$. One has $\int_S \Delta_J(f) = \int_S d(df \circ J) = 0$ by the Stokes Theorem. Comparing co-dimensions shows that the image of Δ_J coincides with the kernel of the integration $\omega \in \Omega^2(S, \mathbb{R}) \mapsto \int_S \omega \in \mathbb{R}$.

The following theorem will be needed. Let $G : \mathbb{C} \to \mathbb{R}$ be the function defined by $G(p) = \frac{-1}{2\pi}\log(|p|)$ and $G(0) = 0$. The function G is an elementary solution of the Poisson equation $\Delta G = \delta$ where δ is the Dirac atomic unit measure at the origine $0 \in \mathbb{C}$. Paul Adrien Maurice Dirac (1902–1984) was a British physicist and mathematician. Siméon Denis Poisson (1781–1840) was a French mathematician and physicist. The idea of using an elementary solution for the Poisson equation is rooted in the early work of George Green (1793–1841), a British miller, physicist and mathematician. For every C^∞ function $u : \mathbb{C} \to \mathbb{C}$ with compact support the function $f = u * G$ obtained by convolution

$$f(p) = \int_{\mathbb{C}} G(q)u(p-q)\,dx \wedge dy$$

is a C^∞-function that satisfies the Poisson equation $\Delta f = u$ with $\Delta = \Delta_J = -\left(\frac{\partial^2}{\partial x^2} + \frac{\partial^2}{\partial y^2}\right)$.

Theorem 7.15 Local inversion of Laplace operator. *Let $u : \mathbb{C} \to \mathbb{C}$ be a C^∞-function with support in the unit disc $D_1 \subset \mathbb{C}$. Then the function $f = u * G$ satisfies $\Delta f = u$. Let M be the integral*

$$M = \int_{D_3} |G(p)|\, dVol(p)$$

over the disc of radius 3. For every monomial $p = \frac{\partial^a}{\partial x^a}\frac{\partial^b}{\partial y^b}$ of partial differ-ential operators the inequality

$$\text{Sup}_{p \in D2} | Pf(p) | \leqslant M \,\text{Sup}_{p \in D1} | Pu(p) |$$

holds.

Proof: The Laplace operator Δ and the partial differential operator P commute, so $Pf = G * Pu$ solves $\Delta Pf = Pu$. Hence for $p \in D_2$ one estimates $| Pf(p) |$ by $M\,\text{Sup}_{p \in D_1} | Pu(p) |$.

It is worth mentioning that the computation of the deRham cohomology of oriented compact connected surfaces of genus g can be completed now.

Theorem 7.16 *The second deRham cohomology group $H^2_{dR}(S)$ of a compact, oriented connected surface S is isomorphic to $\mathbb{R}$.*

Proof: First equip S with a J-field J. Since $H^2_{dR}(S) = \Omega^2(S, \mathbb{R})/d\Omega^1(S, \mathbb{R})$ it suffices to show that the space of exact 2-forms $d\Omega^1(S, \mathbb{R})$ is the kernel of the map $\int_S : \omega \in \Omega^2(S, \mathbb{R}) \mapsto \int_S \omega \in \mathbb{R}$ By Stokes Theorem we have that $d\Omega^1(S, \mathbb{R}) \subset \text{Kern}\left(\int_S\right)$. For $\omega \in \text{Kern}\left(\int_S\right)$ by the Laplace Inversion Theorem there exists a function f with $\Delta_J(f) = \omega$. Put $\alpha \overset{\text{def}}{=} df \circ J$, hence $d\alpha = \omega$ and $d\Omega^1(S, \mathbb{R}) = \text{Kern}\left(\int_S\right)$.

7.6 Topology of the two point Green function

Let $S = (S, J)$ be a Riemann surface. The Green functions $h_{p,q}$, $p, q \in S$, $p \neq q$, are strongly related to the topology of the surface S. The function $h_{p,q} : S \to \mathbb{R} \cup \{\pm\infty\}$ is harmonic on $S \setminus \{p, q\}$. So, $h_{p,q}$ has no local maxima or minima. The function $h_{p,q}$ is locally the real part of a holomorphic function. Near p, q the function is the real part of a function $\frac{f}{z}$ with f holomorphic and z a local holomorphic coordinate at p or q. It follows that the critical points of $h_{p,q}$ are isolated and do not accumulate near p or q. Hence, the number of critical points is finite.

By choosing the points p, q in a general position we may assume that all critical points are non-degenerated and that the function $h_{p,q}$ separates the critical points. So for points p, q in general position the function $h_{p,q}$ is a Morse function.

At a critical point c there exists a local centered holomorphic coordinate $z = x + iy$ with $h_{p,q} = \mathrm{Re} z^2 = x^2 - y^2$. So all critical points are saddle points of $h_{p,q}$.

Theorem 7.17 *Let $S = (S, J)$ be a Riemann surface and let p, q be distinct points in general position. The Green function $h_{p,q}$ is a Morse function. The number of critical points equals the number of critical values and is twice the genus g of S. Let $t_1 < t_2 < \cdots < t_{2g-1}$ be regular values that separate the critical values. The submanifold $h_{p,q}^{-1}(\{t_1, t_2, \cdots, t_{2g-1}\})$ is a union of embedded circles in S. The system of circles is a decomposition of the twice punctured surface $S \setminus \{p, q\}$ and also of the surface S into cylinders and pairs of pants. After removing for each cylinder one boundary curve, decompositions in pairs of pants remain.*

Proof: Let (p, q) be a generic pair of distinct points on a Riemann surface S of genus $g \geqslant 2$. Let $h_{p,q}$ have g' critical points and critical values. Connected components of the complement in S or in $S \setminus \{p, q\}$ of $h_{p,q}^{-1}(\{t_1, \cdots, t_{2g'-1}\})$ are cylinders or a pairs of pants. The number of pairs of pants that appear after having removed one boundary circle for each cylinder on $S \setminus \{p, q\}$ equals $2g' = \chi(S \setminus \{p, q\})$. On S there are two cylinders more and two pairs of pants less, so the final number of pairs of pants on S equals $2g' - 2 = \chi(S) = 2g - 2$.

One concludes $g = g'$.

Genus 3 Green function with 4 cylinders and 6 pairs of pants as shown in figure 25.

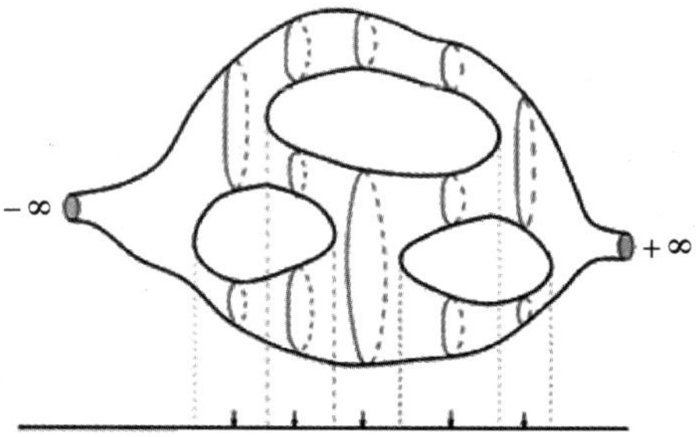

Figure 25 Genus 3 Green function with 4 cylinders and 6 pairs of pants

8 Differential Geometry in Economics and Finance

From this part we select recent applications on the differential and conformal geometry in Economics and finance. Such as the geometry of production models that are usually analyzed in economics, differential and conformal geometry do help in figure out some problems we found in economics and finance, such as SABR model and geometry of no arbitrage.

8.1 SABR model

The SABR model owes its popularity to the fact that it can reproduce comparatively well the market-observed volatility smile and that it provides a closed-form formula for the implied volatility.[6] In fact, because of these two features most practitioners use the SABR model mostly as a smile-interpolation tool rather than a pricing tool.

The dynamics of the forward rate Ft is

$$dF_t = \sum_t C(F_t)\, dW_t,$$

$$d\sum_t = \alpha \sum_t dZ_t.$$

Here Σ_t is the stochastic volatility parameter, $C(F) = F^{\beta}$, and W_t and Z_t are Brownian motions with

$$E[dW_t dZ_t] = \rho dt.$$

We supplement the dynamics with the initial condition $F_0 = f$, $\Sigma_0 = \sigma$.

Special case: normal SABR model

The normal SABR model is a special case in which $\beta = 0$, and $\rho = 0$:

$$dF_t = \sum_t dW_t,$$

$$d\sum_t = \alpha \sum_t dZ_t.$$

and $E[dW_t dZ_t] = 0$.

Backward Kolmogorov's equation reads:

$$\frac{\partial G_{T,F,\Sigma}}{\partial t} + \frac{1}{2}\sigma^2\left(\frac{\partial^2 G_{T,F,\Sigma}}{\partial f^2} + \alpha^2 \frac{\partial^2 G_{T,F,\Sigma}}{\partial \sigma^2}\right) = 0,$$

$$G_{T,F,\Sigma}(t,f,\sigma) = \delta\left(f - F, \sigma - \sum\right), \text{at} t = T.$$

After the transformation $t \rightarrow T - t$:

$$\frac{\partial G_{F,\Sigma}}{\partial t} = \frac{1}{2}\sigma^2\left(\frac{\partial^2 G_{T,F,\Sigma}}{\partial f^2} + \alpha^2 \frac{\partial^2 G_{F,\Sigma}}{\partial \sigma^2}\right),$$

$$G_{F,\Sigma}(0,f,\sigma) = \delta\left(f - F, \sigma - \sum\right).$$

This resembles the heat equation on the Poincare plane!

Normal SABR model and Poincare geometry

Brownian motion on the Poincare plane is described by:

$$dX_t = Y_t dW_t,$$

$$dY_t = Y_t dZ_t,$$

with $E[dW_t dZ_t] = 0$.

This is the normal SABR model if we make the following identifications:

$$X_t = F_{\alpha^2 t},$$

$$Y_t = \frac{1}{\alpha}\sum_{\alpha^2 t}.$$

Geometry of the full SABR model

The state space associated with the general SABR model has a somewhat more complicate dgeometry. Let $\mathbb{S}^2$ denote the upper half plane $\{(x,y) : y > 0\}$, equipped with the following metric g:

$$g = \frac{1}{\sqrt{1 - \rho^2 y^2 C(x)^2}}\begin{pmatrix} 1 & -\rho C(x) \\ -\rho C(x) & C(x)^2 \end{pmatrix}.$$

This metric is a generalization of the Poincare metric: the case of $\rho = 0$ and

$C(x) = 1$ reduces to the Poincare metric.

The metric g is the pullback of the Poincare metric under the following diffeomorphism. We choose $p \geqslant 0$, and define a map $\phi_p : \mathbb{S}^2 \to \mathbb{H}^2$ by

$$\phi_p(z) = \left(\frac{1}{\sqrt{1-\rho^2}} \left(\int_p^x \frac{du}{C(u)} - \rho y \right), y \right).$$

A consequence of this fact is that we have an explicit formula for the geodesic distance $\delta(z, Z)$ on $\mathbb{S}^2$:

$$\cosh \delta(z,Z) = \cosh d(\phi_p(z), \phi_p(Z))$$

$$= 1 + \frac{\left(\int_X^x \frac{du}{C(u)} \right)^2 - 2\rho(y - Y) \int_X^x \frac{du}{C(u)} + (y - Y)^2}{2(1-\rho^2) yY}.$$

We use invariant notation. Let $z^1 = x$, $z^2 = y$, and let $\partial_i = \partial / \partial z^i$, $i = 1, 2$, denote the corresponding partial derivatives. We denote the components of g^{-1} by g^{ij}, and use g^{-1} and g to raise and lower the indices: $z_i = \sum_j g_{ij} z^j$, $\partial^i = \sum_j g^{ij} \partial_j$. Explicitly,

$$\partial^1 = y^2 (C(x)^2 \partial_1 + \rho C(x) \partial_2),$$

$$\partial^2 = y^2 (\rho C(x) \partial_1 + \partial_2).$$

Consequently, the initial value problem can be written in the form:

$$\frac{\partial}{\partial_s} K_Z(s,z) = \frac{1}{2} \varepsilon \sum_i \partial^i \partial_i K_Z(s,z),$$

$$K_Z(0,z) = \delta(z - Z).$$

Except for the normal case, the operator $\sum_i \partial^i \partial_i$ does not coincide with the Laplace-Beltrami operator Δ_g on $\mathbb{S}^2$. One verifies that

$$\sum_i \partial^i \partial_i f = \Delta_g f - \frac{1}{\sqrt{\det g}} \sum_{ij} \frac{\partial}{\partial x^j} (\sqrt{\det g}\, g^{ij}) \frac{\partial f}{\partial x^i}$$

$$= \Delta_g f - \frac{1}{\sqrt{1-\rho^2}} y^2 C C' \frac{\partial f}{\partial x}.$$

We treat the Laplace-Beltrami part by mapping it to the Laplace-Beltrami operator in the Poincare plane. The first order operator is treated as a regular perturbation of the Laplace-Beltrami operator.

Asymptotics of the Green's function

Using the asymptotic expansion of McKean's formula we derive the following asymptotic expansion for the Green's function:

$$K_Z(t,z) = \frac{1}{2\pi\lambda\sqrt{1-\rho^2}\,Y^2C(X)}\exp\left(-\frac{\delta^2}{2\lambda}\right)\sqrt{\frac{\delta}{\sinh\delta}}$$

$$\left[1-\frac{\delta}{\sinh\delta}q-\left(\frac{1}{8}+\frac{\delta\coth\delta-1}{8\delta^2}-\frac{3(1-\delta\coth\delta)+\delta^2}{8\delta\sinh\delta}q\right)\lambda+\cdots\right].$$

Here $\lambda = t\alpha^2$, and

$$q(z,Z) = -\frac{yC'(x)}{2(1-\rho^2)^{\frac{3}{2}}Y}\left(\int_X^x\frac{du}{C(u)}-\rho(y-Y)\right).$$

Probability distribution in the SABR model

STEP 1: We integrate the asymptotic joint density over the terminal volatility variable Y to find the marginal density for the forward x:

$$P_X(t,x,y) = \int_0^\infty K_Z(t,z)\,dY$$

$$= \frac{1}{2\pi\lambda\sqrt{1-\rho^2}\,C(X)}\int_0^\infty e^{-\frac{\delta^2}{2\lambda}}\sqrt{\frac{\delta}{\sinh\delta}}$$

$$\left[1-\frac{\delta}{\sinh\delta}q-\frac{1}{8}\lambda\left(1+\frac{\delta\coth\delta-1}{\delta^2}-\frac{3(1-\delta\coth\delta)+\delta^2}{\delta\sinh\delta}q\right)\right]\frac{dY}{Y^2}.$$

Here again, $\delta(z,Z)$ denotes the geodesic distance on $\mathbb{S}^2$.

STEP 2: We evaluate this integral asymptotically by using the steepest descent method. Assume that $\phi(u)$ is positive and has a unique minimum u_0 in $(0,\infty)$ with $\phi''(u_0) > 0$. Then, as $\varepsilon\to 0$,

$$\int_0^\infty f(u)\,e^{\frac{-\phi(u)}{\epsilon}}du = \sqrt{\frac{2\pi\epsilon}{\phi''(u_0)}}\,e^{\frac{-\phi(u_0)}{\epsilon}}\times$$

$$\left\{f(u_0)+\epsilon\left[\frac{f''(u_0)}{2\phi''(u_0)}-\frac{\phi^{(4)}(u_0)f(u_0)}{8\phi''(u_0)^2}-\frac{f'(u_0)\phi^{(3)}(u_0)}{2\phi''(u_0)^2}+\frac{5\phi^{(3)}(u_0)^2f(u_0)}{24\phi''(u_0)^3}\right]+O(\epsilon^2)\right\}.$$

STEP 3: The exponent:

$$\phi(Y) = \frac{1}{2}\delta(z,Z)^2$$

has a unique minimum at Y_0 given by

$$Y_0 = y\sqrt{\zeta^2 - 2\rho\zeta + 1},$$

where

$$\zeta = \frac{1}{y}\int_X^x \frac{du}{C(u)}.$$

Y_0 is the "most likely value" of Y, and thus $Y_0 C(X)$ (when expressed in the original units) is the leading contribution to the observed implied volatility.

STEP 4: Let $D(\zeta)$ denote the value of $\delta(z, Z)$ with $Y = Y_0$. Explicitly,

$$D(\zeta) = \log\frac{\sqrt{\zeta^2 - 2\rho\zeta + 1} + \zeta - \rho}{1 - \rho}.$$

We also introduce the notation:

$$I(\zeta) = \sqrt{\zeta^2 - 2\rho\zeta + 1} = \cosh D(\zeta) - \rho\sinh D(\zeta).$$

Then, to within $O(\lambda^2)$, we find that

$$P_X(t, x, y) = \frac{1}{\sqrt{2\pi\lambda}}\frac{1}{yC(X)I^{\frac{3}{2}}}\exp\left\{-\frac{D^2}{2\lambda}\right\}$$

$$\left\{1 + \frac{yC'(x)D}{2\sqrt{1-\rho^2}I} - \frac{1}{8}\lambda\left[\begin{array}{l} 1 + \dfrac{yC'(x)D}{2\sqrt{1-\rho^2}I} + \dfrac{6\rho yC'(x)}{\sqrt{1-\rho^2}I^2}\cosh(D) - \\ \left(\dfrac{3(1-\rho^2)}{I} + \dfrac{3yC'(x)(5-\rho^2)D}{2\sqrt{1-\rho^2}I^2}\right)\dfrac{\sinh(D)}{D} \end{array}\right] + \cdots\right\}.$$

In terms of the original variables:

$$P_F(t, f, \sigma) = \frac{1}{\sqrt{2\pi\tau}}\frac{1}{\sigma C(F)I^{\frac{3}{2}}}\exp\left\{-\frac{D^2}{2tv^2}\right\}$$

$$\left\{1 + \frac{\sigma C'(f)D}{2v\sqrt{1-\rho^2}I} - \frac{1}{8}\tau v^2\left[\begin{array}{l} 1 + \dfrac{\sigma C'(f)D}{2v\sqrt{1-\rho^2}I} + \dfrac{6\rho\sigma C'(f)}{v\sqrt{1-\rho^2}I^2}\cosh(D) - \\ \left(\dfrac{3(1-\rho^2)}{I} + \dfrac{3\sigma C'f(5-\rho^2)D}{2v\sqrt{1-\rho^2}I^2}\right)\dfrac{\sinh(D)}{D} \end{array}\right] + \cdots\right\}.$$

8.2 Geometry of no arbitrage

8.2.1 Holonomy and arbitrage

For $\phi \in \Gamma(L)$ there is a 1-form ω such that $\nabla(\phi) = \omega\phi$. If $\phi'(x) = \Lambda(x)\phi(x)$, then

$$\nabla(\phi') = \nabla(\Lambda\phi) = (d\Lambda + \Lambda\omega)\phi,$$

and so

$$\begin{aligned}\omega' &= \Lambda^{-1}d\Lambda + \omega\\ &= d\log\Lambda + \omega.\end{aligned}$$

The absence of arbitrage is related to the flatness of ω, $d\omega = 0$.

8.2.2 LIBOR market model

We are given N LIBOR forwards $L_t^1, \cdots, L_t^N$, expiring at T_j, with the dynamics

$$dL_t^j = \Delta^j(L_t, t)\,dt + C^j(L_t^j, t)\,dW_t^j,$$

with

$$E[dL_t^i dL_t^j] = \rho^{ij}dt.$$

Choose the drifts so that this dynamics is arbitrage free!

The instantaneous Riemannian metric is given by

$$g^{ij}(L) = \rho^{ij}C^i(L^i)\,C^j(L^j).$$

We let $P_j(L)$ denote the price of the zero coupon bond expiring at T_j,

$$p_j(L) = \prod_{1\leqslant i\leqslant j}\frac{1}{1+\delta_i L^i},$$

where δ_i is the day count fraction. Therefore, if

$$\Lambda(L) = \frac{P_k(L)}{P_j(L)},$$

the corresponding connection forms differ by

$$d\log\left(\prod_{j+1\leqslant i\leqslant k}\frac{1}{1+\delta_i L^i}\right).$$

Therefore,

$$\omega_i \begin{cases} -\dfrac{\delta_i}{1+\delta_i L_t^i}, & if \quad j+1 \leqslant i \leqslant k, \\ \dfrac{\delta_i}{1+\delta_i L_t^i}, & if \quad k+1 \leqslant i \leqslant j, \\ 0, & otherwise. \end{cases}$$

and thus

$$\Delta^j = \sum_i g^{ij}\omega_i = C^j \sum_i \rho^{ij} C^i{}_{\omega i}.$$

As a consequence, the dynamics of the LMM has the familiar form:

Under Q^k,

$$dL_t^j = C^j(L_t^j, t) \times \begin{cases} -\sum_{j+1 \leqslant i \leqslant k} \dfrac{\rho_{ji}\delta_i C^i(L_t^i, t)}{1+\delta_i L_t^i} dt + dW_t^j, & if \quad j < k, \\ dW_t^j, & if \quad j = k, \\ \sum_{k+1 \leqslant i \leqslant j} \dfrac{\rho_{ji}\delta_i C^i(L_t^i, t)}{1+\delta_i L_t^i} dt + dW_t^j, & if \quad j > k. \end{cases}$$

8.2.3 Extended LIBOR market model

We consider an extension of the LIBOR market model with stochastic volatility parameters denoted by $\sigma_t^1, \cdots, \sigma_t^N$:

$$dL_t^j = \Delta^j(L_t, \sigma_t, t)\, dt + C^j(L_t^j, \sigma_t^j, t)\, dW_t^j,$$
$$d\sigma_t^j = \Gamma^j(L_t, \sigma_t, t)\, dt + D^j(L_t^j, \sigma_t^j, t)\, dZ_t^j,$$

with

$$E[dW_t^i dW_t^j] = \rho^{ij} dt,$$
$$E[dW_t^i dZ_t^j] = r^{ij} dt,$$
$$E[dZ_t^i dZ_t^j] = \pi^{ij} dt.$$

Choose the drifts so that this dynamics is arbitrage free!

The state space of this model has dimension $2N$ and the instantaneous Riemannian metric is given by:

$$g^{ij}(L,\sigma)=\begin{cases}\rho^{ij}C^i(L^i,\sigma^i)\,C^j(L^j,\sigma^j)\ ,if\quad 1\leqslant i,j\leqslant N,\\ \pi^{ij}C^i(L^i,\sigma^i)\,D^j(L^j,\sigma^j)\ ,if\quad 1\leqslant i\leqslant N,N+1\leqslant j\leqslant 2N,\\ \pi^{ij}D^i(L^i,\sigma^i)\,C^j(L^j,\sigma^j)\ ,if\quad N+1\leqslant i\leqslant 2N,1\leqslant j\leqslant N,\\ \tau^{ij}D^i(L^i,\sigma^i)\,D^j(L^j,\sigma^j)\ ,if\quad N+1\leqslant i,j\leqslant 2N.\end{cases}$$

Calculation of the connection form ω is identical to that of the LIBOR model. Under Q^k ,

$$dL_t^j=C^j(L_t^j,\sigma_t^j,t)\times\begin{cases}-\sum_{j+1\leqslant i\leqslant k}\dfrac{\rho_{ij}\delta_i C^i(L_t^i,\sigma_t^i,t)}{1+\delta_i L_t^i}dt+dW_t^j, & if\quad j<k,\\ dW_t^i, & if\quad j=k,\\ \sum_{k+1\leqslant i\leqslant j}\dfrac{\rho_{ij}\delta_i C^i(L_t^i,\sigma_t^i,t)}{1+\delta_i L_t^i}dt+dW_t^j, & if\quad j>k,\end{cases}$$

$$dL_t^j=D^j(L_t^j,\sigma_t^j,t)\times\begin{cases}-\sum_{j+1\leqslant i\leqslant k}\dfrac{\tau_{ij}\delta_i C^i(L_t^i,\sigma_t^i,t)}{1+\delta_i L_t^i}dt+dZ_t^j, & if\quad j<k,\\ dZ_t^j, & if\quad j=k,\\ \sum_{k+1\leqslant i\leqslant j}\dfrac{\tau_{ij}\delta_i C^i(L_t^i,\sigma_t^i,t)}{1+\delta_i L_t^i}dt+dZ_t^j, & if\quad j>k.\end{cases}$$

9 Conformal Geometry in Economics and Finance

In this section we will discuss conformal symmetries and stochastic time. Market models such as HJM and BJM are too computationally expensive. In addition, they have limited predictive power due to their lack of structure and tractability. Unspanned stochastic volatility models are virtually the only viable alternative to market models. Rate volatilities are deemed unspanned if they cannot be determined by the term-structure of forward rates alone, thus requiring additional state variables. These extra variables should control volatilities without influencing rates themselves. From the risk-management perspective, this idea adheres to the common wisdom that one should not attempt to hedge swaptions or other rate derivatives with bonds and swaps alone. Unspanned models make a subset of the wider class of *separable* models. A model is said to be separable if a strict subset of the parameters is entirely determined by the yield curve. Instruments such as swaptions would normally be used to determine the rest of the parameters. Unspanned models are always separable but not all the separable models are unspanned. For instance, while HJM models are always separable, they still can be spanned if rate volatilities are determined by yields instead of being separate stochastic processes. Separable models allow modification of parameters (usually of the functional form) while preserving the parametric class of yield curves. Usually, separable volatilities can be made unspanned by turning these additional parameters to stochastic processes. Vice versa, unspanned volatilities can be reduced to separable volatilities by being subordinated to yields. These relations are similar to those between stochastic vol and local vol models. Analytically, separability is paramount, as it enables bootstrapping calibration. Market models are separable by construction. Shortrate models generally lack this property. Most of the known finite-dimensional separable models are affine, i.e., with linear relations between instantaneous rates and their drifts and variances. Models of this type appear inconsistent both with market data and empirical behavior. The notable exception is the Cheyette class of unspanned models. However, this class of models remains rather restrictive and high-dimensional. The number of state variables in Cheyette models significantly exceeds the number of random factors①. As it has been demonstrated in, application of conformal symmetry provides a wide class of parsimonious models with separable volatilities. However, the approach still struggles in handling a sustained low-rates environment.

9.1 Models with Zero Instantaneous Spot Rate

Naively, persistently vanishing instantaneous spot rate would lead to vanishing term rates.[41] Indeed, in conventional interest rate models, discount factors can be expressed as the following risk-neutral expectation:

$$B(t,T) = E\left[\exp\left(-\int_t^T r(\tau)\, d\tau\right)\right]. \tag{9.1.1}$$

Therefore,

$$\forall_{s\in[t,T]}\ r(s) = 0 \Rightarrow B(t,T) = 1.$$

The discrete version of the formula (9.1.1):

$$B(t_0,t_N) = \tilde{E}\left[\prod_{i=1}^{N} B(t_{i-1},t_i)\right] = \tilde{E}\left[\exp\left(-\sum_{i=1}^{N} r(t_{i-1},t_i)(t_i - t_{i-1})\right)\right] \tag{9.1.2}$$

does always hold. Here, $\tilde{E}$ denotes expectations in the measure associated with

---

① The number of state variable is a dimension of the space (manifold), fully specifying the market state following some Markovian process under the model's assumptions. The number of factors is the number of random drivers of the process. From the Kolmogorov equation perspective, the number of the state variables determines the dimension of the diffusion equation, while the number of random factors is the rank of the second order coefficients matrix in this equation. For HJM models, the state dimension is infinite while the number of factors remains finite. For BGM models, the number of state variables is finite but grows indefinitely with the number of covered cash-flow dates.

the discretely compounded money market account. This can be proven via a reinvestment strategy. However, the continuous limit in this formula can be taken only if convergence of the term spot rate to the instantaneous spot rate is uniform in t:

$$\lim_{T\to t}\frac{1-B(t,T)}{T-t}=r(t)\,. \tag{9.1.3}$$

9.1.1 Counter examples

1. Discounting with the Running Maximum

Let C_0 be a currency with the zero risk-free rate, i.e, with all the discount factors equal to $B_0(t,T)=1$. Let x be some continuous stochastic process in the risk-neutral measure associated with C_0, e.g.

$$dx=\sigma dW+\mu dt.$$

Consider the running maximum of this process

$$x^{\max}(t)=\sup_{s<t}x(s)\ ,$$

and define the synthetic currency C, such that its exchange rate with the currency C_0 is equal to

$$\frac{C}{C_0}=\exp(-x^{\max})\,.$$

The discount factors for this synthetic currency can be calculated as

$$B(t,T)=E[\exp(x(t)-x^{\max}(T))]\,.$$

The corresponding instantiation rate (9.1.3) vanishes as long as the drawdown of the x-process is positive

$$x^{\max}(t)>x(t)\Rightarrow r(t)=\lim_{T\to t}\frac{1-B(t,T)}{T-t}=0.$$

This happens *almost always*. Nevertheless,

$$B(t,T)<1.$$

Note, that C_0 can be interpreted as the money market account associated with C.

2. Merton Credit Model

In a similarly naive approach to credit models, default probabilities P(t,T) can be expressed as

$$P(t,T) = 1 - B(t,T)\ ,B(t,T) = E\left[\exp\left(-\int_t^T h(\tau)\ d\tau\right)\right].$$

where h is the instantaneous hazard rate. However, in the Merton credit model, the instantaneous hazard rate always vanishes, which does not preclude the event of default. The term hazard rates in the Merton credit model are not vanishing. Moreover, they increase dramatically in the proximity of the Merton boundary. The Merton credit model can be applied to interest rates by interpreting survival probabilities $B(t,T)$ as discount factors, and the measure conditional on survival as the forward T-measure.

9.2 Conformal Symmetries and Lorentz Transformations

To build flexible models that are capable of matching the market data and capturing the empirical market behavior, we shall apply conformal symmetries in dimensions $n>2$. Conformal maps may distort the image, but remain proportional in the small scale limit. Conformal symmetries in n dimensions can be associated with the special type of $n+2$ dimensional hyperbolic rotations known in physics as Lorentz transformations . Similarly to orthogonal rotations, these transformations preserve some inner product. However, this inner product is not positive definite. Instead, it is of the form

$$(x,x) = x_1^2 + \cdots + x_n^2 + x_{n+1}^2 - x_{n+2}^2. \tag{9.2.1}$$

This brings into existence non-trivial zero norm vectors forming the so-called *light cone*:

$$\mathbb{T}_0 = \{x \mid x \in \mathbb{T}, x \neq \mathbb{O}, (x,x) = 0\}.$$

The light cone $\mathbb{T}_0$ is equipped with an inner product on its tangent spaces, inherited from the embedding space $\mathbb{T}$. This inner product is positive semidefinite, degenerate along the scaling dimension $dx \sim x$. This, in turn, induces a positive definite conformal structure on the *projective light cone* X, consisting of light rays:

$$X = \mathbb{T}_0 / \sim (\forall_{\lambda \in \mathbb{R} \setminus \{0\}}\ x \sim \lambda x).$$

Therefore, hyperbolic rotations (*Lorentz transformations*)

$$U:\mathbb{T}\rightarrow\mathbb{T},(Ux,Ux)=(x,x)$$

are associated with conformal transformations in X.

9.2.1 Flat Representation

The projective light cone is conformally equivalent to the compactified flat euclidean space. To demonstrate this, let us use a different (*light cone*) basis in $\mathbb{T}$:

$$(x,x)=x_1^2+\cdots+x_n^2+2\underbrace{\frac{1}{\sqrt{2}}(x_{n+l}+x_{n+2})}_{x+}\underbrace{\frac{1}{\sqrt{2}}(x_{n+l}-x_{n+2})}_{x-}$$

$$=x_1^2+\cdots+x_n^2+2x_+x_-. \tag{9.2.2}$$

Then, for each light ray, we select a single point in T_0 by imposing the condition $x_+=1$ (See figure 26). As a consequence of the zero-norm condition:

$$x\_=-\frac{1}{2}(x_1^2+\ldots+x_n^2).$$

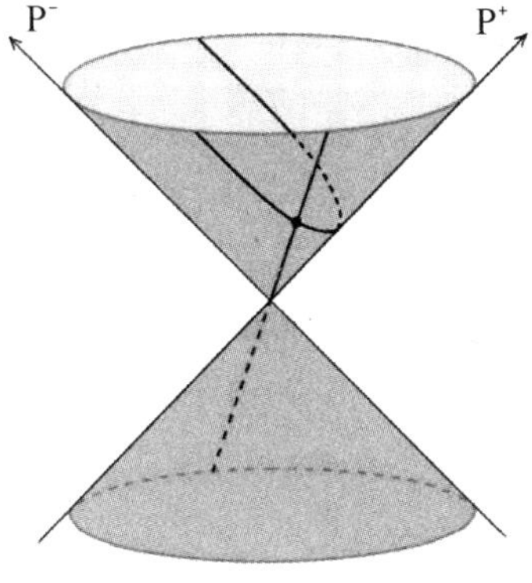

Figure 26 **Isotropic Basis**

The remaining light ray generated by the vector with the vanishing x_+ component

$$e_{-} = \begin{pmatrix} 0 \\ \cdot \\ \cdot \\ \cdot \\ 0 \\ 1 \end{pmatrix}$$

can be associated with $\mathbb{R}^n$ infinity. Thus, we mapped the projective light cone to the compactified euclidean space. To apply a hyperbolic rotation in this representation, we should start by mapping an $\mathbb{R}^n$ vector to the light cone, then performing the rotation, then re-scaling the result to restore the x_+ component back to one, and finally removing the last two components:

$$\begin{pmatrix} x_1 \\ \cdot \\ \cdot \\ \cdot \\ x_n \end{pmatrix} \sim \begin{pmatrix} x_1 \\ \cdot \\ \cdot \\ \cdot \\ x_n \\ 1 \\ -\dfrac{x_1^2 + \cdots + x_n^2}{2} \end{pmatrix} \overset{U}{\mapsto} \begin{pmatrix} x_1' \\ \cdot \\ \cdot \\ \cdot \\ x_n' \\ x_+' \\ x_-' \end{pmatrix} \cong \begin{pmatrix} x_1'/x_+' \\ \cdot \\ \cdot \\ \cdot \\ x_n'/x_+' \\ 1 \\ x_-'/x_+' \end{pmatrix} \sim \begin{pmatrix} x_1'/x_+' \\ \cdot \\ \cdot \\ \cdot \\ x_n'/x_+' \end{pmatrix} \tag{9.2.3}$$

Let us now compute an inner product of a pair of light cone vectors in such *flat* representation:

$$(x, y) = \left(\begin{pmatrix} x_1 \\ \cdot \\ \cdot \\ \cdot \\ x_n \\ 1 \\ -\dfrac{|\boldsymbol{x}|^2}{2} \end{pmatrix}, \begin{pmatrix} y_1 \\ \cdot \\ \cdot \\ \cdot \\ y_n \\ 1 \\ -\dfrac{|\boldsymbol{y}|^2}{2} \end{pmatrix} \right) = \boldsymbol{x} \cdot \boldsymbol{y} - \frac{|\boldsymbol{x}|^2 + |\boldsymbol{y}|^2}{2} = -\frac{|\boldsymbol{x} - \boldsymbol{y}|^2}{2}. \tag{9.2.4}$$

Hereafter, the boldface symbols (e.g., $\boldsymbol{x}$, $\boldsymbol{y}$) refer to euclidean vectors mapped to the projective light cone X. As expected, the right part of the equation is invariant under orthogonal rotations and translations (the Poincaré group). Those are special cases of conformal transformations.

9.3 Conformal Diffusion

9.3.1 Conformally Invariant Generator

Consider the Laplacian operator:

$$\Delta \equiv \partial_{x_1}^2 + \cdots + \partial_{x_n}^2.$$

In two dimensions, $n=2$, it is conformally invariant modulo scaling. This is a special case however. In higher dimensions, such a conformally invariant linear elliptic operator does not exist . To realize the conformal invariance of the Laplacian, we should interpret it differently. Let $\mathfrak{X} \subseteq X$ be an open subset in the projective light cone and $\pi^{-1}\mathfrak{X} \subseteq \mathbb{T}_0$ be the subset in the light cone, which projects into $\mathfrak{X}$. Consider a space $\mathcal{F}_{\mathfrak{X}}^{\gamma}$ of homogeneous functions on $\pi^{-1}\mathfrak{X}$ of the order γ:

$$\mathcal{F}_{\mathfrak{X}}^{\gamma} = \{\psi : \pi^{-1}\mathfrak{X} \to \mathbb{R} \mid \forall_{x \in \pi^{-1}\mathfrak{X}, \lambda \in \mathbb{R}\setminus\{0\}} \psi(\lambda x) = |\lambda|^{\gamma}\psi(x)\}.$$

Homogeneous functions of the trivial order $\gamma=0$ can be thought of as functions on the projective light cone, which we have mapped to the compactified $\mathbb{R}^n$. Homogeneous functions of a nontrivial order can be represented by the homogeneous functions of the trivial order multiplied by x_+^{γ} . For each function $F:\mathbb{R}^n \to \mathbb{R}$ define

$$F_{\gamma} \in \mathcal{F}^{\gamma} : F_{\gamma}(x) \equiv F(\boldsymbol{x})\, \boldsymbol{x}_+^{\gamma}(x \in \mathbb{T}_0).$$

Consider a linear differential operator $\mathcal{F}^{\gamma} \xrightarrow{\diamondsuit} \mathcal{F}^{\gamma'}$, such that

$$\forall_F \diamondsuit F_{\gamma} = (\Delta F)_{\gamma'}. \tag{9.3.1}$$

For $\gamma = 1 - \dfrac{n}{2}, \gamma' = -1 - \dfrac{n}{2}$, this definition appears to be independent on the choice of the light cone basis (9.2.2) . Then the operator $\diamondsuit$ is Lorentz-invariant.

Ⅰ. Wealth Bundle and Numeraire-Free Framework

The conformally invariant generator $\diamondsuit$ does not operate on ordinary functions. Instead, it operates on objects which can be mapped to ordinary functions by choosing a unit, e.g., x_+^γ. However, in financial applications, the backward Kolmogorov equation does not quite operate on functions either. Values of financial products are not just numbers; they also have units. There is no universal unit. Any positive self-financing account can serve as a numeraire. Mathematically, functions taking values measured in units can be interpreted as sections of a line bundle. The line bundle associated with financial products will be called the wealth bundle†. A ratio of two sections is unitless. It can be interpreted as an exchange rate of the associated assets. As the operator $\diamondsuit$ acts on $\mathcal{F}^\gamma\left(\gamma=-1-\frac{n}{2}\right)$, we should interpret elements of $\mathcal{F}_{\mathbb{X}}^\gamma$ as sections of the wealth bundle. The nontrivial value of the order γ reflects the fact that conformal symmetries are accompanied by changes in numeraire. Wealth sections $\Psi \in F_{\mathbb{X}}^\gamma$ satisfying the equation $\diamondsuit\Psi=0$ will be called *harmonic*. They correspond to stationary solutions of the following numeraire independent valuation equation:

$$\left(\partial_t + \frac{1}{2}\sigma_t^2\diamondsuit\right)\Psi_t = 0(\Psi_t \in \mathcal{F}^\gamma, \sigma_t \in \mathcal{F}^1). \qquad (9.3.2)$$

Here, Ψ_t is a time-dependent wealth section associated with some self-financing account.

Ⅱ. Forward Measure and Forward Parameterization

Let us choose, as a numeraire, a zero coupon bond expiring at $T > t$. The value of the bond itself in this numeraire is given by the constant 1-function, which is obviously harmonic:

$$\Delta 1 = 0.$$

According to (9.3.1), it corresponds to the following harmonic wealth section

$$\mathfrak{B}_T(x) \equiv x_+^\gamma = (e_-, x)^\gamma, \diamondsuit\mathfrak{B}_T = 0.$$

Note that the only Lorentz invariant property of $e_- \in T$ is $(e_-, e_-) = 0$. By symmetry, we can associate a similar harmonic section with any other light cone vector:

$$\mathbb{T}_0 \ni b \to \Psi_b \in \mathcal{F}^\gamma : \Psi_b(x) \equiv (b, x)^\gamma, \forall_{b\in\mathbb{T}_0} \diamondsuit\Psi_b = 0.$$

Indeed, according to (9.2.4), in the flat representation such wealth sections becomes

$$\Psi_b(x) = (b,x)^{\gamma} = \left(\frac{1}{2}|b_+ x_+||b - \boldsymbol{x}|^2\right)^{\gamma} = \left(\sqrt{\frac{1}{2}}|b_+ x_+||b - \boldsymbol{x}|\right)^{2-n}.$$

Meanwhile, the function $|\mathbf{b} - \mathbf{x}|^{2-n}$ is known to be harmonic. It is natural to assume that Ψ_b can be related to the zero-coupon bonds of other expirations:

$$\forall_{T \geqslant t} \mathfrak{B}_T = \Psi_{b_T}(b_T \in \mathbb{T}_0). \qquad (9.3.3)$$

Under this assumption, the forward discount factors can be calculated as:

$$B(T,T') = \frac{\mathfrak{B}_{T'}}{\mathfrak{B}_T} = \left(\frac{(b_{T'},x)}{(b_T,x)}\right)^{\gamma}. \qquad (9.3.4)$$

They satisfy the required martingale property as long as the $\boldsymbol{x}$ -process in the forward T-measure is of the form

$$dX_i = \sigma dW_i \qquad (9.3.5)$$

Here, W_i are independent Wiener processes, and σ is some positive scalar process.

Ⅲ. Separability

There are virtually no restrictions on the σ-process. It might be fully subordinated to the $\boldsymbol{x}$ -process $\sigma = \sigma(\boldsymbol{x}, t)$, or governed by any number of additional stochastic factors. The discount factors (9.3.4) are entirely determined by the map $\mathbb{R} \ni T \to b_T \in \mathbb{T}_0$ and is not influenced by the choice of the σ-process. This property is particularly important for bootstrapping calibration to swaptions.

9.4 Time Homogeneity and Hyperbolic (Lorentz) Evolution

Consistency of the forward discount factors (9.3.4) with the forward measure dynamics (9.3.5) can be easily proven without conformal symmetries. However, we also need to understand the conditions which make the model time-homogeneous. In the canonical formulation, time-homogeneity is defined as invariance under the time translations. However, this definition is inapplicable, when, like in our case, the state variables or the numeraire used in the model specification are themselves non-stationary. Indeed, the $\boldsymbol{x}$ -variables are related to the forward discount factors with fixed start dates and maturities. These are not stationary observables. Furthermore, they become undefined after the current time reaches the start date. The same applies to the forward measure, which we used to specify the process. Let us extend the definition of time-homogeneity to such non-stationary parametrization as follows: A model is deemed time homogeneous if it is symmetric under some one-dimensional *evolution* group $\{Us\}_{\{s\in\mathbb{R}\}}$ of transformations accompanied by time translations:

$$t \xrightarrow{U_S} t + s.$$

The map $s \to U_S$ is a homeomorphism, i.e.,

$$U_{S_1} U_{S_2} = U_{S_1+S_2}.$$

The evolution symmetries may involve changes in the numeraire, which affect the drift terms. However, the covariances must remain invariant. Therefore, for the dynamics of the form (9.3.5), the action of the evolution transformations on the state variables **x** should be conformal. As we demonstrated, conformal transformation can be associated with Lorentz rotations. A generic Lorentz evolution can be defined as

$$U_S = e^{\epsilon s}. \tag{9.4.1}$$

Here, ϵ is an infinitesimal hyperbolic rotation. Similarly to infinitesimal orthogonal rotations, it is related to a skew-symmetric form in $\mathbb{T}$:

$$\forall_{x,y\in\mathbb{T}}(x,\epsilon y) + (y,\epsilon x) = 0.$$

Since the model states are associated with elements of the projective light cone X, the Lorentz evolution (9.4.1) can be extended with scaling:

$$U_s = e^{(\epsilon+k)s}(k \in \mathbb{R}). \tag{9.4.2}$$

In application to the zero coupon bond wealth sections (9.3.3), our definition of the time homogeneity yields

$$b_{T+s} = U_s b_T. \tag{9.4.3}$$

The choice of the Lorentz generator ϵ is central to the model. It determines the parametric form of future yield curves and the correlation structure of forward rates. It can be shown, that with the appropriate choice of *light cone* basis (9.2.2), ϵ can always be represented in the following form:

$$
\varepsilon = \begin{pmatrix}
 & & & & & -a_1 & 1 \\
 & & -a_3 & & & -a_2 & \\
 & a_3 & & \cdots & & & \\
 & & \cdots & & -a_n & & \\
 & & & a_n & & & \\
-1 & & & & & k & \\
a_1 & a_2 & & & & & -k
\end{pmatrix}. \tag{9.4.4}
$$

The global model parameters k and $\{a_i\}_{i=1}^{n}$ are normally calibrated to swaptions with short expirations. This is done prior to bootstrapping.

9.4.1 Parametric Yield Curve

The yield curve implied by the model can be specified by the global model parameters k and $\{a_i\}_{i=1}^{n}$, in conjunction with the n-dimensional initial state $\mathbf{x}$. This parametric form covers a wide variety of yield curves. For capturing initial yield curve exactly, the standard fudging technique can be used:

$$
B(t,T) = \frac{\Phi(T)}{\Phi(t)} B_{\text{model}}(t,T).
$$

Here the Φ is a deterministic positive function of time. Fudging can also be used to allow negative rates.

9.4.2 Stationary Parameterization

Until now, we employed parametrization in which forward discount functions with fixed start and maturity dates are independent of time. In the *stationary parametrization*, spot rates with fixed tenors $B(t,t+s)$ should be time independent instead. The stationary parametrization is related to the forward parameterization as follows:

$$
\tilde{\mathbf{x}} = U_{t-T}\,\mathbf{x}. \tag{9.4.5}
$$

Indeed, according to (9.3.4), (9.4.3):

$$
\begin{aligned}
B(t,t+s) &= \left(\frac{(b_{t+s},x)}{(b_t,x)}\right)^{\gamma} = \left(\frac{(U_{t+s-T}b_T,x)}{(U_{t-T}b_T,x)}\right)^{\gamma} = \left(\frac{(U_s b_T, U_{t-T}x)}{(b_T, U_{t-T}x)}\right)^{\gamma} \\
&= \left(\frac{(U_s b_T,\tilde{x})}{(b_T,\tilde{x})}\right)^{\gamma} = \left(\frac{(U_s e_-,\tilde{x})}{(e_-,\tilde{x})}\right)^{\gamma}.
\end{aligned} \tag{9.4.6}
$$

In the stationary parametrization, the process can be naturally described in the risk neutral-measure. Consider a time step $t \to t + \delta t$. According to (9.4.5), the forward parametrization associated with the expiration $t + \delta t$ is related to the stationary parametrization as $x = U_{\delta t}\tilde{x}$. It also coincides with the stationary parametrization after completion of the time step. Therefore, according to (9.3.5), in the forward ($t + \delta t$)-measure, the process $\tilde{\mathbf{x}}$ is of the form

$$\tilde{\mathbf{x}} \to U_{-\delta t}\, \tilde{\mathbf{x}} + \sigma d\, \boldsymbol{W}. \tag{9.4.7}$$

Note, that for the single step, the risk-neutral measure is the same as the forward ($t + \delta t$)-measure. Therefore, the formula (9.4.7) defines the process in the risk neutral measure.

9.4.3 The Process Region

For the bonds of the form (9.3.3), instantaneous forward rates can be calculated as

$$rT(x) = - \gamma \frac{(\dot{b}_T, x)}{(b_T, x)} = \left(\frac{n}{2} - 1\right) \frac{(\dot{b}_T, x)}{(b_T, x)}, \tag{9.4.8}$$

where

$$\dot{b}_T \equiv \frac{d}{dT} b_T = (\epsilon + k)\, b_T.$$

Here, we applied the formulae (9.4.3) and (9.4.2). As b_T are light cone vectors, their derivatives $\dot{b}_T$ must be orthogonal to b_T, which results in positivity of their inner square:

$$(\dot{b}_T, b_T) = 0 \Rightarrow \dot{b}_T^2 > 0.$$

For a given orthogonal pair of b_T, $\dot{b}_T$, we can always choose a light cone basis such that

$$b_T = e_+, \dot{b}_T = |\dot{b}_T| e_1.$$

In the associated flat representation, the formula (9.4.8) becomes

$$r_T = \left(\frac{n}{2} - 1\right) |\dot{b}_T| \mathbf{x}_1$$

Then the area of positive r_T

$$\mathfrak{X}_T = \{x \in X \mid r_T(x) \geqslant 0\}$$

maps to a half space. Generically, when $\dot{b}_T$ has nontrivial light cone components,

$\mathfrak{X}_T$ has a spherical boundary defined by the condition

$$\partial\mathfrak{X}_T = \{x \in X \mid (\dot{b}_T, x) = 0\}.$$

Spheres and hyperplanes are known to be conformally equivalent. In order to avoid negative rates, we should keep the process within the positive rates region

$$x_t \in \mathfrak{X}_t.$$

Then the process volatility must dissipate at the boundary:

$$\lim_{x \to \partial\mathfrak{X}} \sigma = 0. \tag{9.4.9}$$

In addition, the process region $\mathfrak{X}_t$ must extends with time (see Fig. 26)

$$\forall_{t_1 < t_2} \mathfrak{X}_{t_1} \subseteq \mathfrak{X}_{t_1}.$$

To satisfy this condition, we should require

$$(\epsilon^2(\epsilon^2 - k^2)\, b_t, b_t) \leqslant 0.$$

Note, that according to (9.4.3), (9.4.2):

$$(\epsilon^2(\epsilon^2 - k^2)\, b_{t+s}, b_{t+s}) = (\epsilon^2(\epsilon^2 - k^2)\, e^{(\epsilon+k)s} b_t, e^{(\epsilon+k)s} b_t)$$
$$= e^{2ks}(\epsilon^2(\epsilon^2 - k^2)\, b_t, b_t) \leqslant 0.$$

Therefore, it is sufficient to check the condition for a single value of t only. It can be shown that for the hyperbolic generator in ϵ the form (9.4.4), this condition is equivalent to

$$a_i \geqslant 0 (i = 1, 2, \cdots, n).$$

In the stationarity parametrization, the process region is constant and can always be mapped to a hyper plain $\tilde{x}_1 > 0$. Then, the confinement condition (9.4.9) becomes

$$\lim_{\tilde{x}_1 \to 0} \sigma = 0.$$

In this parametrization, the model is specified by the process (9.4.7) and discount factors (9.4.6). It is directly time homogeneous as long as the σ process does not explicitly depend on time. For instance σ can be an arbitrary function of $\tilde{\mathbf{x}}$ defined on the half plane $\tilde{\mathbf{x}}_1 \geqslant 0$ and vanishing at the boundary $\tilde{\mathbf{x}}_1 = 0$. In reality, time homogeneity of the σ process is often broken as a result of bootstrapping.

9.5 The Conformal Model under Stochastic Clock

Consider a function on the projective light cone

$$\mathfrak{T}: X \to \mathrm{R}$$

defined by the condition

$$x \in \partial \mathfrak{X}_{\mathfrak{T}(x)} \tag{9.5.1}$$

The value $\mathfrak{T}(\mathbf{x})$ can be interpreted as the minimum time such that $\mathbf{x}$ is contained within the process region $\mathfrak{X}_{\mathfrak{T}(\mathbf{x})}$. Let us now reinterpret the conformal diffusion (9.3.5) as a process under some stochastic clock τ, and define the physical clock as a running maximum of the $\mathfrak{T}(\mathbf{x}(\tau))$ process

$$t(\tau) = \sup_{\tau' < \tau} \mathfrak{T}(\mathbf{x}(\tau')).$$

Then, under the physical clock t, the processes $\{x_i\}_{i=1}^{N}$ becomes

$$\mathbf{x} = \mathbf{x}(\tau(t)),$$

where

$$\tau(t) = \inf\{\tau \mid \mathfrak{T}(x(\tau)) = t\}.$$

As a consequence of (9.5.1), the physical clock process is confined to the boundary of the positive rates region:

$$x(\tau(t)) \in \partial \mathfrak{X}_t \tag{9.5.2}$$

thus reducing the number of state variables by 1. This keeps the instantaneous spot rate vanishing. However, forward rates in this model are positive pure jump processes.

Due to the scaling symmetry, the stochastic clock version of the model is independent on the choice of the σ process. This helps to provide closed form solutions. Let us demonstrate it by computing the distribution of $\mathbf{x}(T)$ in the forward T-measure. In the forward parametrization associated with the expiration T, the condition (9.5.2) becomes $\mathbf{x}_1 = 0$. Due to the scaling symmetry, we can, without losing generality, assume that σ is constant in this parametrization. Then, the problem is reduced to computing the distribution of the hyperplane intercept point for the standard n-dimensional Brownian process. This distribution is known to be an $n-1$-dimensional student distribution:

$$\rho(\mathrm{x}(T)) = \frac{\Gamma\left(\frac{n}{2}\right)\mathrm{x}_1(t)}{\left(\sqrt{\pi}\,|\mathrm{x}(T) - \mathrm{x}(t)|\right)^n}.$$

9.5.1 Models with Regime Change

In reality, low-rates recession periods alternate with relatively high-rates periods of economic growth. Can we have a model covering both regimes? Define the *physical* time as

$$t = \max(\tau, \sup_{\tau' < \tau} \mathfrak{T}(x(\tau')))$$

When the stochastic clock dominates $t = \tau$, $\mathfrak{T}(x(t)) < t$, the process is continuous and the instantaneous spot rate is positive. When the process reaches the boundary $\mathrm{x}(t) \in \partial\mathfrak{X}(t) \Leftrightarrow \mathfrak{T}(x(t)) = t$, , the regime changes. In the new regime, the stochastic clock diverges from the physical clock $\tau < t$, the instantaneous spot rate vanishes while the forward rates become pure jump processes. When the stochastic clock catches up with the physical clock $\tau = t$, the instantaneous spot rate jumps up and the process returns to the continuous regime.

References

[1] A'CAMPO NORBERT, PAPADOPOULOS ATHANASE. Notes on hyperbolic geometry[J]// Strasbourg Master class on Geometry. IRMA Lectures in Mathematics and Theoretical Physics. Zürich: European Mathematical Society (EMS), 2012(18):1-182.

[2] ALBERT FATHI, FRANçOIS LAUDENBACH, VALENTIN POENARU. Thurston's Work on Surfaces [M]// Mathematical Notes 48. Princeton University Press, Translated by DJUN KIM and DAN MARGALIT from the French edition (1978) Travaux de Thurston, 2012.

[3] ALBIAC FERNANDO, KALTON NIGEL J. Topics in Banach Space Theory[J]. Graduate Texts in Mathematics. New York: Springer, 2006:233.

[4]------. Algebraische Theorie der Körper[M]. New publication with permission by ERNST STEINITZ and with the addition: Abriss der Galoisschen Theorie. by REINHOLD BAER and HELMUT HASSE. Berlin: W. de Gruyter and Co., 1930.

[5] A M POLYAKOV. Quantum geometry of bosonic strings[J]. Phys. Lett., 1981(103B): 211-213.

[6] ANDREW LESNIEWSKI. The Uses of Differential Geometry in Finance [R]. Bloomberg, 2005:15-41.

[7] ARCHIMEDES OF SYRACUSE (BC 225), Περὶ σφαίρας καὶ κυλίνδρου [EB/OL]. http://openn.library.upenn.edu/Data/0014/ArchimedesPalimpsest/.

[8] BAKER H F. Abel's theorem and the allied theory of theta functions [M]. Cambridge, UK : Cambridge University Press, 1897; Reprinted 1995.

[9] BERGER MARCEL. A Panoramic View of Riemannian Geometry [M]. Berlin, Heidelberg, New York: Springer Verlag, 2007.

[10] BIKBOV R, M CHERNOV. Unspanned stochastic volatility in affine

models: Evidence from Eurodollar futures and options [J]. Management Science, 2009 (55): 1292-1305.

[11] BONOLA ROBERTO. Non-Euclidean Geometry, A critical and Historical Study [M]. New Dover Edition, New York : Dover Publications, Inc., 1906.

[12] B OSGOOD, R PHILLIPS, P SARNAK. Extremals of determinants of Laplacians [J]. Journal of Functional Analysis, 1988, 80 (1): 148-211.

[13] BOURBAKI NICOLAS. Livre III, Topologie Générale [M]. Paris: Hermann, 1961 : Chap. 1-2.

[14] BRÄGGER WALTER. A Uniformisation of Weighted Maps on Compact Surfaces [M]. Basel: Modern Birkhäuser Classics, 2001.

[15] BROWDER FELIX E. Mathematical Developments Arising from Hilbert Problems [M]. Proceedings of Symposia in Pure Mathematics XXVIII, American Mathematical Society. A collection of survey essays by experts devoted to each of the 23 problems emphasizing current developments, 1976.

[16] BUSEMANN HERBERT. Spaces with non-positive curvature [J]. Acta Math, 1948 (80): 259-310.

[17] BUSER PETER. Geometry and Spectra of Compact Riemann Surfaces [M]. Basel: Modern Birkhäuser Classics, 1992.

[18] B-Y CHEN. Solutions to homogeneous Monge-Ampere equations of homothetic functions and their applications to production models in economics [J]. Journal of Mathematical Analysis and Applications. 2014, 411 (1): 223-229.

[19] C A IOAN. Applications of the space differential geometry at the study of production functions [J]. Euro Economica, 2007: 1830-1838.

[20] CARTAN ÉLIE. Sur certaines expressions différentielles et le problème de Pfaff [J]. Annales scientifiques de l' École Normale Supérieure. 1899, Sér. 3 (16): 239-332.

[21] CARTAN ÉLIE. Sur une classe remarquable d'espaces de Riemann [J]. Bulletin de la Société Mathématique de France, 1926 (54): 214-216.

[22] CARTAN ÉLIE. Sur une classe remarquable d'espaces de Riemann [J]. Bulletin de la Société Mathématique de France, 1927 (55): 114-134.

[23] CARTAN HENRI. Calcul différentiel [M]. Paris : Hermann, 1967.

[24] CARTAN HENRI. Théorie élémentaire des fonctions analytiques

d'une ou plusieurs variables complexes, Avec le concours de Reiji Takahashi [M]. Paris : Hermann, 1964.

[25] CHOW W - L. On Compact Complex Analytic Varieties [J]. American Journal of Mathematics, 1949, 71 (4): 893-914.

[26] C J EARLE, J EELLS. The diffeomorphism group of a compact Riemann surface [J]. Bulletin of the American Mathematical Society, 1967, 73 (4): 557-560.

[27] Coxeter H S M, Moser W O J. Generators and Relations of Discrete Groups [M]. Berlin: Springer, 1972.

[28] DEAHNA F. Über die Bedingungen der Integrabilitat [J]. Journal Für Die Reine Und Angewandte Mathematik, 1840 (20): 340-350.

[29] DE SAINT-GERVAIS, PAUL HENRI. Le site Analysis Situs [EB/OL]. http://analysissitus. math. cnrs. fr/ et sections: Introductional-Analysis-situs-par-les-surfaces.html, Bibliographie-commentee.html.

[30] DE SAINT-GERVAIS, PAUL HENRI. Uniformisation des Surfaces de Riemann [M]. Lyon : Retour sur un Théorème centenaire, ENS Editions, 2010.

[31] DIEUDONNÉ JEAN. Exposé at the Symposium in honnor of Henri Cartan's 70th birthday [R]. University Paris-Sud at Orsay, 1974.

[32] DIEUDONNé JEAN. Foundations of modern analysis [M]. Boston, MA: Academic Press, 1969.

[33] DONALDSON SIMON. Riemann Surfaces [M]. London: Oxford University Press, 2011.

[34] EINSTEIN ALBERT. Über die von der molekularkinetischen Theorie der Wärme geförderte Bewegung von in ruhenden Flüssigkeiten suspendierten Teilchen [J]. Annalen der Physik, 1905, 322 (8): 549-560.

[35] FISCHER ARTHUR E, TROMBA ANTHONY J. Almost complex principal fiber bundles and the complex structure on Teichmüller space [J]. Journal Für Die Reine Und Angewandte Mathematik, 1984 (352): 151-160.

[36] FROBENIUS, GEORG. Über das Pfaffsche Problem [J]. Journal Für Die Reine Und Angewandte Mathematik, 1877 (82): 230-315.

[37] GABAIX X. Linearity-generating processes: A modelling tool yielding

closed forms for asset prices [M]. Preprint, 2009.

[38] G E VÎLCU. A geometric perspective on the generalized Cobb-Douglas production functions [J]. Applied Mathematics Letters, 2011, 24 (5): 777-783.

[39] GIRONDO, ERNESTO, GONZÁLEZ-DIEZ, GABINO. Introduction to compact Riemann surfaces and dessins d'enfant [M]. London: Mathematical Society Student Texts, Cambridge University Press, 2012.

[40] GRAMAIN ANDRÉ. Topology of surfaces [M]. Moscow, Idaho: BCS Associates, 1984.

[41] GREGORY PELTS. Unspanned Stochastic Volatility, Conformal Symmetries, and Stochastic Time [J]. Social Science Electronic Publishing, 2017: 3-20.

[42] GREGORY PELTS. Unspanned Volatility in Non-Affine Short Rate Models and Conformal Symmetry [J]. Social Science Electronic Publishing, 2012.

[43] GROTHENDIECK, ALEXANDRE. Produits tensoriels topologiques et espaces nucléaires [J]. Memoirs of the American Mathematical Society, 1955 (16).

[44] GROTHENDIECK ALEXANDRE. Résumé des resultats essentials dans la théorie des produits tensoriels topologiques et des espaces nucléaires [J]. Annales de l'Institut Fourier, 1952 (4): 73-112.

[45] GRÜNBAUM BRANKO, SHEPHARD G C. Tilings and Patterns [M]. New York : Freeman and Company, 1986.

[46] - Grundlagen für eine allgemeinen Theorie der Funktionen einer veränderlichen complexen Grösse [M]. Göttingen: Inauguraldissertation, 1851.

[47] HARNACK AXEL. Die Grundlagen der Theorie des logarithmischen Potentiales und der eindeutigen Potentialfunktion in der Ebene [M]. Leipzig: B. G. Teubner, 1887.

[48] HELGASON SIGURDUR. Differential geometry, Lie groups and symmetric spaces [M]. New York: Academic Press, 1978.

[49] H GARLING. Grundlehren der mathematischen Wissenschaften [M]. New York: Springer Verlag, 1971.

[50] HILBERT DAVID, COHN-VOSSEN STEPHAN. Anschauliche Geom-

etrie [J]. Mathematical Gazette, 1932, 36 (317).

– Second edition with extra Appendix, Einfachste Grundbegriffe der Topologie, Alexandroff, Paul, Springer Verlag, 2011.

[51] HODGE W V D. The theory and applications of harmonic integrals [M]. London: Cambridge Mathematical Library, Cambridge University Press, 1941.

[52] HURWITZ ADOLF. Über algebraische Gebilde mit eindeutigen Trans formation in sich [J]. Mathematische Annalen, 1892, 41 (3): 408–442.

[53] IVANOV NIKOLAI V. A Topologist's View of the Dunford-Schwartz Proof of the Brouwer Fix-Point Theorem [J]. The Mathematical Intelligencer, 2000, 22 (3): 55–57.

[54] J MOSER. On the Volume Elements on a Manifold [J]. Transactions of the American Mathematical Society, 1965, 120 (2): 286–294.

[55] KAKUTANI SHIZUO. Two-dimensional Brownian motion and harmonic functions [J]. Proceedings of the Imperial Academy, 1944, 20 (10): 706–714.

[56] KNUS MAX-ALBERT, MERKURJEV, ALEXANDER, ROST MARKUS, TIGNOL JEAN-PIERRE. The Book of Involutions [J]. American Mathematical Society Colloquium Publications of American Mathematical Society, 1998 (3).

[57] KOSZUL JEAN-LOUIS. Lectures on fibre bundles and Differential Geometry [M]. Bombay: Tata Inst. Fund. Research, 1965.

[58] KÖTHE GOTTFRIED. Topologische lineare Räume I [M]. Berlin: Springer, 1960.

[59] KÜRSCHáK J. Über Limesbildung und allgemeine Körpertheorie [J]. Journal für die reine und angewandte Mathematik, 1913 (142): 211 –253.

[60] KÜRSCHÁK J. Über Limesbildung und allgemeine Körpertheorie [J]. Proceedings of the 5th International Congress of Mathematicians Cambridge, 1912 (1): 285–289.

[61] LÉVY PAUL. Le mouvement brownien plan, Amer [J]. Journ. of Math., 1940: 61.

[62] LÓS, JERZY. Quelques remarques, théorèmes et problèmes sur les classes définissables d'algèbres [J]. Symposium by THORALF SKOLEM and WISKUNDIG GENOOTSCHAP on Mathematical interpretation of formal systems, Amsterdam : North-Holland Publishing Co., 1955: 98-113.

[63] MAEHARA RYUJI. The Jordan Curve Theorem Via the Brouwer Fixed Point Theorem [J]. The American Mathematical Monthly, Mathematical Association of America, 1984, 91 (10): 641-643.

[64] MAGNUS, WILHELM. Noneuclidean Tesselations and Their Groups [M]. New York and London: Academic Press, 1974.

[65] MALGRANGE BERNARD. Sur l'intégrabilité des structures presque complexes [M]. Séminaire Jean Leray N. 1, 1969: 1-8.

[66] MALLIAVIN PAUL. Géométrie différentielle intrinsèque [M]. Paris: Hermann, 1972.

[67] MASKIT, BERNARD. Comparison of hyperbolic and extremal lengths [J]. Annales Academiae Scientiarum Fennicae Series A I Mathematica, 1985, 10 (10): 381-386.

[68] MCMULLEN C T. Entropy on Riemann surfaces and the Jacobians of finite covers [J]. Commentarii Mathematici Helvetici, 2013, 88 (4): 953-964.

[69] MILNOR JOHN W. Topology from the differential view point [M]. Charlottesville, USA: The University Press of Virginia, 1965.

[70] MILYUTIN ALEKSEI A. Isomorphism of the spaces of continuous functions over compact sets of the cardinality of the continuum [J]. Teor. Funkcii Funkcional Anal. i Prolozen, 1966 (2): 150-156.

[71] MINSKY YAIR N. Extremal length estimates and product regions in Teichmüller space [J]. Duke Mathematical Journal, 1996 (83): 249-286.

[72] MISCHLER BERNARD (±1975, ...). Private communications, at several occasions of travelling by bicycle.

[73] MORSE MARSTON. The critical points of a function of n variables [J]. Proceedings of the National Academy of Sciences, 1930, 16 (11): 777-779.

[74] NEWLANDER A, NIRENBERG L. Complex analytic coordinates in

almost complex manifolds [J]. Annals of Mathematics. Second Series, 1957, 65 (3): 391-404.

[75] NIJENHUIS ALBERT, WOOLF WILLIAM. Some integration problems in almost-complex and complex manifolds [J]. Ann. Math., 1963 (77): 424-489.

[76] OSTROWSKI, ALEXANDER. Über einige Fragen der allgemeinen Körpertheörie [J]. Journ. f. d. reine u. angewandte Math., 1913 (143): 255-284.

[77] OSTROWSKI ALEXANDER. Untersuchungen zur arthmetischen Theorie der Körper [J]. Math. Z., 1935, 39 (1): 269-404.

[78] PERRON OSKAR. Eine neue Behandlung der ersten Randwertaufgabe Δu=0 [J]. Math. Z., 1923: 18.

[79] PETERSSON HANS, Über eine Metrisierung der automorphen Formen und die Theorie der Poincaréschen Reihen [J]. Math. Ann., 1940 (117): 453-537.

[80] PFLUGER ALBERT. Theorie der Riemannschen Flächen [M]. Berlin, Göttingen, Heidelberg: Springer Verlag, 1957.

[81] PHELPS ROBERT R. Lectures on Choquet's Theorem, Lectures Notes in Mathematics [M]. Heidelberg, Berlin, New York: Springer, First Edition , 1966; Second Edition, N. J.: van Nostrand, Princeton, 2001.

[82] PIERRE COLLIN-DUFRESNE. Robert S. Goldstein Do Bonds Span the Fixed Income Markets? Theory and Evidence for Unspanned Stochastic Volatility [J]. Journal of Finance, 2002, 57 (4): 1685-1730.

[83] POPESCU-PAMPU PATRICK. What is the Genus? Lecture Notes in Mathematics [M]. Berlin: Springer Verlag, 2016.

[84] RADÓ TIBOR. Über den Begriff der Riemannschen Fläche [J]. Acta Szeged, 1925, 2 (2): 101-121.

[85] RADÓ T. Subharmonic Functions [M]. Erg. Math. u. i. Grenzgebiete, Berlin: Julius Springer, 1937.

[86] REVUZ DANIEL, YOR MARC. Continuous martingales and Brownian motion [M]. Berlin: Springer Verlag, 1999.

[87] RIEMANN BERNARD. Gesammelte Mathematische Werke und wissenschaftlicher Nachlass [M]. Herausgegeben unter Mitwirkung von R. DEDEKIND von H. WEBER, Leipzig: Druck und Verlag von B. G. Teubner, 1876.

[88] ROSENFELD B A. A history of non-euclidean geometry. Evolution of

the concept of a geometric space, Translated from the Russian by Abe Shenitzer. Studies in the History of Mathematics and Physical Sciences [M]. New York, Berlin: Springer Verlag, 1988.

[89] ROZENFELD B A. Istori neevklidovoui geometrii. Razvitie ponti o geometriqeskom prostranstve [M]. Nauka, Moscow: Izdat, 1976.

[90] SAMELSON HANS. Differential Forms, the Early Days; or the Stories of Deahna's Theorem and of Volterra's Theorem [J]. The American Mathematical Monthly, 2001, 108 (6): 522-530.

[91] SARD ARTHUR. The measure of the critical values of differentiable maps [J]. Bulletin of the American Mathematical Society, 1942, 48 (12): 883-890.

[92] SCHOUTENS HANS. The Use of Ultraproducts in Commutative Algebra [M]. Lecture Notes in Mathematics, Heidelberg, Springer Verlag, 2010.

[93] SCHWARTZ LAURENT. Théorie des distributions, Publications de l'Institut de Mathématique de l'Université de Strasbourg, No. IX-X [M]. Nouvelle édition, entiérement corrigée, refondue et augmentée. Paris: Hermann, 1966.

[94] SERRE JEAN-PIERRE. Géométrie algébrique et géométrie analytique [J]. Annales de l'Institut Fourier, 1956 (6): 1-42.

[95] SERRE JEAN-PIERRE. Un théorème de dualité [J]. Commentarii Mathematici Helvetici, 1955, 29 (1): 9-26.

[96] STEINITZ ERNST. Algebraische Theorie der Körper [J]. Journal für die reine und angewandte Mathematik, 1910 (137): 167-309.

[97] TITS JACQUES. Sur les analogues algébriques des groupes semisimples complexes [M]. Colloque d'algèbre supérieure, tenu à Bruxelles du 19 au 22 décembre 1956, Centre Belge de Recherches Mathématiques, Établissements Ceuterick, Louvain, Paris: Librairie Gauthier-Villars, 1957: 261-289.

[98] TROMBA ANTHONY J. On a natural algebraic affine connection on the space of almost complex structures and the curvature of Teichmüller space with respect to its Weil-Petersson metric [J]. Manuscripta Mathematica, 1986, 56 (4): 475-497.

[99] -Über das Verschwinden der Theta-Functionen [M]. 1865.

[100] VOISIN CLAIRE. Hodge Theory and Complex Algebraic Geometry [M]. London: Cambridge University Press, 2007.

[101] WEIL ANDRÉ. Sur les courbes algébriques et variétés qui s'en déduisent, Hermann and Cie, 6, rue de la Sorbonne, Paris: Publications de l'Institut de Mathématiques de l'Université de Strasbourg, 1948.

[102] WEYL HERMANN. Das asymptotische Verteilungsgesetz der Eigenwerte linearer partieller Differentialgleichungen (mit einer Anwendung auf die Theorie der Hohlraumstrahlung) [J]. Mathematische Annalen, 1912, 71 (4): 441-479.

[103] WEYL HERMANN. Die Idee der Riemannschen Fläche [M]. Leipzig: Teubner, 1913.

[104] WIENER NORBERT. Generalized harmonic analysis [J]. Acta Mathematica, 1930, 55 (1): 117-258.

[105] W MUELLER, K WENDLAND. Extremal Kaehler metrics and Ray-Singer analytic torsion, Geometric aspects of partial differential equations (Roskilde, 1998) [M]. 242 AMS, Providence, RI, USA: Contemp. math., 1999: 135-160.

[106] WOLPERT SCOTT A. Chern forms and the Riemann tensor for the moduli space of curves [J]. Inventiones Mathematicae, 1986, 85 (1): 119-145.

[107] - Work on Surfaces, Mathematical Notes 48 [M]. Princeton University Press, Translated by DJUN KIM and DAN MARGALIT from the French edition (1978) Travaux de THURSTON, 2012.

[108] YAMADA SUMIO. Local and global aspects of Weil-Petersson geometry [J]. HANDBOOK of Teichmüller Theory, 2014 (IV): 44-107.

[109] YAMADA SUMIO. Weil-Petersson convexity of the energy functional on classical and universal Teichmüller space [J]. Journal of Differential Geometry, 1999 (51): 35-96.

[110] YOR MARC. Some Aspects of Brownian Motion. Part I: Some Special Functionals [M]. BIRKHAEUSER, 1992; Some Aspects of Brownian Motion. Part II: Some Recent Martingale Problems [M]. Birkhaeuser, 1997.

后　记（Postscript）

出版一部纯英文学术专著，需要面临许多挑战，所幸一路遇到各种助力，终于达成所愿。本书能够顺利成稿，要感谢许多前辈与相关领域学者的提携和帮助，在这里谨致以最衷心的谢意！

限于篇幅，本书议题内尚有部分内容不能完全展开，诸如 Uniformisation by Spectral Determinant，Functions on Riemann Surfaces，Line Bundles and Cohomology，Dimensions of Spaces of Holomorphic Sections；Riemann Surfaces and Algebraic Curves，The Jacobian of a Riemann Surface，Fundamental Group and Coverings，等等。还有一些更加深入的思考有待继续推进，让我们共同期待后续完善提高的机会。

本书能够顺利出版，感谢相关学术资助，感谢西南财经大学出版社编辑和我的学生们的敬业工作。

朱南丽

2021 年 6 月于昆明